T5-BSG-701

THE UNITED STATES FLAG & TOUCH FOOTBALL LEAGUE 2008-2009 RULE BOOK & OFFICIAL'S MANUAL

U.S.F.T.L.
9th Edition
Official Flag & Touch Football Rules

Adopted, Published and Distributed by:

THE UNITED STATES FLAG & TOUCH FOOTBALL LEAGUE

7709 Ohio St.
Mentor, Ohio 44060
Phone: (440) 974-8735
Fax: (440) 974-8441
E-Mail: usftl@usftl.com
Website: www.usftl.com

No part of this book may be reproduced or utilized in any form or by any means without the written permission from the publisher. Copyright 1988, by the United States Flag & Touch Football League. Reprinted: 1992, 1994, 1996, 1998, 2000, 2002, 2004, 2006. Printed in the United States of America. All Right Reserved.

TABLE OF CONTENTS

The United States Flag & Touch Football League Story 6
How The U.S.F.T.L. Operates 7
Playing Rules Committee 8
State, Section and Region Structure 10
Executive Board of Directors and Officers 11
Executive Committee 11
Officials Committee 12
Rules of Conduct 13
Rule Changes 14

RULE BOOK

RULE 1:	Definitions 16
RULE 2:	The Games 23
RULE 3:	The Playing Fields 26
RULE 4:	Equipment 30
RULE 5:	Periods, Time Factors & Overtime 32
RULE 6:	Substitutions 37
RULE 7:	Ball in Play, Dead Ball, Out of Bounds 37
RULE 8:	Series of Downs, Number of Downs, Zone Line to Gain & Team Possession After Penalty 39
RULE 9:	The Scrimmage, Snapping, Handing & Passing the Ball 41
RULE 10:	The Kicking Game 47
RULE 11:	Scoring 56
RULE 12:	Conduct of Players & Others Subject to the Rules 59
RULE 13:	Enforcement of Penalties 66
RULE 14:	Formula for Identical Records (Tie Breaker) 72
RULE 15:	Protests 73
RULE 16:	Ranking System 74
RULE 17:	Communicable Disease Procedures 76
RULE I 8:	Men's Program 76
RULE 19:	Women Is Program 78
RULE 20:	Co-Recreation (Co-Rec) Program 79
RULE 21:	Youth Program 82
RULE 22:	Masters Program 83
RULE 23:	4 on 4 Program 84
RULE 24:	Corporate Program 89
RULE 25:	Church Program 91
RULE 26:	Armed Forces Program 92
RULE 27:	Law Enforcement Program 94
RULE 28:	Indoor Rules 95
RULE 29:	5 on 5 Program 96
RULE 30:	Paid Bids 100
Play Ruling	101

CONSTITUTION

ARTICLE 1:	Organization.	105
ARTICLE 2:	Membership.	105
ARTICLE 11:	Team Eligibility	107
ARTICLE 12:	Individual Player Eligibility	108
ARTICLE 13:	World Championship	112
ARTICLE 15:	Acts of Disbarment	112
ARTICLE 23:	Copyrights, Telecast & Broadcast Rights	113
ARTICLE 26:	Tournament Procedures, By-Laws & Guidelines	114

OFFICIAL'S MANUAL

MANUAL PURPOSE

PART I –	*U.S.F.T.L. Duties, Principles & Procedures*	126
	for Good Officiating	
SECTION 1 –	Knowledge of the Rules	126
SECTION 2 –	Physical Condition	126
SECTION 3 –	Judgment	126
SECTION 4 –	Duties & Responsibilities	126
SECTION 5 –	Signals	126
SECTION 6 –	Hustle	127
SECTION 7 –	Cooperation & Communication	127
SECTION 8 –	Do Not Discuss	127
SECTION 9 –	Pre-Game Duties & Procedures	127
SECTION 10 –	Toss of Coin	128
SECTION 11 –	Sounding Your Whistle	128
SECTION 12 –	Stopping & Starting the Clock	129
SECTION 13 –	Declaring Ball Ready-For-Play	130
SECTION 14 –	Operating Down Marker	130
SECTION 15 –	Measuring for 1st Downs	131
SECTION 16 –	Time-Out Procedure	131
SECTION 17 –	Enforcement of Fouls	132
SECTION 18 –	Coach-Referee Conference	133
SECTION 19 –	After a Touchback, Safety, Try-For-Point or Field Goal	133
SECTION 20 –	Disqualification of Players or Coaches	134
SECTION 21 –	Administering Penalties	135
SECTION 22 –	Between Halves Procedure	137
SECTION 23 –	End Of Game Procedure	137
SECTION 24 –	Protest Procedure	137
SECTION 25 –	U.S.F.T.L. Official's Uniform &	
	Equipment Requirements	137
SECTION 26 –	U.S.F.T.L. Official's Code of Ethics	138

U.S.F.T.L. Official's Mechanics

PART II –	*2 Person Crew Mechanics*	140
SECTION 1 –	Kickoff (Free Kick) - Positions & Responsibilities	140
SECTION 2 –	Pass/Run Plays from Scrimmage -	
	Positions & Responsibilities	143
SECTION 3 –	Protected Scrimmage Kick (Protected Punt) -	

	Positions & Responsibilities 147
SECTION 4 –	Try-For-Point (Extra Point Kick) & Field Goal Kick Attempt - Positions & Responsibilities 148
SECTION 5 –	Goal Line & Try-For-Point Plays (Scrimmage Plays, No Kick- Positions & Responsibilities 150

PART III –	*3 Person Crew Mechanics* 151
SECTION 1 –	Kickoff (Free Kick) - Positions & Responsibilities 151
SECTION 2 –	Pass/Run Plays from Scrimmage - Positions & Responsibilities 154
SECTION 3 –	Protected Scrimmage Kick (Protected Punt) - Positions & Responsibilities 159
SECTION 4 –	Try-For-Point (Extra Point Kick) & Field Goal Kick Attempt - Positions & Responsibilities 160
SECTION 5 –	Goal Line & Try-For-Point Plays (Scrimmage Plays, No Kick) - Positions & Responsibilities 162

PART IV –	*4 Person Crew Mechanics* 164
SECTION 1 –	Kickoff (Free Kick) - Positions & Responsibilities 164
SECTION 2 –	Pass/Run Plays from Scrimmage - Positions & Responsibilities 167
SECTION 3 –	Protected Scrimmage Kick (Protected Punt) - Positions & Responsibilities 173
SECTION 4 –	Try-For-Point (Extra Point Kick) & Field Goal Kick Attempt - Positions & Responsibilities 175
SECTION 5 –	Goal Line & Try-For-Point Plays (Scrimmage Plays, No Kick) - Positions & Responsibilities 177

Code of Official Football Signals 179
Summary of Penalties and Fouls 181
Index to Rules 184

NOTE: Use of the word "he" in this publication is intended to include both masculine and feminine genders unless otherwise noted!

NOTE: All new changes are screened throughout this publication.

NOTE: An Official's Signal (S) refers to the U.S.F.T.L. Code of Official Football Signals 1 through 47.

The U.S.F.T.L. Rules committee wishes to acknowledge the National Federation of State High School Associations, The National Collegiate Athletic Association and N.I.R.S.A. for rulebook interpretations, specific rules and rulebook format. Full credit is given for materials used herein.

Any rule interpretation not discussed in this rulebook will be covered by the National Federation of State High School Association's Football Rule Book and Casebook.

Approved by the voting delegates at the National Meeting of the U.S.F.T.L.

FLAG FOOTBALL INSURANCE
ENDORSED BY USFTL
Available 1-01-08 to 12-31-08

Teams and Leagues	* Maximum # of Players per Team	$100,000 Medical Only	$100,000 Medical And $2,000,000 Gen. Liability.		$2,000,000 General Liability Only (Waiver Required)	
Teams - Youth	25	$48 per team	$162 per team		Not Available	
Teams - Adult	25	$92 per team	$195 per team		$166 per team	
TOURNAMENTS ARE LIMITED TO 3 DAYS OR LESS			1-24 TEAMS	25-50 TEAMS	1-24 TEAMS	25-50 TEAMS
Tournaments - Youth	25	Not Available	$459 per team	$565 per team	Not Available	Not Available
Tournaments – Adult	25	Not Available	$524 per team	$640 per team	$355 per team	$529 per team

"Looking To The Future"
Sportsplex Operators & Developers Association
Office: (585) 426-2215   Fax: (585) 247-3112
www.amateursportsinsurance.com

THE UNITED STATES FLAG & TOUCH FOOTBALL LEAGUE STORY

The United States Flag & Touch Football League (U.S.F.T.L.) is a non-profit, 501(c)(3) membership based organization that was founded in 1988, in Cleveland, Ohio, by Executive Director Michael Cihon. The sports of Flag & Touch football were in desperate need of some type of organization because of the vast number of different rules that were being used by different local groups around the country. The U.S.F.T.L. was the first organization to address all versions of Flag & Touch Football in one clear, concise Rule Book. Due to the differing opinions on how the game should be played, the U.S.F.T.L. did an exhaustive 5 year study of all the different types of Flag & Touch Football and concluded that there were 4 basic fundamental styles of play ("Games"). Those "Games" are Contact Flag Football, Touch Football, Screen Flag Football and Ineligible Lineman Flag Football.

The U.S.F.T.L. is dedicated to promoting the games of Flag & Touch Football to all people, regardless of gender, race, age, religious affiliation or natural ability.

Its mission is to establish uniform rules and regulations in order to ensure safe and enjoyable participation for everyone. The organization encourages sportsmanship and fair play at all levels, while educating all who are interested in the proper skills necessary for safe and rewarding play. This is accomplished through the creation of rules, conducting clinics, training and certifying officials and producing educational aids (video tapes, training manuals, etc.) for the continuing education in the sports of Flag & Touch Football.

In closing, the U.S.F.T.L. motto is "It's Time To Give The Game To The Players."

U.S.F.T.L. MISSION STATEMENT

The Mission Statement of the U.S.F.T.L. shall be to promote the games of Flag & Touch Football to all people regardless of race, religion, sex, nationality or age. To establish uniformity in Flag & Touch Football rules and regulations making the game safe and enjoyable for everyone. To encourage sportsmanship and fair play at all levels. To educate and teach the proper skills of Flag & Touch Football through the creation of rules, promoting, organizing, conducting clinics, seminars and training courses.

U.S.F.T.L. VISION STATEMENT

"IT'S TIME TO GIVE THE GAME TO THE PLAYERS."

HOW THE U.S.F.T.L. OPERATES

Each state operates its own organization through a State Director affiliated with the U.S.F.T.L. Each State Director reports to a Sectional Vice President, who in turn reports to a Regional President. Directors are appointed by the U.S.F.T.L. to coordinate and administer the programs and activities in each state. The State Director is responsible for appointing Local Directors, Local Directors of Officials and a State Director of Officials. These Local and State Directors help coordinate U.S.F.T.L. activities and give the players, officials and sponsors a full range of programs from which to choose.

Individual teams wishing to join and participate in U.S.F.T.L. events and activities register through their Local and State Directors. Upon registering, the team coach shall receive a Rule Book and Constitution, a U.S.F.T.L. membership card, a yearly subscription to the U.S.F.T.L. Newspaper, "First & Twenty" and permission to participate in all U.S.F.T.L. sanctioned events. A number of N.I.T.'S (National Invitational Tournaments), state, sectional and regional tournaments are offered to these sanctioned participants leading to national and even world championship competition. Teams can also purchase insurance for accident and liability protection at greatly reduced rates.

Officials have the same opportunity to affiliate with the U.S.F.T.L. through a membership program that provides a number of benefits. They receive a Rule Book and Constitution, a U.S.F.T.L. membership card, a yearly subscription to the U.S.F.T.L. newspaper, "First & Twenty", a U.S.F.T.L. patch and permission to officiate in all U.S.F.T.L. sanctioned events. Medical and Liability insurance is offered to players, teams, officials, directors, leagues, complexes and recreation departments that are affiliated with the U.S.F.T.L.

The U.S.F.T.L. Executive Board of Directors meets annually at the U.S.F.T.L. National Meeting to discuss rule changes, equipment, awards, eligibility and National Tournament sites, to name a few of the more important issues that are discussed. Proposals are brought before the Executive Board of Directors, composed of the Executive Director, National President, National Vice President, National Secretary, National Treasurer, Legal Counsel, four Regional Presidents, International Region President, International Region Vice President and a representative from the U.S.F.T.L. Board of Trustees. These Proposals are reviewed and either approved or rejected by a majority vote of the Executive Board of directors. This is all administered by a full time National Headquarters staff for whom Flag & Touch Football is top priority 365 days a year.

Michael Cihon
Executive Director & President
U.S.F.T.L.

PLAYING RULES COMMITTEE OF THE UNITED STATES FLAG & TOUCH FOOTBALL LEAGUE

NATIONAL VICE PRESIDENT - CHAIRMAN

NATIONAL DIRECTOR OF OFFICIALS
(National Playing Rules Interpreter)

EXECUTIVE DIRECTOR

NATIONAL PRESIDENT

NATIONAL SECRETARY

4 REGIONAL DIRECTORS OF OFFICIALS

8 SECTIONAL DIRECTORS OF OFFICIALS

51 STATE DIRECTORS OF OFFICIALS

NATIONAL SECRETARY OF OFFICIALS

ALL INQUIRIES PERTAINING TO PLAYING RULE INTERPRETATIONS
SHOULD BE SENT TO:
National Director of Officials
C/O U.S.F.T.L. National Headquarters
7709 Ohio St., Mentor, Ohio 44060 or
Email: usftl@usftl.com

IF AN UNUSUAL OR DISPUTED PLAY OCCURS IN A GAME, write it out in detail in order to receive an answer or interpretation. Please enclose a self-addressed stamped envelope. Should you wish a U.S.F.T.L. RULE BOOK and OFFICIAL'S MANUAL, place your order at www.usftl.com. You may also email your request to usftl@usftl.com.

All inquiries pertaining to matters
other than rule interpretations should be sent to:
U.S.F.T.L. NATIONAL HEADQUARTERS
7709 OHIO ST.
MENTOR, OHIO 44060 or
Email: usftl@usftl.com
Website: www.usftl.com

GREAT AMERICAN AWARDS INC.
TROPHIES • PLAQUES • ENGRAVINGS • GIFTS

10958 Kinsman Road • P.O. Box 305 • Newbury, OH 44065

(440) 564-5560
Fax (440) 564-5561

"Official Awards Supplier of the USFTL"

OFFICIAL SUPPLIER OF REFEREE'S EQUIPMENT TO THE USFTL

800-468-3284
www.honigs.com

-MAILING-	-TELEPHONE-	-SHIPPING-
PO BOX 1711	800-468-3284, 734-761-2244	7136 JACKSON RD
ANN ARBOR, MI 48106	FAX 877-869-4783	ANN ARBOR, MI 48103

UNITED STATES FLAG AND TOUCH FOOTBALL LEAGUE

STATE, SECTION AND REGION STRUCTURE

EASTERN REGION

NORTHEASTERN SECTION
Maine
New Hampshire
Massachusetts
Rhode Island
Connecticut
Vermont
New York
New Jersey
Pennsylvania

ATLANTIC SECTION
Delaware
Maryland
Washington D.C.
Virginia
North Carolina
South Carolina
West Virginia

SOUTHERN REGION

SOUTHEASTERN SECTION
Georgia
Florida
Alabama
Tennessee
Mississippi

SOUTHWESTERN SECTION
Texas
Oklahoma
Arkansas
Louisiana

NORTHERN REGION

GREAT LAKES SECTION
Michigan
Ohio
Kentucky
Indiana
Illinois
Wisconsin

CENTRAL SECTION
Minnesota
North Dakota
South Dakota
Iowa
Nebraska
Kansas
Missouri

WESTERN REGION

NORTHWESTERN SECTION
Washington
Oregon
Montana
Idaho
Wyoming
Utah
Colorado
Alaska

PACIFIC SECTION
California
Nevada
Arizona
Hawaii
New Mexico

INTERNATIONAL REGION

All Foreign Countries

U.S.F.T.L. EXECUTIVE BOARD OF DIRECTORS AND OFFICERS

EXECUTIVE DIRECTOR - CHAIRMAN

NATIONAL PRESIDENT

NATIONAL VICE PRESIDENT

NORTHERN REGION PRESIDENT

SOUTHERN REGION PRESIDENT

WESTERN REGION PRESIDENT

EASTERN REGION PRESIDENT

INTERNATIONAL REGION PRESIDENT

INTERNATIONAL REGION VICE PRESIDENT

NATIONAL SECRETARY

NATIONAL TREASURER

LEGAL COUNSEL

BOARD OF TRUSTEES REPRESENTATIVE

EXECUTIVE COMMITTEE

NATIONAL PRESIDENT - CHAIRMAN

EXECUTIVE DIRECTOR

NATIONAL VICE PRESIDENT

NATIONAL TREASURER

NATIONAL SECRETARY

EIGHT SECTIONAL VICE PRESIDENTS

FIFTY-ONE STATE DIRECTORS

11 NATIONAL PROGRAM DIRECTORS:

Women	Youth	Masters
Men	Co-Rec	Corporate
4 on 4	5 on 5	Church
Armed Forces	Law Enforcement	

NATIONAL OFFICIALS COMMITTEE

NATIONAL DIRECTOR OF OFFICIALS - CHAIRMAN

NATIONAL SECRETARY OF OFFICIALS

FOUR REGIONAL DIRECTORS OF OFFICIALS

ONE INTERNATIONAL REGION DIRECTOR OF OFFICIALS

ONE INTERNATIONAL REGION ASSISTANT DIRECTOR OF OFFICIALS

EIGHT SECTIONAL DIRECTORS OF OFFICIALS

FIFTY-ONE STATE DIRECTORS OF OFFICIALS

LOCAL DIRECTOR OF OFFICIALS REPRESENTATIVE
(4 - One from each Region)

LOCAL OFFICIAL REPRESENTATIVE
(4 - One from each Region)

UNITED STATES FLAG & TOUCH FOOTBALL LEAGUE
U.S.F.T.L. RULES OF CONDUCT

It is the purpose of the United States Flag & Touch Football League to conduct the best possible Tournaments from all aspects. To achieve this objective the U.S.F.T.L. must have the cooperation of each player, coach and sponsor. We are guests in the city in which the tournament is conducted and nothing should occur that would reflect adversely on your team, players, our host city, or the United States Flag & Touch Football League. Therefore, it is required that all teams in the tournament comply with the following rules:

1. Team coaches must have full control of their players at all times. This means "on" and "off" the field.

2. In case of a disputed play or decision, team coaches or captains may consult the game officials. The other players and coaches or sponsors are to be kept out of the discussion.

3. Coaches and players are not to fraternize with spectators while on the playing field. At no time will players be allowed to smoke on the field or on the sidelines.

4. At no time will players be allowed to drink or have in their possession any alcoholic beverage while on the sidelines or on the playing field during the course of any game.

5. Coaches are to report any unsportsmanlike or derogatory acts by players or spectators to the tournament director. The purpose here is to prevent any serious situation developing that would be harmful to the tournament.

6. Coaches, players, sponsors and teams are liable for suspension by not adhering to the tournament rules in effect. This could mean suspension for a game, games, tournament or a longer duration depending on the act of violation.

7. A player, coach, or sponsor may be suspended for fighting, abusive tactics or unbecoming acts that are detrimental and not in the best interest of the United States Flag & Touch Football League and tournament play.

8. Be careful of your conduct. Be sure that no action occurs that could reflect adversely on your sponsor, team or region. Remember that the wrong actions of even one player can reflect upon your entire team and the game of Flag & Touch Football.

9. Any report of destruction of property or abuse of the host hotel or motel property by a U.S.F.T.L. team player during a tournament will be dealt with very sternly. Team coaches and sponsors will not be warned other than through this notice. Failure to pay hotel or motel bills can result in team disbarment from future U.S.F.T.L. play.

10. Any team submitting a bad check to the U.S.F.T.L. will be subject to disbarment.

UNITED STATES FLAG & TOUCH FOOTBALL LEAGUE
U.S.F.T.L. CHANGES FOR 2006-2007

RULE BOOK:
(RULE-SECTION-ARTICLE)

Note: All references to Flag Football are now referred to as Contact Flag Football

2-1-1	Screen Flag Football - Number of players on field.
3-1-1	The Field - Zone Markings
3-1-1	The Field - 4 on 4 and 5 on 5 Field size
4-2-1	Flag Specifications
5-2-3C-1	Extension on Period
5-2-3G	Extension of Period
10-7-4	Next Play after Kick-Off
10-8-2	Next Play after Field Goal
11-1-1F-1	Co-Rec Female - Extra Point - 2 points
11-1-1F-2	Co-Rec Female - Extra Point - 3 points
12-6-1	Batting a Free Ball
12-8-3f	Illegal Participation
12-9-1	Ejection Fee
12-10-1	Last Man Rule
12-11-1	Team Not Leaving Field of Play
13-3-11e	Loss of Down - Flag Guarding
16-1-1c	National Ranking Point Breakdown
16-2-1	National Ranking Point Explanation
16-3-1	Tournament Seeding
16-4-1	Procedure for Changing Division Ranking
18-1-5b	Men's Program - Screen Flag Football - Number of Players on Field
19-1-5b	Women's Program - Screen Flag Football - Number of Players on Field
20-1-9	Co-Rec Scoring
21-1-5b	Youth Program - Screen Flag Football - Number of Players on Field
22-1-5b	Master's Program - Screen Flag Football - Number of Players on Field
23-1-8	4 on 4 Program - Playing Field Size
23-1-9F-1	4 on 4 Program - Co-Rec Female - Extra Point - 2 points
23-1-9F-2	4 on 4 Program - Co-Rec Female - Extra Point - 3 points
23-2-2	4 on 4 Program - The Field
23-2-4A	4 on 4 Program - Scoring and Overtime - Co-Rec Female player
23-2-5C	4 on 4 Program - Running Plays - Laterals
23-2-5G	4 on 4 Program - Running Plays - No Run Zone
23-2-6A	4 on 4 Program - Passing - Backward Passes and Laterals
23-2-11A-8	4 on 4 Program - Penalty Enforcement - Batting the Ball
24-1-5b	Corporate Program - Screen Flag Football - Number of Players on Field
25-1-5b	Church Program - Screen Flag Football - Number of Players on Field
26-1-5b	Armed Forces Program - Screen Flag Football - Number of Players on Field
27-1-5b	Law Enforcement Program - Screen Flag Football - Number of Players on Field
29-1-8	5 on 5 Program - Playing Field Size
29-1-9F-1	5 on 5 Program - Co-Rec Female - Extra Point - 2 points
29-1-9F-2	5 on 5 Program - Co-Rec Female - Extra Point - 3 points
29-2-2	5 on 5 Program - The Field
29-2-4A	5 on 5 Program - Scoring and Overtime - Co-Rec Female player
29-2-4C	5 on 5 Program - Sudden Death Overtime
29-2-5C	5 on 5 Program - Running Plays - Laterals

UNITED STATES FLAG & TOUCH FOOTBALL LEAGUE
U.S.F.T.L. CHANGES FOR 2006-2007

RULE BOOK:
(RULE-SECTION-ARTICLE)

29-2-5F	**5 on 5 Program** - Running Plays - No Run Zone
29-2-6A	**5 on 5 Program** - Passing - Backward Passes and Laterals
29-2-11A-8	**5 on 5 Program** - Penalty Enforcement - Batting the Ball
30-1-1	**Paid Bids** - Paid Bids Chart
30-1-2	**Paid Bids** - Travel Expense Explanation

CONSTITUTION;
(ARTICLE-SECTION)

26-15	**Playing Field** - 4 on 4 and 5 on 5 field dimensions.

U.S.F.T.L. 2008-2009 RULEBOOK

RULE 1 - DEFINITIONS

SECTION 1 - BALL=LIVE, DEAD, LOOSE AND POSSESSION:

ARTICLE 1 - LIVE AND DEAD BALL: A live ball is a ball in play and a dead ball is a ball not in play. A pass, kick, or fumble which has not yet touched the ground is a live ball in flight and therefore recoverable by either team.

ARTICLE 2 - LOOSE BALL: A loose ball is a live ball not in player possession during:
  A. A running play
  B. A scrimmage or free kick before possession is gained, regained, or the ball is dead by rule.
  C. The interval after a legal forward pass is touched, and before it becomes complete, incomplete or intercepted.

ARTICLE 3 - WHEN THE BALL IS READY FOR PLAY. A dead ball is ready for play when the Referee:
  A. If time is in, sounds the whistle and signals "ready for play"
  B. If time is out, sounds the whistle and signals either "start the clock" or "ball ready for play."

ARTICLE 4 - IN POSSESSION: "In possession" is an abbreviation meaning "in possession of a live ball." A player is in possession when he/she is holding or controlling the ball. A team is in possession:
  A. When one of its players is in possession.
  B. While a punt, or place kick is being attempted.
  C. While a forward pass thrown by one of its players is in flight.
  D. When it was last in possession during a loose ball.

SECTION 2 - BLOCKING:

ARTICLE 1 - CONTACT BLOCKING: Contact Blocking is legally hindering the progress of an opponent in a fair and safe manner. Blockers must be on their feet before, during and after contact is made with their opponent. You may not dive to block. 2 on 1 blocking is permitted. Under no conditions shall a high-low block, cross body block, or rolling block be permitted. The blocker is allowed to contact only that portion of the opponent's body between the waist and shoulders. An open hand, straight arm block, within the framework of the blocker's body, is the ideal block to avoid unnecessary rough play. You may not grab the jersey of an opponent while attempting to block. The blocker's hands may not be locked together. The blocker may not swing, throw or flip the elbow or forearm. There shall be no contact of any kind to the head and/or shoulders in the attempt to block an opponent. The main concept to keep contact blocking under control is to stress safe, clean, sportsmanlike contact between opponents.

ARTICLE 2 - SCREEN BLOCKING:

A. Screen blocking is legally obstructing an opponent without contacting his/-her with any part of the screen blocker's body. The offensive screen block shall take place without contact. The screen blocker shall have his/her hands and arms at his/her side or behind his/her back. Any use of the arms, elbows, or legs to initiate contact during an offensive player's screen block is illegal. A blocker may use his/her hand or arm to break a fall or to retain his/her balance. A player must be on his/her feet before, during and after screen blocking.

PENALTY: Personal Foul, 10 yards. (S38).

B. Screen Blocking Fundamentals. A player who screens shall not:
1. When he/she is behind a stationary opponent, take a position closer than a normal step from him or her.
2. When he/she assumes a position at the side or in front of a stationary opponent, make contact with him/her.
3. Take a position so close to a moving opponent that his/her opponent cannot avoid contact by stopping or changing direction. The speed of the player to be screened will determine where the screener may take his/her stationary position. This position will vary and may be 1 or 2 normal steps or strides from the opponent.
4. After assuming him/her legal screening position move to maintain it, unless he/she moves in the same direction and path as his/her opponent. If the screener violates any of these provisions and contact results, he/she has committed a personal foul.

C. Blocking and Interlocked Interference. Teammates of a runner or passer may interfere for hini/her by screen blocking, but shall not use interlocked interference by grasping or encircling one another in any manner.

PENALTY: Personal Foul. 10 yards. (S38).

D. Use of Hands or Arms by the Defense. Defensive players must go around the offensive player's screen block. The arms and hands may not be used as a wedge to contact the opponent. The application of this rule depends entirely on the judgment of the official. A blocker may use his/her arms or hands to break a fall or retain his/her balance.

PENALTY: Personal Foul, 10 yards. (S38).

SECTION 3 - CASH PRIZES:

ARTICLE 1: A "CASH PRIZE" shall mean prizes in cash that are awarded to players or teams based on the final standings of an event. Paid Bids and Travel Expense Monies are not considered "CASH PRIZES."

SECTION 4 - CATCH, INTERCEPTION, RECOVERY, SIMULTANEOUS CATCH & FAIR CATCH:

ARTICLE 1 - CATCH: A catch is an act of establishing player possession of a live ball in flight.
ARTICLE 2 - INTERCEPTION: A catch of an opponents pass or fumble in

flight is an interception.

ARTICLE 3 - LEGAL CATCH OR INTERCEPTION: If a player attempts a catch, interception, or recovery while in the air, the player must contact the ground in bounds with the ball in his/her possession prior to touching out of bounds, unless an opponent's contact causes him/her to first touch out of bounds. Catching is always preceded by touching of the ball: thus, if touching causes the ball to become dead, securing possession of the ball has no significance.
- A. If one foot first lands inbounds and the receiver has possession and control of the ball, it is a catch or interception even though a subsequent step or fall takes the receiver out-of-bounds.
- B. A catch by any kneeling or prone inbounds player is a completion or interception.
- C. A loss of ball simultaneously with returning to the ground is not a catch or interception.
- D. If there is a doubt, the catch, interception or recovery is not valid.

PLAY: A pass from QB A-1 is near the sideline and receiver A-2, moving toward the goal line, leaps and possesses the pass at the 3 yard line. B-1 attempts to intercept the ball and A-2 and B-1 make legal contact with each other so that A-2's first contact with the ground is out-of-bounds at the 3 yard line.

RULING: Completed pass. The contact by B-1 changed the direction of A-2 and forced A-2 out-of-bounds. A-2 would have landed inbounds if the contact had not occurred.

ARTICLE 4 - RECOVERY: Securing possession of a live ball after a fumble is "recovering" it. If a fumble hits the ground, the ball is dead at the spot, with no "recovery" possible. If a fumble is caught in the air, the ball remains a live ball, and is "recoverable". A punt or free kick following a safety is considered dead when it strikes the ground after a player touches the ball beyond the line of scrimmage. The ball then becomes a dead ball, belonging to the recovering team.

ARTICLE 5 - SIMULTANEOUS CATCH: A catch in which there is joint possession of a live ball by opposing players inbounds. On a simultaneous catch, possession goes to the offense.

ARTICLE 6 - FAIR CATCH (LEGAL): A fair catch is a catch of a free or protected scrimmage kick (punt), which is beyond the scrimmage line, by a player of the receiving team. The player must signal intention by extending one arm above his head and waving it laterally from side to side more than once.

ARTICLE 7 - FAIR CATCH (ILLEGAL): An Illegal Fair Catch signal is any signal given by a runner:
- A. After the kick has been caught;
- B. After the kick has been recovered.

ARTICLE 8 - FAIR CATCH (INVALID): An Invalid Fair Catch Signal is any signal by a receiver before the kick is caught or recovered:
- A. That does not meet the requirements of a valid signal.
- B. After the kick has touched a receiver.
- C. After the kick has touched the ground.

SECTION 5 - CLIPPING:

ARTICLE 1 - CLIPPING: Clipping is running or diving into the back, or throwing or dropping the body across the back of the leg or legs of an opponent or pushing an opponent in the back.

SECTION 6 - CONTACT BLOCKING:

ARTICLE 1 - CONTACT BLOCKING: Contact blocking is legally hindering the progress of an opponent in a fair and safe manner. Blockers must be on their feet before, during and after contact is made with their opponent.

SECTION 7 - DEFLAGGING:

ARTICLE 1: Deflagging is the legal removal of a flag from an opponent in possession of the ball. Pushing, striking, holding, slapping, or tripping when attempting to pull a flag is not permitted. Defensive players may leave their feet to pull a flag. Offensive players are not permitted to protect or guard their flags.

SECTION 8 - DOWN AND BETWEEN DOWNS:

ARTICLE 1: A down is a unit of the game which starts, after the ball is ready for play, with a snap or free kick and ends when the ball next becomes dead. Between downs is the interval during which the ball is dead.

SECTION 9 - ENCROACHMENT:

ARTICLE 1: Encroachment denotes the position of a player, except the snapper or the kicker, who is illegally beyond their line of scrimmage.

SECTION 10 - FOUL:

ARTICLE 1: A foul is a rule infraction for which a penalty is prescribed.

SECTION 11 - FUMBLE, MUFF, BATTING, TOUCHING BALL:

ARTICLE 1 - FUMBLE: A fumble is loss of player-possession other than by handing off, passing or kicking the ball that is still in the air and has not hit the ground. A fumble which hits the ground is immediately considered dead.

ARTICLE 2 - MUFF: A muff is an unsuccessful attempt to catch or recover a ball, the ball being touched in the attempt. All muffs which then strike the ground are dead.

ARTICLE 3 - BATTING: Batting is intentionally striking or slapping with the hand or arm:
A. A loose ball.
B. A ball in player possession by a player of the team in possession.

ARTICLE 4 - TOUCHING THE BALL: Touching refers to any contact with the ball.

SECTION 12 - GOAL LINES:

ARTICLE 1: Each goal line is a vertical plane separating the end zone from the field of play.

SECTION 13 - HANDING THE BALL:

ARTICLE 1: Handing the ball is transferring player possession from one teammate to another without throwing or kicking it.

SECTION 14 - HUDDLE:

ARTICLE 1: A huddle is two or more offensive players grouped together after the ball is ready for play and before assuming scrimmage formation prior to the snap.

SECTION 15 - HURDLING:

ARTICLE 1: Hurdling is an attempt by a player to jump over another player.

SECTION 16 - KICKS:

ARTICLE 1 - FIELD GOAL: A field goal must be a place kick. A field goal, if successful, is worth 3 points.

ARTICLE 2 - FREE KICK: A free kick is a kick made under restrictions which prohibit either teams from advancing beyond established restraining lines until the ball is kicked.

EXAMPLE: Kick-off following a field goal, touchdown or after a safety.

ARTICLE 3 - KICKER: The kicker is any player who punts, or place kicks. The kicker is a runner until he/she actually kicks the ball. Players of his/her team are known as kickers and any opponent is a receiver.

ARTICLE 4 - KICKOFF: A Kickoff is a free kick which starts each half and follows each try-for-point, safety, or field goal. A kickoff following a try-for-point must be a place kick. A kickoff following a field goal must be a place kick. A kick-off following a safety may be a place kick or a punt. The ball is dead as soon as it contacts a player and then touches the ground.

ARTICLE 5 - LEGAL AND ILLEGAL KICKS: A legal kick is a punt or place kick by a player of the team in possession when such a kick is permitted by rule. Kicking the ball in any other manner is illegal. Any kick continues to be a kick until it is caught or recovered by a player or becomes dead.

ARTICLE 6 - PLACE KICK: A place kick is kicking the ball from a fixed position either on the ground or on a tee. The ball may be held in position by any player of the kicking team. If a tee is used it may not elevate the ball's lowest point more than two inches above the ground.

ARTICLE 7 - PROTECTED SCRIMMAGE KICK: A protected scrimmage kick is made by Team A under restrictions which prohibits either team from advancing beyond their scrimmage lines until the ball is kicked. A protected scrimmage kick must be a punt.

ARTICLE 8 - PUNT: A punt is kicking the ball by the player who drops it and kicks it before it strikes the ground.

SECTION 17 - LOSS OF A DOWN:

ARTICLE 1: "Loss of a down" is an abbreviation meaning: "loss of the right to repeat the down."

SECTION 18 - NEUTRAL ZONE:

ARTICLE 1: The neutral zone is the space between the two free kick lines during a free kick and on the line of scrimmage during a scrimmage down and is established when the ball is ready for play.

SECTION 19 - PASSER:

ARTICLE 1 - PASSING: Passing the ball is throwing it. In a pass, the ball travels in flight. A pass continues to be a pass until caught, intercepted, or the ball becomes dead. The initial direction determines whether a pass is forward or backward.

ARTICLE 2 - FORWARD AND BACKWARD PASS: A forward pass is a live ball thrown towards the opponent's end line. A backward pass is a live ball thrown toward or parallel to the passer's end line. A pass continues to be a pass until it is caught or strikes the ground. A backward pass that hits the ground is ruled the same as a fumble. It will be dead at the spot where it strikes the ground.

SECTION 20 - PENALTY:

ARTICLE 1: A penalty is a loss imposed by Rule upon a team which has comniitted a foul.

SECTION 21 - PROFESSIONAL FOOTBALL PLAYERS (FLAG, TOUCH OR TACKLE FOOTBALL):

ARTICLE 1 - If a player participates in an event that gives away cash as prizes, they are considered "PROFESSIONAL." Travel Expense Monies and Paid Bids are not considered Cash Prizes.

SECTION 22 - REMOVING THE FLAG-

ARTICLE 1 - FLAG REMOVAL: When the flag is clearly taken from the runner the down shall end and the ball is declared dead. A player who removes the flag ftom the runner should immediately hold the flag above his/her head to assist the official in locating the spot where the capture occurred. If a flag inadvertently falls to the ground, a two hand tag between the shoulders and knees constitutes capture. A player who removes the flag may leave his/her feet.

ARTICLE 2 - CONTACT: In an attempt to remove a flag from a ball carrier, defensive players may contact the body and shoulders of an opponent with their hands, but not their face or any part of their neck or head. A defensive player may not hold, push, or knock the ball carrier down in an attempt to remove the flag.

ARTICLE 3 - DROPPED FLAG: The flag may be dropped at the spot of capture by the defense with no penalty.

SECTION 23 - SCREEN BLOCKING:

ARTICLE 1: Very simply, screen is football with no contact. It is a very fast moving, aerobic style game, ideally suited for the fitness wave of the future.

SECTION 24 - SCRIMMAGE:

ARTICLE 1 - SCRIMMAGE: A scrimmage is the interplay of the two teams during a down in which play begins with a snap and ends when the ball next becomes dead.

ARTICLE 2 - SCRIMMAGE LINE: The scrimmage line for each team is the yard line and its vertical plane which passes through the point of the ball nearest its own goal line. To be on the line of scrimmage an offensive lineman's head must break the plane of the line drawn through the waistline of the snapper

ARTICLE 3 - BACKFIELD LINE: To be legally in the backfield a Team A player's head must not break the plane of the line drawn through the waistline of the nearest Team A player, except the snapper, on the line of scrimmage.

SECTION 25 - SHIFT:

ARTICLE 1: A shift is the action of one or more offensive players who, after a huddle or after taking set positions, moves to a new set position before the ensuing snap.

SECTION 26 - SNAPPING THE BALL:

ARTICLE 1: Snapping the ball (a snap) is handling or passing it back from the position on the ground through the legs. In a legal snap, the movements must be a quick and continuous motion of the hand or hands during which the ball actually leaves the hand or hands. The long axis of the ball must be at right angles to the scrimmage line.

SECTION 27 - SPOTS:

ARTICLE 1 - DEAD BALL SPOT: The dead ball spot is the point at which the ball last became dead.

ARTICLE 2 - ENFORCEMENT SPOT: An enforcement spot is the point from which the penalty for a foul is enforced.

ARTICLE 3 - INBOUNDS SPOT: The inbounds spot is the intersection of the nearer inbounds line and the yard-line passing through the dead ball spot, or the spot where the ball is left in a side zone by a penalty.

ARTICLE 4 - OUT-OF-BOUNDS SPOT: The out-of-bounds spot is the point at which the ball becomes dead because of going or being declared out-of-bounds.

ARTICLE 5 - PREVIOUS SPOT: The previous spot is the point from which the ball was last put in play.

ARTICLE 6 - SPOT OF THE FOUL: The spot of the foul is the point at which that foul occurs. If out-of-bounds between the goal lines it shall be the intersection of the nearer inbounds line and the yard-line extended through the spot of the foul.

ARTICLE 7 - SUCCEEDING SPOT: The succeeding spot, as related to a foul, is the point at which the ball would have been put in play if that foul had not occurred.

SECTION 28 - TEAM AND PLAYER DESIGNATIONS:

ARTICLE 1 - BALL CARRIER: The ball carrier is a player in possession of a live ball. Once a player catches or intercepts a pass, he/she becomes a ball carrier.

ARTICLE 2 - DISQUALIFIED PLAYER: A disqualified player is one who becomes ineligible from further participation in the game.

ARTICLE 3 - KICKER: The kicker is any player who makes a punt, or place kick. The kicker is a runner until he/she actually kicks the ball.

ARTICLE 4 - LINEMAN AND BACKFIELDMAN: A lineman is any player on his/her scrimmage line when the ball is snapped; a back is any player who is legally behind that line when the ball is snapped.

ARTICLE 5 - OFFENSIVE AND DEFENSIVE TEAM: The offensive team is the team in possession, of the team to which the ball belongs, the defensive team is the opposing team.

ARTICLE 6 - PASSER: The passer is the player who has thrown a legal forward pass. He/she remains the passer while the ball is in flight.

ARTICLE 7 - PLAYER: A player is any one of the participants in the game at any particular time.

ARTICLE 8 - SNAPPER: The snapper is the player who snaps the ball.

ARTICLE 9 - SUBSTITUTE: A substitute is a replacement for a player or a player vacancy.

ARTICLE 10 - TEAM A AND B: Team A is the team which puts the ball in play. The opponent of Team A is Team B. A player of Team A is A-1 and teammates are A-2 and A-3. Other abbreviations are B-1 for a player of Team B, K-1 for a player of the kicking team and R-1 for a player of the receiving team.

SECTION 29 - TOUCHING:

ARTICLE 1: Touching is a simultaneous placing of both hands anywhere between the shoulders and knees of an opponent, with the ball. This includes the ball in ball-carrier possession. The feet of the toucher may leave the ground to make a touch. Pushing, striking, slapping and holding are not permitted. If the player trips the ball carrier in his/her attempt to make a diving tag, it is a penalty.

SECTION 30 - TRIPPING:

ARTICLE 1: Tripping is using the lower leg, foot, or arm extended in an obvious manner to obstruct an opponent (including the ball carrier) below the knees.

SECTION 31 - YARD LINE:

ARTICLE 1: A yard line is a line in the field of play parallel to the end line and between the goal lines.

SECTION 32 - ZONE-LINE-TO-GAIN:

ARTICLE 1: The zone line to gain is the next line on the playing field in the direction of, and parallel to, the opponents goal line. The down box shall be stationed at the zone line to gain.

RULE 2 - THE GAMES

SECTION 1 - THE TYPE OF GAMES PLAYED (OFFERED):

ARTICLE 1 - CONTACT FLAG FOOTBALL: The game of Contact Flag Football shall be played between 2 teams of 8 players each. 6 players are required to avoid a forfeit. The type of blocking that is used shall be contact blocking. All players shall be eligible receivers. The game of Contact Flag Football shall be offered to men, women, co-rec and youth. In the men, women, and co-rec Contact Flag Football Programs, competition classification of SUPER, A, B, C & D shall be offered. In the youth program, boys and/or girls will be offered Contact Flag Football programs in the following age classification: 6 & under, 8 & under, 10 & under, 12 & under, 14 & under, 16 & under and 18 & under. The adult age classifications shall be 2 types: 18 & Over and 35 & Over. The game of Contact Flag Football shall use the scoring system found in Rule 11 of this book. The game of Contact Flag Football shall use a Licensed Football of the U.S.F.T.L., with men using the regular size ball and the women and youth using any size ball - regular, intermediate, junior or youth. The game of Contact Flag Football shall use a Licensed Flag of the U.S.F.T.L. The game of Contact Flag Football shall be played on the regular size field (53 1/3yd x 100yd) or the abbreviated size field (40yd x

80yd). Any playing rule not specifically covered in Rule 2, Section 1, Article 1 - Contact Flag Football, of this book, shall be governed by the other rules as outlined in Rules 1 through 17 of this book.

ARTICLE 2 - SCREEN FLAG FOOTBALL: The game of Screen Flag Football shall be played between 2 teams of 7 players each. 5 players are required to avoid a forfeit. The type of blocking that is used shall be screen blocking. All players shall be eligible receivers. The game of Screen Flag Football shall be offered to men, women, co-rec and youth. In the men, women and co-rec Screen Flag Football Programs, competition classifications of SUPER, A, B, C & D shall be offered. In the youth program, boys and/or girls will be offered Screen Flag Football programs in the following age classifications: 6 & under, 8 & under, 10 & under, 12 & under, 14 & under, 16 & under and 18 & under. The adult age classifications shall be 2 types: 18 & over and 35 & over. The game of Screen Flag Football shall use the scoring system found in Rule 11 of this book. The game of Screen Flag Football shall use a Licensed Football of the U.S.F.T.L., with men using the regular size ball and women and youth using any size ball - regular, intermediate, junior or youth. The game of Screen Flag Football shall use a Licensed Flag of the U.S.F.T.L. The game of Screen Flag Football shall be played on the regular size field (53 1/3yd x 100yd) or the abbreviated size field (40yd x 80yd). Any playing rule not specifically covered in Rule 2, Section 1, Article 2 - Screen Flag Football, of this book, shall be governed by the other rules as outlined in Rules 1 through 17 of this book.

ARTICLE 3 - INELIGIBLE LINEMAN FLAG FOOTBALL: The game of Ineligible Lineman Flag Football shall be played between 2 teams of 9 players each. 7 players are required to avoid a forfeit. The type of blocking that is used shall be contact blocking. The center and the 2 players on either side of the center, (guards) are ineligible to receive a forward pass or run with the ball. All other players are eligible to receive. The game of Ineligible Lineman Flag Football shall be offered to men, women, co-rec and youth. In the men, women and co-rec Ineligible Lineman Flag Football Programs, competition classifications of SUPER, A, B, C & D shall be offered. In the youth program, boys and/or girls will be offered Ineligible Lineman Flag Football progrwns in the following age classifications: 6 & under, 8 & under, 10 & under, 12 & under, 14 & under, 16 & under and 18 & under. The adult age classifications shall be 2 types: 18 & over and 35 & over. The game of Ineligible Lineman Flag Football shall use the scoring system found in Rule I I of this book. The game of Ineligible Lineman Flag Football shall use a Licensed Football of the U.S.F.T.L., with men using the regular size ball and women and youth using any size ball - regular, intermediate, junior or youth. The game of Ineligible Lineman Flag Football shall use a Licensed Flag of the U.S.F.T.L. The game of Ineligible Lineman Flag Football shall be played on the regular size field (53 1/3yd x 100yd) or the abbreviated size field (40yd x 80yd). Any playing rule not specifically covered in Rule 2, Section 1, Article 3 -Ineligible Lineman Flag Football, of this book, shall be governed by the other rules as outlined in Rules 1 through 17 of this book.

ARTICLE 4 - TOUCH FOOTBALL: The game of Touch Football shall be played between 2 teams of 7 players each. 5 players are required to avoid a forfeit. The type of blocking that is used shall be contact blocking. All players shall be eligible receivers. The game of Touch Football shall be offered to men, women, co-rec and youth. In the men, women and co-rec Touch Football Programs, competition classifications of SUPER, A, B, C & D shall be offered. In the youth program, boys and/or girls will be offered Touch Football programs in the following age classifications: 6 & under, 8 & under, 10 & under, 12 & under, 14 & under, 16 & under and 18 & under. The adult age classifications shall be 2 types: 18 & over and 35 & over. The game of Touch Football shall use the scoring system found in Rule 11 of this book. The game of Touch Football shall use a Licensed Football of the U.S.F.T.L., with men using the regular size ball and women and youth using any size ball - regular, intermediate, junior or youth. The game of Touch Football shall be played on the regular size field (53 1/3yd x 100yd) or the abbreviated size field (40yd x 80yd). Any playing rule not specifically covered in Rule 2, Section 1, Article 4 - Touch Football, of this book, shall be governed by the other rules as outlined in Rules 1 through 17 of this book.

SECTION 2 - GENERAL PROVISIONS:

ARTICLE 1 - SUPERVISION: The game shall be played under the supervision of 2 to 4 officials. The officials are: Referee, Line Judge, Back Judge and Field Judge. In U.S.F.T.L. Championship Games of Leagues and Tournaments, 3 or 4 officials are recommended. Positions and responsibilities for each official can be found in the U.S.F.T.L. Official's Manual.

ARTICLE 2 - TEAM CAPTAINS: Each coach shall designate to the Referee the team captain or captains. If more than one player is designated, a speaking captain must be selected to make all decisions. The captain's first choice of any penalty option shall be irrevocable. Decisions involving penalties shall be made before any charged time-out is granted to either team.

ARTICLE 3 - PERSONS SUBJECT TO THE RULES: Team representatives, including players, substitutes, replaced players, coaches, trainers, and other persons affiliated with the team are subject to the rules of the game, and shall be governed by decisions of officials assigned to the game.

ARTICLE 4 - WINNING TEAM: The teams shall be awarded points for scoring according to Rule 11 and unless the game is forfeited; the team having the larger score at the end of the game shall be the winning team.

ARTICLE 5 - GOAL LINES: Goal lines for each team shall be established at opposite ends of the field, and each team shall be allowed the opportunity to advance the ball across their opponent's goal line by running, passing, or kicking it on a field with goal posts.

ARTICLE 6 - NUMBER OF PLAYERS NEEDED TO AVOID A FORFEIT: The number of players that needed to start a game to avoid a forfeit shall be:

2 Man Team -	2 players needed to avoid forfeit
3 Man Team -	2 players needed to avoid forfeit
4 Man Team -	2 players needed to avoid forfeit
5 Man Team -	3 players needed to avoid forfeit
6 Man Team -	4 players needed to avoid forfeit
7 Man Team -	5 players needed to avoid forfeit
8 Man Team -	6 players needed to avoid forfeit
9 Man Team -	7 players needed to avoid forfeit
10 Man Team -	8 players needed to avoid forfeit
11 Man Team -	9 players needed to avoid forfeit

ARTICLE 7 - ROSTERS: 30 players per team. **EXCEPTION:** 10 players per team in 5 on 5 Program. 8 players per team in 4 on 4 Program.

ARTICLE 8 - CLASSIFICATION OF TEAMS: When a team wins a State or National Championship in a particular division, they must move up a division the following year. **EXAMPLE:** Class "D" Champions move to Class "C"; Class "C" Champions move to Class "B"; Class "B" Champions move to Class "A".

RULE 3 - THE PLAYING FIELDS

SECTION 1 - THE FIELD:

ARTICLE 1 - ZONE MARKINGS: The field shall be a rectangular area with lines and zones shown in the accompanying diagram. However, in case of facility limitations, distances of field length and width can be modified. The width of the field should be lined at 20 yard intervals from goal line to goal line. These zone markings may be changed according to field dimensions. There shall be one inbounds hash mark dividing the field into halves. The hash mark shall run parallel with each sideline. The 3, 5 and 10 yard try-for-point lines shall be 1 yard wide. The regulation field shall be 100 yards long and 53 1/3 yards wide with 10 yard end zones. The abbreviated field size shall be 80 yards long and 40 yards wide with 10 yard end zones. The 4 on 4 field size and the 5 on 5 field size shall be 46 yards long and 25 yards wide with 7 yard end zones. Indoor fields vary by facility limitations.

ARTICLE 2 - TEAM AREA: On each side of the field a team area is designated for the teams, coaches, and authorized team attendants. This team area shall be located 2 yards from the sideline and between the 20 yard lines. When the playing area is modified, so should the team area. If teams cannot agree on a sideline, the Referee will conduct a coin toss.

ARTICLE 3 - INBOUNDS/OUT-OF-BOUNDS: The lines bounding the sidelines and the end zones are out-of-bounds in their entirety, and the inbounds area is bound by the lines. The entire width of each goal shall be a part of the end zone.

ARTICLE 4 - GOAL POSTS: Each goal shall consist of two uprights, extended 20 ft above the ground and 23 feet 4 inches apart, measured inside to inside and no more than 24 feet apart measured outside to outside. The two uprights shall be connected by a horizontal bar, the top of which is 10 feet above the ground.

ARTICLE 5 - BALL SPOTTER: A spotter is used to mark the line of scrimmage.

ARTICLE 6 - DOWN MARKER: A down marker shall be used to indicate the number of the down and placed at the zone line-to-gain. It shall be positioned 2 yards out-of-bounds and operated under the jurisdiction of the Line Judge for 3 and 4 person crews and the referee for a 2 person crew.

ARTICLE 7 - PYLONS: Soft, flexible pylons shall be placed at the inside corner of each of the intersections of the sideline with the goal lines and the end lines, and at the intersections of the end lines and inbounds line extended, and at the middle of the end line.

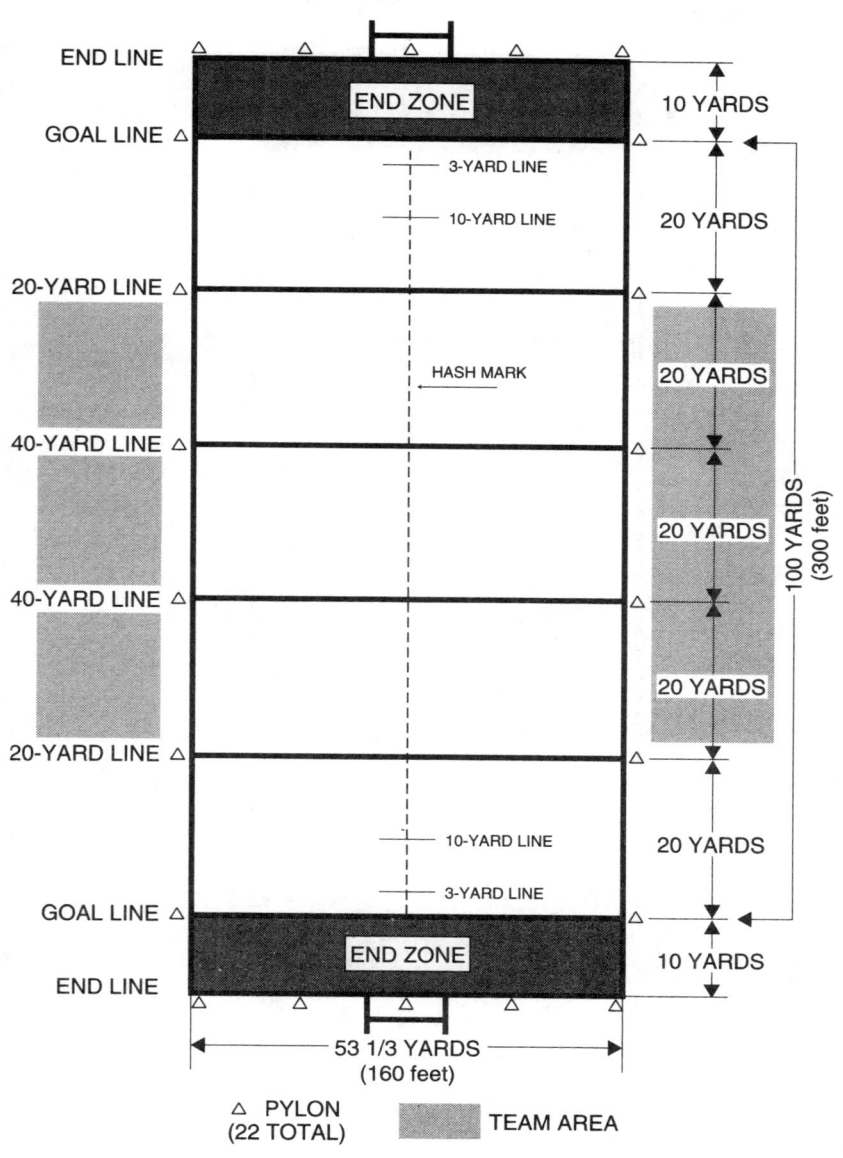

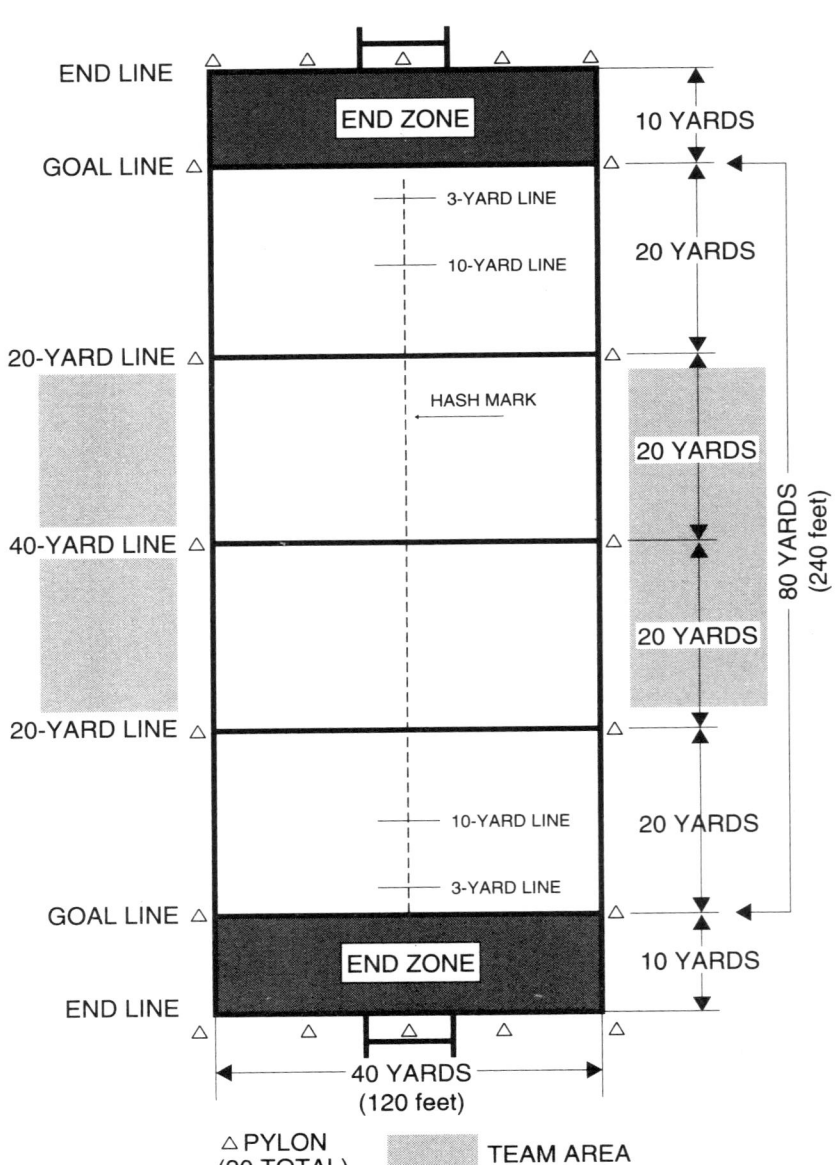

4 ON 4 FIELD/5 ON 5 FIELD

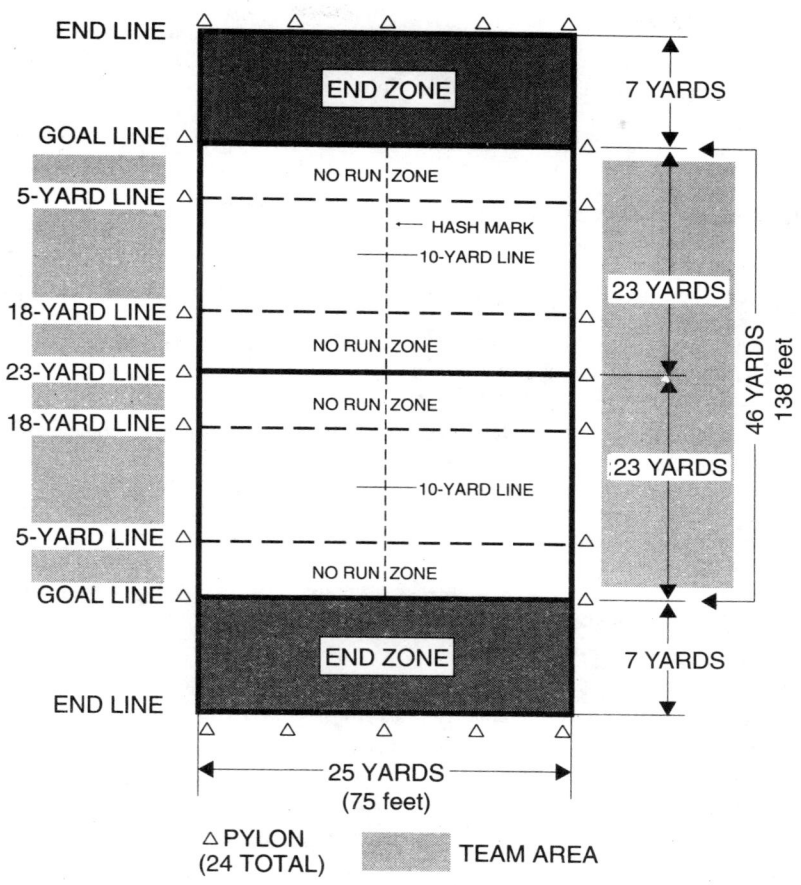

RULE 4 - EQUIPMENT

SECTION 1 - THE BALL:

ARTICLE 1 - SPECIFICATIONS: The official ball shall be pebble-grained leather or rubber covered and shall meet the recommendations of size and shape for a regulation football. There are no requirements regarding ball pressure and markings. Men shall use the regular size while women and youth may use any size ball (regular, intermediate, junior or youth size). The regular, intermediate, junior or youth size football shall be used for Co-recreational games.

Size	Length	Short Circumference	Long Circumference	Weight
1) Youth	9 1/2" to 10"	17 3/4" to 18"	23 7/8" to 24 1/8"	9 1/2 oz. to 10 1/2 oz.
2) Junior	9 1/2" to 10 1/2"	18" to 19"	25" to 26"	11 oz. to 13 oz.
3) Intermediate	10" to 11"	19" to 20"	26" to 27"	12 oz. to 14 oz.
4) Regular	10 7/8" to 11 7/16"	20 3/4" to 21 1/4"	27 3/4" to 28 1/2"	14 oz. to 15 oz.

ARTICLE 2 - ADMINISTRATION:

a) The Tournament Director or League Director shall specify a U.S.F.T.L. Licensed Football for play.

b) The Referee shall enforce any Licensed ball offered for play and may change the ball during play at his or her discretion. During the game each team must use a legal ball of its choice when in possession.

ARTICLE 3 - LICENSED FOOTBALL: U.S.F.T.L. Licensed Footballs displaying the U.S.F.T.L. approval and logo must be used in all U.S.F.T.L. Tournaments. Approval of footballs to be used as Officially Required Footballs in the U.S.F.T.L. program must be made by executing an Official Licensing and Royalties Agreement, prepared by the U.S.F.T.L. Legal Counsel, and signed by the U.S.F.T.L.'s Executive Director. All Licensed balls shall be voted upon by a majority vote of the Executive Board of Directors at the National Meeting. The description and dimensions shall appear in the U.S.F.T.L. Rule Book.

SECTION 2 - THE FLAGS:

ARTICLE 1 - SPECIFICATIONS: The flags should be a minimum of 1.5 inches wide and 14 inches long. The flags must be of a contrasting color to their opponents' flags. The flags may not be altered in any way. The flags must be of a contrasting color to the players pants or shorts.

ARTICLE 2 - ADMINISTRATION:

a) The Tournament Director or League Director shall specify a U.S.F.T.L. Licensed Flag for play.

b) The Referee shall enforce any Licensed Flag used, and may require a player to change flags at his or her discretion.

ARTICLE 3 - LICENSED FLAG BELTS: U.S.F.T.L. Licensed Flag Belt displaying the U.S.F.T.L. approval and logo must be used in all U.S.F.T.L. Tournaments. Approval of flag belts to be used as Officially Licensed Flag Belts in the U.S.F.T.L. program must be made by executing an Official Licensing and Royalties Agreement, prepared by the U.S.F.T.L.'s Legal Counsel and signed by the U.S.F.T.L. Executive Director. All Licensed Flag Belts shall be voted upon by a majority vote of the Executive Board of Directors at the National Meeting. The description and dimensions shall appear in the U.S.F.T.L. Rule Book.

SECTION 3 - PLAYER EQUIPMENT REQUIRED:

ARTICLE 1 - JERSEY: Players of opposing teams must wear contrasting colored jerseys, numbered on the front and rear. Jerseys must be tucked into pants or shorts, no waist-length jerseys or shimmel length jerseys allowed. The visiting team is responsible for avoidance of similarity of colors, but if there is doubt, the Referee may request the home team to change.

ARTICLE 2 - PANTS/SHORTS: Each player must wear pants or shorts. The pants or shorts must be a different color than the flags.

ARTICLE 3 - SHOES: Each player must wear shoes. They must be made of soft, pliable upper material (canvas, leather, or synthetic) which covers the foot. A one piece molded bottom type of shoe is allowed. Screw-in cleats are allowed if the screw is part of the cleat.

SECTION 4 - PLAYER EQUIPMENT OPTIONAL:

ARTICLE 1 - HEADWEAR: Any type of hat is allowed, as long as there is no hard, unyielding material in it's composition. Baseball style hats with bills must be turned around, facing backwards, to be legal.

ARTICLE 2 - PADS: No pads are allowed to be worn on the upper body. Players may wear soft, pliable pads on the leg, knee and/or ankle. Women players may wear breast protectors as long as they are made from a soft pliable material. Decisions on pads to protect injuries shall be left up to the discretion of the Referee.

ARTICLE 3 - ACE BANDAGE: Players may use an ace bandage no more than two turns thick in any given area. It can be anchored at each end by tape not to exceed two turns.

ARTICLE 4 - MOUTH AND TOOTH PROTECTOR: It is MANDATORY that a mouth piece be worn by all players.

ARTICLE 5 - GLOVES: Players may wear gloves which must consist of a soft, pliable and nonabrasive material.

ARTICLE 6 - STICK-UM: Spray stick-um is acceptable. Paste stick-um is illegal.

SECTION 5 - PLAYER EQUIPMENT ILLEGAL:

ARTICLE 1: A player wearing illegal equipment shall not be permitted to play. This applies to any equipment which, in the opinion of the Referee, is dangerous or confusing. Types of equipment or substances which shall always be declared illegal include:

A. Headgear containing any hard, unyielding material.
B. Jewelry.
C. Pads or braces worn above the waist.
D. Shoes with metal, ceramic, screw-in, or detachable cleats.

EXCEPTION: Screw-in cleats are allowed if the screw is part of the cleat.
E. Shirts or jerseys which do not remain tucked in.
F. Leg and knee braces made of hard, unyielding material, unless covered on both sides and all edges overlapped, and any other hard substance is covered with at least 1/2 inch of closed cell slow recovery rubber or other material of similar thickness and physical properties.
G. Any slippery or sticky foreign substance on any equipment or exposed part

of the body.

EXCEPTION: Spray stick-um is allowed.

H. Eyewear: Sunglasses are illegal. Only prescription glasses or prescription sunglasses are legal. Clear, protective eyeguards/goggles are legal. They may not be dark or tinted.

SECTION 6 - PLAYER EQUIPMENT MISSING OR ILLEGAL:

ARTICLE 1: When any required player equipment is missing or when illegal equipment is found on any incoming substitute or player, correction must be made before participation. An official's time-out shall be declared to permit prompt repair of equipment which becomes illegal or defective through use.

PLAY: A-1 breaks the huddle not wearing a flag belt or the jersey is untucked as the 25 second count is running: (a) The Referee informs A-1 of the problem and as A-1 secures a flag belt or tucks in the jersey the 25 second count expires; or (b) the Referee points out the problem to A-1 who refuses to acquire a flag belt or tuck in the jersey; or (c) the Referee does not see A-1 without a flag belt as the ball is snapped and A-1 advances 35 yards before tagged by B-4.

RULING: In (a), penalize A for delay of game, In (b), penalize A for unsportsmanlike conduct. In (c), B can take the result of the play or penalize A 5 yards from the previous spot for not wearing required equipment.

RULE 5 - PERIODS, TIME FACTORS AND OVERTIME

SECTION 1 - THE START OF EACH PERIOD:

ARTICLE 1 - COIN TOSS: Each half shall start with a kickoff. Three minutes before the start of the game, the Referee shall toss a coin in the presence of the opposing Field Captains, after first designating which captain shall call the fall of the coin.

A. The captain winning the toss shall choose one of the following options:
  1. to kickoff,
  2. to receive,
  3. to designate which goal his/her team will defend,
  4. to defer choice to the 2nd half.

B. The loser of the toss shall make a choice of the remaining options.

C. Before the start of the second half, the choice of options shall be reversed.

ARTICLE 2 - FORFEIT TIME: Game time is forfeit time.

SECTION 2 - GAME TIME:

ARTICLE 1 - PLAYING TIME AND INTERMISSIONS: Playing time shall be 48 minutes, divided into two halves of 24 minutes each. The intermission between halves shall be 1 minute. When overtime is used, there will be a 1 minute intermission.

ARTICLE 2 - SHORTENING PERIOD: Before the start of the game, if darkness threatens, playing time may be shortened by mutual agreement of the field captains and the Referee. Anytime during the game, the playing time of any remaining period(s) may be shortened by mutual agreement of the opposing captains and the Referee.

ARTICLE 3 - EXTENSION OF PERIOD: A half may be extended by an

untimed down only when during the last timed down, one of the following occurred:
- A. If a touchdown was scored, the try-for-point is attempted as a part of the same half.
- B. If there was an inadvertent whistle and the down is to be replayed, the down must be replayed as part of that half.
- C. If there was a foul by either team, and the penalty is accepted.
  1. In the judgement of the Official, if the penalty is an illegal forward pass or lateral to achieve an extra play at the end of the half or game, the game shall be over.
- D. If there was fair catch interference and (1) if the offended team accepts an awarded fair catch, the half may be extended and the ball put in play by a free-kick or a snap or if this occurs at the end of the half, the offended team may choose to start the next quarter by a free-kick or a snap; or (2) if the offended team accepts the distance penalty, the half must be extended and down replayed.
- E. If there was a deliberate foul by the kicking team and the penalty is not declined, the half must be extended.
- F. If there was a double foul. If in (b), (c), (d), (e) or (f) there was an inadvertent whistle, or a foul by the defense only, or fair catch interference during the untimed down, the outlined procedure is repeated.
- G. In the judgement of the Official, if the Team with possession of the ball tries to extend the period with no time left on the clock and commits a penalty during a live ball play, the period shall end.

ARTICLE 4 - GAME TIMER: Playing time shall be kept on a football timer operated by the Referee and or on a scoreboard field clock, operated by a designated timer, under the supervision of the Referee.

ARTICLE 5 - FIRST 22 MINUTES OF EACH HALF: The clock will start when the kickoff is legally touched. It will run continuously for the first 22 minutes of each half unless it is stopped for a:
- A. Team time-out: starts on the snap.
- B. Referee's time-out: starts on the ready for play.

ARTICLE 6 - TWO MINUTE WARNING: With 2 minutes remaining in each half, the Referee shall stop the clock and inform both captains of the playing time remaining in the half. The clock starts on the snap. The Referee will announce to the captains the remaining time and status of the clock whenever it is stopped or when it is requested during the final 2 minutes of each half.

ARTICLE 7 - LAST 2 MINUTES: During the final 2 minutes of each half, the clock will stop for:
- A. Incomplete pass - starts on the snap.
- B. Out-of-Bounds - starts on the snap.
- C. Score (touchdown, field goal or safety) - starts when the kickoff is legally touched, other than by the kicker.
- D. Team time-out - starts on the snap.
- E. First down - dependent on the previous play.
- F. Fair catch or an awarded fair catch - starts on the snap.
- G. Penalty and administration - dependent on the previous play.

EXCEPTION: Delay of game - starts on the snap.

- H. Referee's time-out - starts at his/her discretion.

I. Touchback - starts on the snap.
J. Change of possession - dependent on the previous play.
K. Team attempting to conserve time illegally - starts on the ready.
L. Team attempting to consume time illegally - starts on the snap.
M. Inadvertent Whistle - starts on the ready.

PLAY: Inside the final two minutes of the second half, A-1: a) advances the ball across the zone line-to-gain and runs five more yards and guards his/her flag before going out of bounds; or b) advances the ball across the zone line-to-gain and is deflagged inbounds.

RULING: In (a), the clock stops for the out-of-bounds and will start on the snap regardless of whether or not the penalty is accepted. In (b), the clock stops for the first down and will start when the Referee marks the ball ready-for-play.

ARTICLE 8 - CORRECT TIMING ERRORS: The Referee shall have authority to correct obvious timing errors if discovery is prior to the second live ball following the error unless the period has officially ended.

ARTICLE 9 - ENDING OF PERIOD: Following delay to insure that:
A. No foul has occurred.
B. No obvious timing error has occurred.
C. No request for a Coach-Referee conference has occurred.
D. No other irregularity has occurred.

The Referee shall hold the ball in one hand overhead to indicate the period has officially ended. (S14).

SECTION 3 - TIME OUTS:

ARTICLE 1 - HOW CHARGED: The Referee shall declare a time-out when he/she suspends play for any reason. Each time-out shall be charged either to the Referee or one of the teams.

ARTICLE 2 - OFFICIAL'S TIME-OUT: The Referee shall declare an official's time-out whenever a touchdown, field goal, touchback, or safety is made within the last 2 minutes of each half; when an excess time-out is allowed or when the game clock is stopped to complete a penalty.

ARTICLE 3 - DISCRETIONARY TIME-OUT. The Referee may declare an official's time-out for any contingency not covered elsewhere by the rules. If a time-out is for repair or replacement of player equipment which becomes illegal through play and is considered dangerous to other players, the Referee shall charge himself/herself. The Referee shall charge himself/herself when an injured player is designated.

ARTICLE 4 - CHARGED TIME-OUTS: Each team is entitled to 3 charged timeouts during each half. Successive charged time-outs may be granted each team during a dead ball period. If the ball is dead and a team has not exhausted its charged time-outs, the Referee shall allow a time-out and charge that team. A team is entitled to only 2 time-outs during the last two minutes of each half.

ARTICLE 5 - LENGTH OF TIME-OUTS: A charged time-out requested by any player shall not exceed 30 seconds. Other time-outs may be longer only if the Referee deems it necessary to remove an injured player.

ARTICLE 6 - WARNING AND NOTIFICATION: The Referee shall warn both teams 5 seconds before a charged time-out expires. The team then has 25 seconds to put the ball in play. When 3 time-outs have been charged to a team in the same half, the Referee shall notify the field captain and the head coach of that team.

ARTICLE 7 - INJURED PLAYER: An injured or apparently injured player who is discovered by an official while the ball is dead and the clock is stopped, shall be replaced for at least one down unless the halftime or overtime intermission occurs. A player who is bleeding, has an open wound, or has blood on the uniform shall be considered an injured player. (NOTE - See RULE 6 - SECTION 1 - ARTICLE 4 "Continued Participation Due to Injury, Bleeding or Open Wound" and also see RULE 17 - "Communicable Disease Procedures".

ARTICLE 8 - COACH - REFEREE CONFERENCE: When a team requests a charged time-out for a rule interpretation, the Referee will confer with the team captain or coach. If the Referee changes his/her ruling, it is an official's time-out. If the ruling is not changed, it is a charged time-out. If the team has used its 3 time-outs, a delay of game penalty will be assessed.

ARTICLE 9 - AUTHORIZED CONFERENCES: There are two types of authorized conferences permitted during charged time-outs and television/radio time-outs:
  A. One or more players and one or more coaches may meet directly in front of the team box within 5 yards of the sideline; or
  B. One coach may enter the field at his/her team's huddle on the inbounds hash mark to confer with his/her players.

SECTION 4 - DELAYS:

ARTICLE 1 - DELAYING THE START OF A HALF: Each team shall have its players on the field for the opening play at the scheduled time for the beginning of each half. All . players must have their flags in legal position (flag only).

PENALTY: Delay of half, 10 yards from the spot of the kickoff. (S27).

ARTICLE 2 - DELAY OF GAME: The ball must be put in play promptly and legally and any action or inaction by either team which tends to prevent this is delay of game. This includes:
  A. Failure to snap or free kick within 25 seconds after the ball is ready for play.
  B. Putting the ball in play before it is declared ready for play.
  C. Deliberately advancing the ball after it has been declared dead.
  D. A Coach-Referee Conference after all permissible charged time- outs for the coach's team have been used, and during which the Referee is requested to reconsider the application of a rule and no change results.
  E. Failure to kick the ball immediately after receiving the snap on a protected scrimmage kick(protected punt).

PENALTY: Delay of Game, 5 yards from spot of the snap. (S7 & S21).

ARTICLE 3 - UNFAIR TACTICS: The Referee may order the game clock started or stopped whenever, in his/her opinion, either team is trying to conserve or consume playing time by tactics obviously unfair.

PENALTY: Delay of game, 5 yards. (S7 & S21).

PLAY: As the game clock is running near the end of the game, Team A stalls and allows the 25 second count to expire.

RULING: Delay of game penalty and the Referee shall order the clock started on the next snap or legally touched if free kicked.

SECTION 5 - OVERTIME:

ARTICLE 1 - PRE-TOSS: In case of a game ending in a tie score, the officials must bring all players and coaches of both teams to the center of the field. They will discuss the tie breaker procedures and answer all questions prior to the coin toss. After this meeting the field captains will stay while the remaining players and coaches return to their respective sidelines.

ARTICLE 2 - THE COIN TOSS: A coin will be flipped by the Referee to determine the options as in the start of the game. The home team captain shall call the toss. There will be only one coin flip during the overtime. If additional overtime periods are played, field captains will alternate choices. The winner of the toss shall be given options of offense, defense, or direction. The loser of the toss shall make a choice of the remaining options. ALL OVERTIME PERIODS ARE PLAYED TOWARD THE SAME GOAL LINE.

ARTICLE 3 - TIE BREAKER: Unless moved by penalty, each team will start 1st and goal from the Team B 20 yard line. The object will be to score a touchdown or field goal. An overtime period consists of one possession by each team. If the score is still tied after one period, they go to a second period or as many as needed to determine a winner. If the first team which is awarded the ball scores, the opponent will still have a chance to win the game. Unless moved by penalty, they will start 1st and goal from the Team B 20 yard line. Try-for-points will be attempted and scored as indicated in Rule 11. If the defense intercepts the ball and returns it for a touchdown, they win the game. If they do not return the interception for a touchdown, the ball will be placed at the Team B 20 yard line to begin their series of 4 downs, if available. Each team is entitled to one time-out per overtime period.

ARTICLE 4 - U.S.F.T.L. SUDDEN DEATH: In U.S.F.T.L. Championship Games, (League and Tournament Championship Games only), a U.S.F.T.L. SUDDEN DEATH overtime is used. In U.S.F.T.L. SUDDEN DEATH, the procedure is exactly the same as the beginning of the game: The captain has 3 choices - offense, defense, or direction. Each team shall receive 1 possession, starting by kickoff, punt, turnover or turnover on downs. After each team receives one possession, and the game is still tied, the first team to score wins. Actual game conditions exist. The U.S.F.T.L. SUDDEN DEATH starts with kick-off (free kick), and proceeds like a regular game. If the defense intercepts the ball and returns it for a touchdown, they win the game. Each team is entitled to one time-out per overtime period. The Turnover Rule does not apply in U.S.F.T.L. SUDDEN DEATH.

ARTICLE 5 - FOULS AND PENALTIES: They are administered similar to the regular game. Team A shall be awarded a new series of 4 downs when the penalty for defensive pass interference or roughing the passer is accepted. Dead ball fouls following a touchdown are penalized on the try-for-point. Dead Ball Fouls following a successful try-for-point will be penalized from the succeeding spot, the Team B 20 yard line, if accepted. Dead ball fouls following a field goal or safety will be penalized from the succeeding spot, the Team B 20 yard line, if accepted. All fouls and penalties during a U.S.F.T.L. SUDDEN DEATH overtime game are administered to as in a regular game.

RULE 6 - SUBSTITUTIONS

SECTION 1:
ARTICLE 1 - ELIGIBLE AND LEGAL SUBSTITUTIONS: No substitute shall enter during a down. Between downs any number of eligible substitutes may replace players provided the substitution is completed by having the replaced players off the field before the ball becomes alive. An incoming substitute must enter the field directly from his/her team area. A replaced player must leave the field at the sideline nearest his/her team area prior to the ball being snapped.

PENALTY: Substitution infraction, 5 yards. (S22). If it is a dead ball foul, 5 yards from the succeeding spot. (S7 & S22).

PLAY: Ineligible Lineman Flag Team A has 10 players on the field. Ineligible Lineman Flag player A-1 realizes this and; (a) runs toward his end line after the ball is snapped; or (b) he steps over the end line prior to the snap.

RULING: Substitution Infraction. In (a) Live Ball Foul and (b) Dead Ball Foul.

ARTICLE 2 - LEGAL SUBSTITUTIONS: During the same dead ball interval, no substitute shall become a player and then withdraw, and no player shall withdraw and then re-enter as a substitute unless a dead ball foul occurs, there is a charged time-out, or a period ends.

PENALTY: Substitution infraction, 5 yards from previous spot. (S22).

ARTICLE 3 - SUBSTITUTES IN UNIFORM: Each substitute shall be in uniform, ready to play, with flags in position as directed by Rule 4, Section 2 & 3.

PENALTY: Substitution infraction, 5 yards from previous spot. (S22).

ARTICLE 4 - CONTINUED PARTICIPATION DUE TO INJURY, BLEEDING OR OPEN WOUND:

a) A player, substitute, coach, trainer or other team member or official who is bleeding or who has an open wound shall be prohibited from participating fur the in the game until the bleeding is stopped and the wound covered.
   1. He/she must be replaced for at least 1 down until the bleeding is stopped or the wound covered.
   2. If there is an excessive amount of blood on the uniform or if a bandage becomes blood soaked, in the judgment of the Referee, the uniform/bandage must be changed before the individual may participate. (NOTE: see RULE 17 "Communicable Disease Procedures".)

RULE 7 - BALL IN PLAY, DEAD BALL, OUT-OF-BOUNDS

SECTION 1 - BALL IN PLAY, DEAD BALL:

ARTICLE 1 - DEAD BALL BECOMES ALIVE: A dead ball, after having been declared ready for play, becomes a live ball when it is snapped or free kicked legally.

ARTICLE 2 - BALL DECLARED DEAD: A live ball becomes dead and an official shall sound the whistle or declare it dead:
   A. When it goes out-of-bounds.
   B. When any part of the ball carrier other than a hand or foot touches the ground.

PLAY: QB A-1 rolls out and slips, but regains his/her balance as the ball in contact with his/her hand touches the ground.

RULING: Play is ruled dead when the ball touches the ground, the ball is dead at the spot.

C. When a touchdown, touch back, safety, field goal or successful try-for-point is made.
D. When a player of the kicking team catches and/or downs a free kick or scrimmage kick or protected scrimmage kick, or recovers any muffed free kick which is beyond the neutral zone; when a protected scrimmage kick or scrimmage kick comes to rest on the ground and no player attempts to secure it:
    1. When a forward pass strikes the ground or is caught simultaneously by opposing players.
    2. When a backward pass or fumble by a player touches the ground. (NOTE: A ball snapped from scrimmage, which hits the ground before or after getting to the intended receiver, is dead at the spot at which it hits the ground. If the snap ball hits the ground in the end zone or touches the end line, or beyond, it is a safety).
    3. When a forward pass is legally completed, or a loose ball is caught or recovered by a player on, above, or behind the opponent's goal line.
    4. Touch Football only: When a ball carrier is legally touched with 2 hands simultaneously between the shoulders and knees, including the hand and arm.
    5. Flag Football Only: When a ball carrier has a flag removed legally by a defensive player.
    6. Flag Football Only: When the flag has fallen off inadvertently with no legal pull of the flag being completed, then a ball carrier must be legally touched with 2 hands simultaneously between the shoulders and the knees, including the hand and arm.
    7. When a player is deflagged/touched prior to releasing the ball.

PLAY: QB A-1 is touched or deflagged when
a) his/her arm is moving forward in an attempt to throw the ball;
b) the ball has already left the hand.

RULING: In **a)** A-1 is down at the spot of the touch or deflagged. In **b)** the ball remains alive, since the ball left the passer's hand before he/she was touched or deflagged.

    8. When a muff of a protected scrimmage kick or scrimmage kick strikes the ground.
    9. Following a valid or invalid fair catch signal when the kick is caught or recovered between the goal lines by any receiver beyond K's line, unless the kick has been touched by one of the kickers beyond the line.

ARTICLE 3 - INADVERTENT WHISTLE: When an official sounds his/her whistle inadvertently, during a down or during a down in which the penalty for a foul is declined, when:
  A. The ball is in player possession - the team in possession may elect to put the ball in play where declared dead or replay the down.
  B. The ball is loose from a fumble, backward pass, illegal kick, or illegal forward pass - the team in possession may elect to put the ball in play where possession was lost or replay the down.

C. During a legal forward pass or a free or protected scrimmage kick - the ball is returned to the previous spot and the down replayed. If a foul occurs during any of the above downs, an accepted penalty shall be administered as in any other play situation. When the foul is accepted, disregard the inadvertent whistle.

SECTION 2 - OUT OF BOUNDS:

ARTICLE 1 - PLAYER OUT OF BOUNDS: A player or other person is out of bounds when any part of him/her touches anything, other than another player or a game official which is on or outside the sideline or end line.

ARTICLE 2 - PLAYER IN POSSESSION OUT OF BOUNDS: A ball in player possession is out of bounds when the runner or the ball touches anything, other than another player or game official, which is on or outside a sideline or end line.

ARTICLE 3 - LOOSE BALL OUT OF BOUNDS: A loose ball other than a kick which scores a field goal or extra point is out of bounds when it touches the ground, a player, or anything else which is on or outside a boundary line.

ARTICLE 4 - OUT OF BOUNDS AT CROSSING POINT: If a live ball or loose ball crosses a boundary line and is then declared out of bounds, it is out of bounds at the crossing point.

RULE 8 - SERIES OF DOWNS, NUMBER OF DOWNS, ZONE LINE-TO-GAIN AND TEAM POSSESSION AFTER PENALTY

SECTION 1 - A SERIES - HOW STARTED, HOW BROKEN, RENEWED:

ARTICLE 1 - A DOWN IS A UNIT: A down is a unit of the game which starts with a legal snap or legal free kick, and ends when the ball next becomes dead. Between downs is any period when the ball is dead.

ARTICLE 2 - SERIES OF DOWNS: A team, in possession of the ball, shall have 4 consecutive downs to advance to the next zone by scrimmage. Any down may be repeated or lost if provided by the rules.

ARTICLE 3 - ZONE LINE-TO-GAIN: The zone line-to-gain in any series shall be the zone in advance of the ball, unless distance has been lost due to penalty or failure to gain. In such case, the original zone in advance of the ball at the beginning of the series of downs is the zone line-to-gain. The most forward point of the ball, when declared dead between the goal lines, shall be the determining factor.

ARTICLE 4 - MEASUREMENT OF DISTANCE: The most forward point of the ball when declared dead between the goal lines shall be the determining point in establishing distance gained or lost by either team in a down. The position of the ball and not the players body when touched or the position of the flag when deflagged, shall determining the spot of the succeeding down.

ARTICLE 5 - AWARDING A NEW SERIES: A new series of downs shall be awarded when a team moves the ball into the next zone on a play free from penalty; or a penalty against the opponents moves the ball into the next zone; or an accepted penalty against the opponents involves an automatic 1st down; or either team has obtained legal possession of a ball as a result of a penalty, free kick, scrimmage kick, protected scrimmage kick, touchback, pass interception, roughing the kicker or holder, or failure to gain the zone in advance of the ball.

SECTION 2 - DOWN AND POSSESSION AFTER A PENALTY:

ARTICLE 1 - FOUL DURING A FREE KICK: When a scrimmage follows the penalty for a live ball foul committed during a free kick, the down and distance established by the penalty shall be first down with the next zone line-to-gain.

ARTICLE 2 - PENALTY RESULTING IN FIRST DOWN: After a penalty which leaves the ball in possession of a team beyond its zone line-to-gain, or when a penalty stipulates a first down, the down and distance established by that penalty shall be first down with next zone line-to-gain.

PLAY: Third and 5 from Team A's 15 yard line. A-1 throws an illegal forward pass beyond the Team A scrimmage line:
 a) at Team A's 23 yard line and the ball hits the ground.
 b) at Team A's 26 yard line and the ball hits the ground.

RULING: In a), Team A is penalized 5 yards for illegal forward pass and loss of down, which places the ball on the 18 yard line - fourth down and 2. In b), Team A is penalized 5 yards and loss of down which puts the ball on the 21 yard line - first down and 19. Even though an illegal forward pass carries a loss of down, since the 5 yard penalty enforcement places the ball beyond the 20 yard line, it is first down for Team A.

PLAY: On fourth down and 5 on Team A:s 15 yard line, A- I runs to its own 23 yard line and throws an illegal forward pass.

RULING: Team B's ball on Team A's 18 yard line, first down and goal to go. Since the 5 yard penalty puts Team A 2 yards short of the zone line-to-gain on fourth down, the loss of down awards the ball to Team B.

ARTICLE 3 - FOUL BEFORE CHANGE OF TEAM POSSESSION: After a distance penalty between the goal lines incurred during a down and before any change of team possession during that down, the ball belongs to Team A and the down shall be repeated unless the penalty also involves loss of down, or leaves the ball on or beyond the zone line-to-gain. If the penalty involves loss of down, the down shall count as one of the four in that series.

ARTICLE 4 - FOUL AFTER CHANGE OF TEAM POSSESSION: After a distance penalty for a foul committed during a down and after team possession has changed during that down, the ball belongs to the team in possession when the foul occurred and, the down and distance established by that penalty shall be first down with zone line-to-gain.

PLAY: B-4 intercepts a pass by A-1 and returns it to the Team A 25 yard line. During the run by B-4, B-2 makes illegal contact with A-6 at the Team A 29 yard line.

RULING: B is penalized 10 yards utilizing the three-and-one principle from the Team A 29 yard line - the end of the run. It is Team B's ball, first down and 19. Team B obtained the ball with "clean hands."

ARTICLE 5 - FOUL BETWEEN DOWNS: After a distance penalty incurred between downs, the number of the next down shall be the same as that established before the foul occurred unless enforcement for a foul by Team B leaves the ball on or beyond the zone line-to-gain.

ARTICLE 6 - FOUL BETWEEN SERIES: A scrimmage following a penalty incurred after a series ends and before the next series begins shall be first down, but the zone line-to-gain shall be established before the penalty is enforced.

PLAY: Team A's protected scrimmage kick goes out-of-bounds at Team B's 25 yard line after which Team B player commits illegal contact.
RULING: This is a dead ball foul. First down and 25 on the Team B 15 yard line.

ARTICLE 7 - FOUL BY BOTH TEAMS: If offsetting fouls occur during a down, that down shall be repeated.

EXCEPTION: If each team fouls during a down in which there is a change of team possession, the team last gaining possession may retain the ball, provided its foul was not prior to the final change of possession and it declines all penalties for its opponent's fouls, other than unsportsmanlike. This is known as the "clean hands" rule on double fouls.

ARTICLE 8 - PENALTY DECLINED: If a penalty is declined the number of the next down shall be whatever it would have been if that foul had not occurred.

ARTICLE 9 - RULE DECISION FINAL: No rule decision may be changed after the ball is next legally snapped or free kicked.

RULE 9 -THE SCRIMMAGE, SNAPPING, HANDING AND PASSING THE BALL

SECTION 1 - THE SCRIMMAGE:

ARTICLE 1 - THE START: All plays from scrimmage must be started by a legal snap from a point between the inbounds lines, unless the rules provide for a free kick.

ARTICLE 2 - BALL RESPONSIBILITY: Team A players are responsible for retrieving the ball after a scrimmage down. The snapper will bring it from the huddle to the Team A scrimmage line. A towel may be placed under the ball.

ARTICLE 3 - STANCES AND EXCEPTION: Stances - Players may use a 2, 3, or 4 point stance.

EXCEPTION: On kicking plays (extra point attempts and field goal attempts), 3 or 4 point stances are not allowed.

SECTION 2 - PRIOR TO THE SNAP:

ARTICLE 1 - ENCROACHMENT: After the ball is ready for play and until the snap, no player on defense may encroach, touch the ball, nor may any player contact opponents or in any other way interfere with them. This includes standing in the neutral zone to give defensive signals, or shifting through the zone. After the snapper has made his/her final ball adjustment, it is encroachment for any player to break the scrimmage line plane, except for the snapper's right to be over the ball.

PENALTY: Dead ball foul, encroachment, 5 yards from the previous spot. (S7 & S1 8). During the interval between scrimmage downs when two or more consecutive encroachment fouls are committed by the defensive team, the penalty will be

10 yards for the second encroachment foul.

PLAY: After the ball is marked ready for play by the Referee, B-4 charges into the neutral zone beyond B's scrimmage line, to give Team A a first down.

RULING: Dead ball foul for encroachment, 5 yards. The penalty is declined by Team A. Team B is informed by the Referee that if this occurs again during the same dead ball interval, a 10 yard penalty will be enforced, if accepted.

ARTICLE 2 - FALSE START: No offensive player shall make a false start. A false start includes simulating a charge or start of play. An infraction of this rule may be penalized whether or not the ball is snapped and the penalty for any resultant encroachment shall be canceled.

PENALTY: Dead ball foul, illegal procedure, 5 yards from the previous spot. (S7 & S19).

ARTICLE 3 - THE SNAP: The snapper, after assuming position for the snap and adjusting the ball, may neither move nor change the position of the ball in a manner simulating the beginning of a play until it is snapped. An infraction of this provision may be penalized, whether or not the ball is snapped, and the penalty for any resultant encroachment or contact foul by an opponent shall be canceled. When over the ball the snapper shall have his/her feet on or behind his/her scrimmage line. The snapper shall pass the ball back between his/her legs from its position on the ground with a quick and continuous motion of the hand(s). The ball shall leave the hand(s) in this motion. The ball must be touching the ground when snapped.

PENALTY: Dead ball foul, illegal procedure, 5 yards.(S7 & S19).

ARTICLE 4 - LINE OF SCRIMMAGE: No players shall interlock their legs at the line of scrimmage.

SECTION 3 - POSITION AND ACTION DURING THE SNAP:

ARTICLE 1 - LEGAL POSITION: Offensive players cannot be within five (5) yards of the sidelines when the ball is snapped.

PENALTY: Illegal Procedure, 5 yards. (S 19).

ARTICLE 2 - MINIMUM LINE PLAYERS: When the ball is snapped:
A. At least 1 player on the offensive line with 2 and 3 players, 2 with 4 players, 3 with 5, 6, and 7 players, 4 with 8 players, 5 with 9 players, 6 with 10 players and 7 with 11 players must be on their scrimmage line. The remaining players must be either on their scrimmage line or behind their backfield line.
B. All players must be inbounds.

ARTICLE 3 - MOTION: One offensive player may be in motion, but not in motion toward the opponent's goal line. If a player starts in motion from their backfield or their scrimmage line, that player may not be in motion toward the opponent's goal line when the ball is snapped. Other offensive players must be stationary in their positions without movement of the feet, body, head, or arms. The offensive team must have at least 1 player in 2 and 3 man, 2 players in 4 man, 3 players in 5, 6, or 7 man, 4 players in 8 man, 5 players in 9 man, 6 players in 10 man and 7 players in 11 man on their scrimmage line at the snap.

PENALTY: Illegal motion; 5 yards. (S20)

PLAY: After a huddle, all A players come to a stop and remain stationary for a full second, then a) A-2 goes in motion legally and the ball is snapped. b) A-1 goes in motion legally as A-2 moves to a new position in the backfield, sets, and the ball is snapped.

RULING: a) Legal b) Illegal Motion, Live Ball Foul, 5 yards.

ARTICLE 4 - CHUCKING THE CENTER (FLAG, TOUCH & INELIGIBLE LINEMAN FLAG ONLY):
There shall be no contact with the center until after the ball has been snapped and the center has attained an upright position and has assumed a blocking position or has proceeded into a pass receiving pattern by at least one full step. The essence of this rule is to protect the center, who is vulnerable in the snapping position. The contact of the center shall consist of one chuck at the line of scrimmage, after the center assumes a blocking position or fires out into his pattern by one full step. Open hand contact is recommended. No chucks above the shoulders are allowed. The defense can chuck the center one time until 5 yards.

ARTICLE 5 - CHUCKING THE RECEIVER (FLAG, TOUCH & INELIGIBLE LINEMAN FLAG ONLY):
There shall be one chuck at the line of scrimmage allowed by the defense. The defense can chuck a receiver one time until 5 yards. Open hand contact is recommended. No chucks above the shoulders are allowed.

ARTICLE 6 - CHUCKING THE CENTER AND RECEIVER (SCREEN FLAG ONLY):
No contact is allowed, anywhere, anytime, to any player, by any player, in screen flag football.

ARTICLE 7 - DIRECT SNAPS:
Direct snaps from the center to anyone in the backfield are allowed. Direct snaps on protected scrimmage kicks, (declared punts), are not allowed. The punter must be at least 5 yards behind the center to receive a snap on a protected kick.

PENALTY: Illegal Procedure, 5 yards.(SI9).

ARTICLE 8 - SNAPS TO LINEMEN:
No offensive player, while on the scrimmage line, may receive a snap.

ARTICLE 9 - SHIFT:
In a snap preceded by a huddle or shift, all offensive players must come to a complete stop and remain stationary in legal position without movement of feet, body, head, or arms for at least one full second before the snap.

PENALTY: Illegal Shift, 5 yards. (S20).

PLAY: Following a huddle or shift one offensive player takes a preliminary position, then advances or drops into final position.

RULING: Such movement constitutes a shift; all players must hold their final positions for one second before a snap.

SECTION 4 - HANDING THE BALL:

ARTICLE 1 - HANDING FORWARD:
No player may hand the ball forward except as follows: a Team A player who is behind the scrimmage line may hand the ball forward to a backfield teammate who is also behind the line; or to a teammate who was on the scrimmage line when the ball was snapped, provided that teammate

left the line of position, faced his or her own end line and was at least one yard behind the scrimmage line when player received the ball. On a scrimmage play, the center, while on the line of scrimmage, cannot receive a forward handoff.

PENALTY: Illegal Handing, 5 yards and loss of down if by Team A before possession change during a scrimmage down. (S35 & S9).

ARTICLE 2 - HANDING BACKWARD: A ball carrier may hand the ball backward at anytime except if intentionally thrown out-of-bounds to conserve time or prevent from being deflagged or tagged. Referee's discretion as to starting or stopping the clock.

ARTICLE 3 - HANDING DURING FREE KICK DOWN: During a free kick down, a player may not hand the ball forward to a teammate, but may hand the ball backward to a teammate at any time.

SECTION 5 - BACKWARD PASS AND FUMBLE:

ARTICLE 1 - ANYTIME: A runner may pass the ball backward or lose player possession by a fumble at anytime except if intentionally thrown out-of-bounds to conserve time or to avoid being deflagged/tagged.

PENALTY: Illegal Pass, 5 yards and loss of down. (S35 & S9). Referee will start the clock on the ready for play.

ARTICLE 2 - CAUGHT OR INTERCEPTED: A backward pass or fumble may be caught in flight inbounds by any player and advanced.

ARTICLE 3 - OUT OF BOUNDS: A backward pass or fumble which goes out-of bounds between the goal lines belongs to the team last in possession at the out-of bounds spot. If out-of-bounds behind a goal line, it is a touchback or safety.

ARTICLE 4 - BALL DEAD WHEN IT HITS THE GROUND: A backward pass or fumble which touches the ground between the goal lines is dead at the spot where it touches the ground and belongs to the team last in possession unless lost on downs.

PLAY: A-1 running with the ball at Team B's 3 yard line slips and fumbles the ball into the end zone.

RULING: Touchback. Team B's ball, first and 20 on B20.

SECTION 6 - LEGAL AND ILLEGAL FORWARD PASS:

ARTICLE 1 - LEGAL FORWARD PASS (CONTACT FLAG FOOTBALL, TOUCH FOOTBALL & SCREEN FLAG FOOTBALL): All players are eligible to touch or catch a pass. During a scrimmage down and before team possession has changed a forward pass may be thrown provided the passer's feet are behind Team A's scrimmage line when the ball leaves the passer's hand. Only one forward pass can be thrown per down.

ARTICLE 2 - LEGAL FORWARD PASS (INELIGIBLE LINEMAN FLAG FOOTBALL): The players that are not eligible to touch or catch a pass, or run with the ball in the game of Ineligible Lineman Flag Football, are the following: The center and 2 lineman on the offensive lines. These players must line up as an offensive line does in regular tackle football. All other players are eligible to catch a pass or run with the ball. All other rules apply as in Rule 9, Section 6, Article 1.

ARTICLE 3 - LINEMAN ELIGIBLE (INELIGIBLE LINEMAN FLAG
FOOTBALL): Lineman are not eligible to catch a pass, run with the ball or throw the ball in Ineligible Lineman Flag Football.

ARTICLE 4 - ILLEGAL FORWARD PASS: A forward pass is illegal:
- **A.** If the passer's foot is beyond Team A's scrimmage line when the ball leaves his/her hand. (S35 & S9).
- **B.** If thrown after team possession has changed during the down. (S35).
- **C.** If intentionally thrown to the ground or out-of-bounds to save loss of yardage. (S36 & S9).
- **D.** If a passer catches his/her untouched forward or backward pass. (S35 & S9).
- **E.** If there is more than one forward pass per down.
- **F.** If a passer crosses the line of scrimmage, then comes back behind the line of scrimmage and throws a pass, it is an illegal forward pass.

PENALTY: 5 yards from the spot of the foul and a loss of down if by Team A before possession changes during a scrimmage down.

PLAY: A-1 throws a short forward pass: (S35 & S9).
- **a.)** A-1 catches; or
- **b.)** the ball is tipped by A-4, or B-3, then A-1 catches; or
- **c.)** A-6 catches pass and throws a backward pass to A-1.

RULING: In (a) illegal forward pass. In (b) and (c) the play is legal as another player touched the ball before A-1 again possessed it. However, Team A cannot throw a second forward pass during the down.

PLAY: QB A- I catches a snap from center and IMMEDIATELY throws the ball into the ground to stop the clock during the last 2 minutes of the 2nd half.

RULING: This play is legal provided the QB is not trying to avoid a loss of yardage and that it happened during the last 2 minutes of the 2nd half.

ARTICLE 5 - ILLEGAL FORWARD PASS (INELIGIBLE LINEMAN
FLAG FOOTBALL): You may not throw a forward pass to a center and the 2 linemen on either side of the center in the game of Ineligible Lineman Flag Football. All other rules apply as in Rule 9, Section 6. Article 4.

ARTICLE 6 - INTENTIONAL GROUNDING: A passer may not intentionally throw the ball into the ground to avoid a loss of yardage.

EXCEPTION: In the last 2 minutes of each half, a passer may throw the ball into the ground to stop the clock and conserve time for his/her team. This play is legal, provided the passer is not trying to avoid a loss of yardage.

ARTICLE 7 - AFTER ILLEGAL FORWARD PASS: When an illegal forward pass touches the ground or goes out-of-bounds the ball becomes dead and belongs to the passing team, at the spot from where the pass was thrown, unless a new series of downs has been created. In such a case the ball belongs to the passing team if, after the enforcement of the penalty, the ball is left in advance of the zone line-to-gain, or belongs to the opponents if the ball, after the penalty, did not make the next zone line-to-gain and the foul occurred during the fourth down. If a player catches an illegal forward pass, the ball continues in play until declared dead.

ARTICLE 8 - ELIGIBLE RECEIVERS: In Touch Football, Contact Flag Football and Screen Flag Football, all players are eligible to catch a pass, throw a pass or run with the ball.

ARTICLE 9 - INELIGIBLE RECEIVERS: In the game of Ineligible Lineman Flag Football, everyone is eligible to catch a pass, throw a pass or run with the ball except the following players: the center and the 2 lineman on the offensive line.

ARTICLE 10 - ELIGIBILITY LOST BY GOING OUT-OF-BOUNDS: An offensive player who goes out-of-bounds on his/her own volition during a passing down loses eligibility until the ball has been touched by an opponent. If an offensive player is pushed out-of-bounds by a defensive player, he/she may return to the playing field, and once again be considered eligible to catch a pass or run with the ball. Penalty: Illegal participation or offensive pass interference.

SECTION 7 - COMPLETED OR INTERCEPTED PASSES:

ARTICLE 1 - PASS CAUGHT OR INTERCEPTED: A forward pass is completed when caught by a member of the passing team inbounds. It is counted as a completion as long as the first part of the person to make contact with the ground after the catch touches inbounds. It is an interception when caught inbounds by a member of the defensive team. A player must have one foot inbounds for a legal catch or interception.

ARTICLE 2 - SIMULTANEOUS CATCH BY OPPOSING PLAYERS: If a legal forward pass is caught simultaneously by members of opposing teams, the ball becomes dead and belongs to the team that snapped the ball, the offensive team.

SECTION 8 - INCOMPLETE PASSES:

ARTICLE 1 - BECOMES DEAD: When a legal forward pass touches the ground or anything out-of-bounds, it becomes dead.

SECTION 9 - FORWARD PASS INTERFERENCE:

ARTICLE 1 - CONTACT: During a down in which a legal forward pass is thrown, contact which interferes with an eligible receiver who is beyond the 5 yard legal chuck area, is pass interference unless it occurs: a) When two or more eligible receivers make a simultaneous and bonafide attempt to reach, catch or bat a pass. b) When opposing lineman immediately following the snap, engage each other as the ball is snapped. It is also pass interference if an eligible receiver is deflagged or touched prior to touching the ball on a pass thrown beyond the scrimmage line.

PLAY: A-1 throws a legal forward pass toward A-4 who is beyond Team A's scrimmage mage line. Before A-4 touches the pass, B-2 deflags A-4.

RULING: Defensive Pass Interference - Automatic 1st down at spot of infraction.(S33 & S8).

ARTICLE 2 - CONTACT (SCREEN FLAG FOOTBALL): During a down in which a legal forward pass is thrown, no contact is permitted by the defense against an offensive player. During a down in which a legal forward pass is thrown, contact which interferes with an eligible receiver who is beyond the scrimmage line is pass interference unless it occurs: a) When two or more eligible receivers make a simultaneous and bonafide attempt to reach, catch or bat a pass. b) It is also pass interference if an eligible receiver is deflagged or touched prior to touching the ball on a pass thrown beyond the scrimmage line.

ARTICLE 3 - LEGAL CONTACT: No contact may be made beyond 5 yards of the neutral zone by either offensive or defensive players prior to the ball being released by the passer on passes which cross the neutral zone.

PENALTY: Spot of the foul and first down if on the defense. 10 yards and loss of down if by the offense.

ARTICLE 4 - LEGAL CONTACT (SCREEN FLAG FOOTBALL): There is no legal contact anywhere, or at anytime on the field in the game of screen flag football.

ARTICLE 5 - OFFENSIVE PASS INTERFERENCE: After the ball is snapped, and until it has been touched by a receiver, there shall be no offensive pass interference beyond the line of scrimmage while the ball is in flight.

EXAMPLE: Blocking downfield when the ball is in the air is an offensive pass interference penalty and it does not matter if the ball is behind or beyond the line of scrimmage. PENALTY. Offensive Pass Interference, 10 yard penalty from the previous spot and loss of down. (S33 & S9).

ARTICLE 6 - DEFENSIVE PASS INTERFERENCE: After the pass is thrown by the passer, and until it is touched, there shall be no defensive pass interference beyond the line of scrimmage while the ball is in flight.

PENALTY: Spot of the foul and automatic first down. (S33 & S8). If the pass interference by either player is intentional or unsportsmanlike, his/her team shall be penalized an additional 10 yards. (S27).

PLAY: B-1 defending against a legal forward pass beyond Team A's scrimmage line, Waves his/her arms in the face of A-2 who is attempting to catch the pass.

RULING: Defensive pass interference. (S33 & S8).

RULE 10 - THE KICKING GAME

SECTION 1 - FREE KICK (KICK-OFFS):

ARTICLE 1 - PUTTING THE BALL IN PLAY: A free kick begins each half of a game and begins play following a touchdown, field goal, or safety. The ball shall be put in play by a place kick from some spot on or behind the kicker's free kick line and between, the inbounds lines. Unless relocated by penalty the kicking team's free kick line on kick offs after touchdowns and field goals shall be its 20 yard line on a field 80 yards long and the 40 yard line on a field 100 yards long. A ball ready for a kickoff must be placed on a legal 2" tee or held or placed on the ground or holder's toe. However, the sole of the holder's shoe must be in contact with the ground. After a safety, the free kick line shall be the 20 yard line on both the 80 yard and 100 yard fields. A free kick after a safety can be either a place kick or punt.

ARTICLE 2 - FORMATION: When the ball is legally kicked, all players of the kicking team must be inbounds and all players, except the holder and kicker of a place kick must be behind their free kick line. At least 3 players of the receiving team with 7 players, 4 with 8 players and 5 with 9 players must be within 5 yards of their free kick line after the ball is ready for play and until the ball is kicked.

They must also be 5 yards in from the nearest sideline.

PENALTY: Dead Ball Foul, Illegal Procedure, 5 yards from the previous spot. (S7 & S19).

ARTICLE 3 - FREE KICK LINES: For any free kick formation the kicking team's free kick line shall be the yard line through the forward most point from which the ball may be kicked. The receiving team's free kick line shall be the yard line 10 yards beyond that point. It is encroachment for any player other than the kicker and the holder to be beyond the free kick line after the ball is ready for play and until it is kicked.

PENALTY: Dead ball foul, Encroachment, 5 yards from the previous spot. (S7 & S18).

ARTICLE 4 - CROSSING THE NEUTRAL ZONE (FIRST TOUCHING): If any kicker touches a free kick before it crosses R's free kick line and before it is touched there by any R player, it is referred to as "first touching." R may take the ball at that spot or may choose to have the ball put in play as determined by the action which follows first touching. The right of R to take the ball at the spot of first touching by K is canceled if R touches the kick and thereafter during the down commits a foul or if the penalty is accepted for any foul committed during the down. (S16).

PLAY: K-1 touches a rolling free kick before it reaches R's restraining line and the ball hits the ground.

RULING: The ball is dead where it hit the ground following K-1's touching. It is R's ball at the spot of first touching or where the ball was declared dead, whichever is most advantageous.

ARTICLE 5 - RECOVERY OF A FREE KICK (ONSIDE KICKS): There are no onside kicks. The kicking team cannot recover an onside kick.

EXCEPTION: If the Free Kick is touched by R and the ball does not touch the ground, K may gain possession if the ball is possessed by K before the ball strikes the ground.

PLAY: a) K-3 picks up a rolling free kick beyond R's restraining line and advances the ball.
b) Free kick hits R-1 inflight, bounces in the air and K-2 catches it.

RULING: a) The ball is dead where K-3 downs it;
b) Award the ball to K-2, first down and Zone line-to-gain.

ARTICLE 6 - FREE KICK CAUGHT OR TOUCHED BY K (KICKING TEAM): If any member of the kicking team catches or touches a free kick before the ball is touched by R or hits the ground, it is fair catch interference.

PENALTY: 10 yards previous spot or awarded fair catch. (S33).

ARTICLE 7 - FREE KICK CAUGHT OR TOUCHED BY R (RECEIVING TEAM): If any member of the receiving team catches the ball it may be advanced. If the kick is fumbled, then strikes the ground, it is dead at that spot. If muffed and touches ground, it is dead at that spot.

ARTICLE 8 - FREE KICK AT REST: If an inbounds free kick comes to rest and no player of either team attempts to secure it, the ball is dead at that spot and belongs to the receiving team.

ARTICLE 9 - FREE KICK INTO THE END ZONE: Free kicks that cross the goal line may be brought out of the end zone and returned. If the free kick goes out of the end zone, it shall be a touchback, with the ball brought out to the twenty yard line.

ARTICLE 10 - FREE KICK REPEATED OR NOT REPEATED: A free kick is not repeated unless a foul occurs prior to a change of possession and the penalty is accepted or there is a double foul.

ARTICLE 11 - FREE KICK AFTER A SCORE: After a score, the kicking team has 30 seconds to put the ball in play by a free kick (kickoff).

PENALTY: Delay of Game - 5 yards (S21).

ARTICLE 12 - KICK -OFF OPTION: At the beginning of each half, and after every score, teams shall be asked if they want to kick-off or start from their 35 yard line, first down and the next zone line-to-gain. Both teams must agree to start at the 35 yard line or there shall be a kick-off.

SECTION 2 - FREE KICK OUT-OF-BOUNDS:

ARTICLE 1 - OUT-OF-BOUNDS UNTOUCHED BETWEEN THE RESTRAINING LINES: If a free kick goes out-of-bounds untouched between the restraining lines, the receiving team will put the ball in play on the inbounds spot where the ball went out-of-bounds.

ARTICLE 2 - OUT-OF-BOUNDS UNTOUCHED BEYOND THE RESTRAINING LINES AND BETWEEN THE GOAL LINES: If a free kick goes out-of bounds untouched beyond the receiving team's restraining line, but before the 35 yard line, the ball is put in play at the point where the ball left the field of play. If the ball goes out-of-bounds untouched between the 35 yard line and the goal line the ball is put in play at the 35 yard line.

ARTICLE 3 - OUT-OF-BOUNDS BEHIND THE GOAL LINE: If a free kick goes out-of-bounds behind a goal line, it is a touchback and the ball belongs to the team defending that goal line at their 20 yard line.

SECTION 3 - SCRIMMAGE KICKS (PUNTS):

ARTICLE 1 - LEGAL KICK: A legal scrimmage kick is a punt made in accordance with the rules.

ARTICLE 2 - PROTECTED SCRIMMAGE KICK: Prior to making the ball ready for play on fourth down, the Referee must ask the Team A captain if he/she wants a protected scrimmage kick. The Referee must communicate this decision to the Team B captain and the other officials. The Team A captain may request a protected scrimmage kick on any down. After such announcement, the ball must be kicked.

EXCEPTION:

a) If a Team A time out is called, or

b) a foul occurs anytime prior to or during this down after the Team A captain's decision which results in the kicking team having the right to repeat the down again, the Referee must again ask the Team A captain whether or not he/she wants a protected scrimmage kick and communicate this decision to the Team

B captain. The kicker (punter) must start at least 5 yards behind the center to receive the snap. No direct snaps are allowed on protected scrimmage kicks. The Punter must punt the ball immediately.
  c) NO DECLARED PUNT IN INELIGIBLE LINEMAN FLAG:
    1) Rushing the punter is allowed in Ineligible Lineman Flag,
    2) You may not rush between center-guard gap,
    3) Roughing the punter is a 10 yard penalty and automatic 1st down,
    4) Only the 2 outside players on the punting team may release at the snap. All other players on punt team must wait until ball is punted.

ARTICLE 3 - PROTECTED SCRIMMAGE KICK FORMATION: Both teams must have and maintain at least 3 players on the line of scrimmage in 7 man, 4 players on the line of scrimmage in 8 man; and 5 players on the line of scrimmage in 9 man, who cannot cross the line of scrimmage until the ball has been kicked. Linemen on the defensive line may raise their arms, and or jump to distract, or try and block the kick. If the kicker (punter) drops the snap, the ball is dead at the spot.

ARTICLE 4 - KICKING THE BALL: The kicker must be at least 5 yards behind the line of scrimmage when receiving the snap. After receiving the snap, the kicker must kick the ball immediately and in a continuous motion

PENALTY: Delay of Game - 5 yards. (S21). If repeated, Unsportsmanlike Conduct 10 yards and loss of down. (S27 & S9). (NOTE: Some teams may wish to kick with no protection or announcement on scrimmage kicks. When exercising this option, rough contact with the kicker results in a penalty).

PENALTY: Roughing the Kicker - 10 yards and automatic first down. (S30 & S8).

ARTICLE 5 - FAILURE TO CROSS THE NEUTRAL ZONE: A scrimmage kick which fails to cross the scrimmage line continues in play and all players are eligible to catch or recover the ball and advance.

ARTICLE 6 - CROSSING THE KICKER'S LINE OF SCRIMMAGE: If any kicker touches a protected scrimmage kick before or after it crosses K's scrimmage line and before it is touched there by any R player, it is referred to as "first touching." R may take the ball at that spot or may choose to have the ball put in play as determined by the action which follows first touching. The right of R to take the ball at the spot of first touching by K is canceled if R touches the kick and thereafter during the down commits a foul or if the penalty is accepted for any foul committed during the down. (S16).

ARTICLE 7 - ELIGIBLE: When a scrimmage kick which has crossed the neutral zone touches a player from either team and then hits the ground the ball is dead and belongs to the receiving team. If it hits a player of the receiving team and is recovered in the air it can be advanced by the receiving team and only recovered by the kicking team, with no advancement allowed.

PLAY: R-3 attempting to catch a scrimmage kick (punt), muffs the ball. K-4 catches the ball before it hits the ground and runs for a touchdown.

RULING: K's ball at the spot where the ball was caught. During a scrimmage kick (punt), K can advance an airborne fumble by R because the kick has ended with possession

ARTICLE 8 - CATCH BY RECEIVING TEAM: If a scrimmage kick is caught by the receiving team on either side of the neutral zone it may be advanced. If muffed, it becomes dead at the spot where it hits the ground after the muff and belongs to the receiving team.

ARTICLE 9 - CATCH BY KICKING TEAM: If a player of the kicking team catches a scrimmage kick behind K's scrimmage line, the ball is dead at that spot and belongs to the receiving team. If a player of the kicking team catches a scrimmage kick beyond K's scrimmage line, provided such kick has been touched by a member of the receiving team who was clearly beyond the scrimmage line at the time of touching, the ball is dead at the spot and belongs to the kicking team. The kicking team may not advance with the ball. The ball must be caught in the air to be recovered by K. If the ball, which has been touched by the receiving team, hits the ground, the ball is immediately dead at that spot.

ARTICLE 10 - SCRIMMAGE KICK OUT-OF-BOUNDS BETWEEN THE GOAL LINES OR AT REST: If a scrimmage kick goes out-of-bounds between goal lines or comes to rest inbounds untouched and no player attempts to secure it, the ball becomes dead and belongs to the receiving team at that spot.

ARTICLE 11 - SCRIMMAGE KICK INTO THE END ZONE: Scrimmage kicks that cross the goal line may be brought out of the end zone and returned. If the scrimmage kick goes out of the end zone, it shall be a touchback, with the ball brought out to the 20 yard line.

ARTICLE 12 - SCRIMMAGE KICKS HITTING THE GROUND: Scrimmage kicks, which after being kicked, hit the ground and roll, are advanceable by the receiving team.

ARTICLE 13 - PROTECTED SCRIMMAGE KICK GENERAL GUIDE LINES:

A. On any down, the offense may request protection for a protected scrimmage kick.
B. The punter must receive the snap, at least 5 yards behind the center and immediately punt the ball. The penalty for not punting the ball immediately shall be a 5 yard Illegal Procedure penalty. (S 19).
C. A fair catch of a declared scrimmage kick - the receiving team may request a free kick for 3 points (field goal), and the defense may not rush the kicker. A kicking tee or block may be used.
D. If the clock has been stopped for some reason and then there is a request for a protected scrimmage kick, the clock will start at the snap.
E. If a protected scrimmage kick has been announced and then there is a time out, then the kicking team must re-declare it's intentions with the Referee.
F. If a protected scrimmage kick has been announced and the kicking team purposely runs an offensive play, other than the punt, the penalty shall be a dead ball foul Unsportsmanlike Conduct penalty,10 yards and loss of down. (S7, S27 & S9).

SECTION 4 - FAIR CATCH:

ARTICLE 1 - SIGNAL: Any receiver may signal for a fair catch while any kick is in flight and is beyond the kicker's free kick line for a free kick or the K's scrimmage line for a scrimmage kick.

ARTICLE 2 - INVALID OR ILLEGAL SIGNALS: The runner shall not give an invalid or illegal fair catch signal.

PENALTY: Invalid or Illegal Fair Catch Signal, 5 yards. (S32).

ARTICLE 3 - VALID CATCH: If any receiver gives a valid signal for a fair catch and catches the kick beyond K's line and between the goal lines, it is a fair-catch and the ball becomes dead.

ARTICLE 4 - NO ADVANCE: After a valid or invalid fair catch signal, by any member of the receiving team, no receiver may advance the ball.

SECTION 5 - FAIR CATCH INTERFERENCE:

ARTICLE 1 - INTERFERENCE WITH FAIR CATCH: While any free kick is in flight or any protected scrimmage kick is in flight beyond K's scrimmage line, K shall not touch the ball or R, nor obstruct R's path to the ball. This prohibition applies even when no signal is given but it does not apply if the act is after the kick has been touched by R.

PENALTY: Fair catch interference, 10 yards. (S33). R may choose a 10 yard penalty from the previous spot with K retaining the football and the down replayed, or they may accept an awarded fair catch from the spot of the foul.

PLAY: A player of the receiving team, attempting to catch a protected scrimmage kick, touches the ball which is then caught by an opponent before striking the ground.

RULING: No interference. Protection against fair catch interference ceases when any player of the receiving team touches the ball. It is dead where caught and belongs to kicking team, first down and zone line-to-gain.

PLAY: A free kick is in flight and
a) K-1 touches the ball,
b) K-3 is in the path of R-2's attempt to catch the ball,
c) K-4 tags or deflags R-2 before he/she touches the ball.

RULING: In a), b) and c) fair catch interference.

SECTION 6 - TOUCHBACK:

ARTICLE 1 - SCRIMMAGE KICK OR FREE KICK: Any kick that goes out of the end zone is a touchback and shall be put into play by the receiving team on the 20 yard line.

ARTICLE 2 - BALL DOWNED IN END ZONE ON FREE KICK: If a player, on the receiving team, receives a free kick in the end zone, possesses it, and then kneels down, this is a touchback, and the ball is brought out to the 20 yard line.

ARTICLE 3 - BALL DOWNED IN END ZONE ON A SCRIMMAGE KICK: If a player on the receiving team, receives scrimmage kick in the end zone, and then kneels down, this is a touchback and the ball is brought out to the 20 yard line.

ARTICLE 4 - BALL DOWNED IN END ZONE ON A FIELD GOAL ATTEMPT: If a player on the receiving team, receives a field goal attempt in the end zone that is short, and then kneels down, this is a touchback and the ball is brought out to the 20 yard line.

ARTICLE 5 - BALL IN END ZONE: The ball is out of bounds behind Team A's own goal line (except from an incomplete forward pass), when the ball becomes dead in possession of a player on, above or behind the player's own goal line, or when the ball not in possession on, above or behind the team's own goal line, and the attacking team is responsible for downing the ball.

PLAY: B-4 kicks off to A-3, who touches the ball in flight at his/her 4 yard line. The ball bounces off his/her hands and lands in the end zone.

RULING: Touchback. Although the ball is dead where it hits, this is not a safety. The initial force was imparted by the kicking team and the ball never was in possession of A-3.

SECTION 7 - TRY-FOR-POINT (EXTRA POINT):

ARTICLE 1 - 1 OR 2 POINTS: An opportunity to score 1 point from the 3 yard line or 2 points from the 10 yard line shall be granted the team scoring a touchdown. There shall be one scrimmage play or kick, unless changed by penalty.

ARTICLE 2 - REFEREE'S RESPONSIBILITY - The Referee must speak to the field captain only, asking him/her whether the extra point shall be from the 3 or 10 yard line. Once the Team A captain makes the choice, he/she may change the decision only by taking a charged team time-out. A team's choice cannot be changed if a penalty should occur. Enforcement of yardage penalties does not change the value of the extra point. The point(s) shall be awarded if the extra point results in what would have been a touchdown.

PLAY: Team A scores a touchdown and elects to attempt a 1 point conversion. Then after calling a charged time-out, selects to change and attempt a 2 point conversion.

RULING: Legal. A Team A charged time-out only can buy a change on an extra point option.

ARTICLE 3 - FOUL DURING EXTRA POINT: If a double foul occurs during the down, the down shall be replayed. When a distance penalty is incurred by Team A during a successful try-for-point, the down will be repeated, if accepted. However, if a Team A penalty carries a loss of down, the try-for-point has ended and will not be repeated. No points are scored for Team A, if accepted.

PLAY: Team A during a try-for-point throws two forward passes which results in a score.

RULING: Since the penalty carries a loss of down, the try-for-point by Team A has ended with no points scored.

ARTICLE 4 - NEXT PLAY: After a try-for-point, the next play shall be a kick-off or 1st and 5 at the 35 yard line.

ARTICLE 5 - THE CENTER (CONTACT FLAG, TOUCH AND INELIGIBLE LINE-MAN FLAG ONLY) - (KICKING EXTRA POINTS ONLY): The center cannot be touched and the center cannot touch anyone on an extra point kick attempt. If there is a fake kick extra point attempt, and the center fires out into a pass pattern, then the defense can legally chuck the center one time, after he takes a full step into his pass pattern. If the extra point attempt is a scrimmage play, then the center can be chucked 1 time after assuming a blocking position or firing out into his/her pass pattern by 1 full step.

ARTICLE 6 - THE CENTER (SCREEN FLAG FOOTBALL ONLY): No offensive player, including the center, is allowed to be touched or blocked in screen flag football. An attempted extra point, either by kicking or on a play from scrimmage shall have no contact involved in any way.

ARTICLE 7 - MINIMUM NUMBER OF PLAYERS ON THE LINE OF SCRIMMAGE: On an extra point attempt, there must be at least 3 players on the line of scrimmage in 7 man, 4 players on the line of scrimmage in 8 man and 5 players on the line of scrimmage in 9 man.

ARTICLE 8 - RUSHING BETWEEN THE CENTER AND GUARD (EXTRA POINT KICK ATTEMPTS ONLY): There shall be no rushing between the center and guard on an extra point kick attempt. The center's foot must be in contact with the guard's foot and the guard's foot must be in contact with the tackle's foot. NO GAPS are allowed on the offensive line.

ARTICLE 9 - STANCES: There shall be no 3 or 4 stances on any kick attempt, including extra point kick attempts.

ARTICLE 10 - POSITION OF HOLDER'S KNEES: The holder of an extra point kick attempt may have his/her knee on the ground, and after receiving the snap, may hold for the kick attempt, or get up and run or pass the ball.

ARTICLE 11 - ROUGHING THE KICKER, HOLDER OR CENTER (EXTRA POINT KICK ATTEMPTS):

a.) Any roughing of the kicker, holder or center is (S30 & S8):
  1. Automatic 10 yard penalty on the kickoff, whether the extra point was good or not;
  2. Choice of 1 point or 2 points from the 1 yard line;
  3. You may run, pass or kick from the 1 yard line for 1 or 2 points;
  4. If a choice for 1 or 2 points has been declared, the only way to change that choice is by requesting a time out;
  5. If the Kicker, Holder or Center is roughed after a kick attempt has been blocked, it is considered a personal foul - Roughing the Kicker, Center or Holder (S30 & S8).

SECTION 8 - FIELD GOAL:

ARTICLE 1 - WHEN SCORED: A field goal shall be scored for the kicking team, when a place kick in flight, other than a try for a point or a kickoff, passes between the uprights of the receiving team's goal before touching the ground or member of the kicking team, and no penalty incurred during the down is inflicted.

ARTICLE 2 - NEXT PLAY: The play following the scoring of a field goal shall be a kickoff or 1st and 5 at the 35 yard line.

ARTICLE 3 - FOUL DURING A FIELD GOAL ATTEMPT: If a double foul occurs during the field goal attempt, the down shall be replayed. When a distance penalty is incurred by Team A during a successful field goal, the down will be repeated, if accepted. However, if a Team A penalty carries a loss of down, the field goal attempt has ended and will not be repeated. No points are scored for Team A, if accepted.

ARTICLE 4 - THE CENTER (CONTACT FLAG, TOUCH AND INELIGIBLE LINE-MAN FLAG FOOTBALL): The center cannot be touched and the center cannot touch anyone on a field goal attempt. If there is a fake field goal attempt, and the center fires out into a pass pattern, then the defense can legally chuck the center one time, after he takes a full step into his pass pattern.

ARTICLE 5 - THE CENTER (SCREEN FLAG FOOTBALL ONLY): No

offensive player, including the center is allowed to be touched or blocked in screen flag football. An attempted field goal shall have no contact involved in any way.

ARTICLE 6 - MINIMUM NUMBER OF PLAYERS ON THE LINE OF SCRIMMAGE: On a field goal attempt, there must be at least 3 players on the line of scrimmage in 7 man, 4 players on the line of scrimmage in 8 man and 5 players on the line of scrimmage in 9 man.

ARTICLE 7 - RUSHING BETWEEN THE CENTER AND GUARD (FIELD GOAL ATTEMPTS): There shall be no rushing between the center and guard on a field goal attempt. The center's foot must be in contact with the guard's foot and the guard's foot must be in contact with the tackle's foot. NO GAPS are allowed on the offensive line.

ARTICLE 8 - STANCES: There shall be no 3 or 4 point stances on any kick attempt, including field goal attempts.

ARTICLE 9 - POSITION OF HOLDER'S KNEE: The holder of a field goal attempt may have his/her knee on the ground, and after receiving the snap, may hold for the kick attempt, or get up and run or pass the ball.

ARTICLE 10 - ROUGHING THE KICKER, HOLDER OR CENTER (FIELD GOAL ATTEMPT): Roughing the kicker, holder or center on a field goal attempt is an automatic 1st down and a 10 yard PENALTY: (S30 & S8).

ARTICLE 11 - WHEN A FIELD GOAL IS MISSED OR BLOCKED:

A. Missed Field Goals:

1. Field goals that are missed inside the 20 yard line shall be brought out to the 20 yard line,

2. Field goals that are missed outside the 20 yard line shall be placed at the original scrimmage line,

3. The receiving team may return a missed field goal attempt from the end zone of the field of play,

4. If the receiving team fumbles or muffs an attempted return of a missed field goal attempt, the ball is dead at the spot where it hits the ground.

B. Blocked Field Goals:

1. If an attempted field goal is blocked and hits the ground, the ball is dead,

2. Field goals that are blocked inside the 20 yard line shall be brought out to the 20 yard line,

3. Field goals that are blocked outside the 20 yard line shall be placed at the original line of scrimmage,

4. The kicking team may advance a blocked field goal attempt that is legally caught behind or beyond the line of scrimmage, as long as the ball has not yet touched the ground,

5. The receiving team may advance a blocked field goal attempt that is legally caught behind or beyond the line of scrimmage, as long as the ball has not yet touched the ground,

6. If the receiving team fumbles or muffs an attempted return of a blocked field goal attempt, the ball is dead at the spot where it hits the ground.

ARTICLE 12 - FIELD GOAL ATTEMPTS ON 1ST, 2ND OR 3RD DOWN: A Field Goal attempt on 1st, 2nd or 3rd down that is blocked by the receiving ream behind the line of scrimmage, and is caught by the kicking team shall be counted as a scrimmage play and the kicking team shall receive the next succeeding down.

SECTION 9 - THE TURNOVER RULE:

ARTICLE 1 - CHANGE OF POSSESSION DURING LAST 2 MINUTES OF SECOND HALF: During the last 2 minutes of the second half ONLY, all Free Kicks that follow a score MUST be returned by R to R's 20 yard line or further (after all penalties that occur have been assessed), or K shall receive the ball at the 50 yard line, 1st down and the next zone line-to-gain. **Applies to losing team only.**

ARTICLE 2 - FOUL DURING A RETURN IN THE LAST 2 MINUTES OF THE SECOND HALF: All fouls that occur on a return, during the last 2 minutes of the 2nd half, must result in the ball being brought to or past the 20 yard line, or K shall receive the ball on the 50 yard line, 1st down and the next zone line-to-gain. **Applies to losing team only.**

ARTICLE 3 - TOUCHBACK: If a Touchback occurs during the last 2 minutes of the second half, it shall be R's ball on R's 20 yard line, 1st down and the next zone line-to-gain.

RULE 11 - SCORING

SECTION 1 - SCORING VALUES:

ARTICLE 1 - SCORING CHART: The following chart shall be used in scoring a game:
- **A:** Touchdown = 6 points
- **B:** Touchdown (female) = 9 points (Co-Rec Only)
- **C:** Field Goal = 3 points
- **D:** Safety = 2 points
- **E:** Forfeited Game = 1 point
- **F:** Extra Point:
    1. By running, passing, or kicking from 3 yards = 1 point (2 points - female, Co-Rec only).
    2. By running, passing or kicking from 10 yards = 2 points. (3 points - female, Co-Rec only)(NOTE: A team is given one choice which cannot be changed even if a penalty should occur. If you declare you are going for 2 points, the ball is placed at the 10 yard line and even if a penalty shall occur the team will only be able to run, pass or kick and if successful no matter from what distance the value of the try is 2 points).
- **G:** Return of Extra Point Attempt by Defense = 2 points

SECTION 2 - TOUCHDOWN:

ARTICLE 1 - HOW SCORED: A touchdown shall be scored when a legal forward pass is completed or a fumble or backward pass is caught on or behind the opponents' goal line and when a player is legally in possession of the ball while any part of the ball is on, above or behind his/her opponents' goal line.

ARTICLE 2 - TOUCHDOWN VALUES: If a female scores a touchdown, the point value is 9 (Co-Recreation rule only). All other touchdowns are 6 points.

ARTICLE 3 - PLAYER RESPONSIBILITY (CONTACT FLAG, SCREEN FLAG AND INELIGIBLE LINEMAN FLAG FOOTBALL ONLY): The player scoring the touchdown must raise his/her arms so the nearest official can deflag the player. If the player is not deflagged with one pull, and the official determines the flag belt has been secured illegally, the touchdown is disallowed. The player is disqualified.

PENALTY: Unsportsmanlike conduct, 10 yards from the previous spot and a loss of down. (S47, S27 & S9).

SECTION 3 - EXTRA POINT (1 OR 2 POINTS):

ARTICLE 1 - 1 OR 2 POINTS: An opportunity to score 1 point from the 3 yard line or 2 points from the 10 yard line shall be granted the team scoring a touchdown. There shall be one scrimmage play or kick, unless changed by penalty. A run, pass or kick attempt is allowed.

ARTICLE 2 - REFEREE'S RESPONSIBILITY: The Referee must speak to the field captain only, asking him/her whether the extra point shall be from the 3 or 10 yard line. Once the Team A captain makes the choice, he/she may change the decision only by taking a charged team time-out. A team's choice cannot be changed if a penalty should occur. Enforcement of yardage penalties does not change the value of the extra point. The point(s) shall be awarded if the extra point results in what would have been a touchdown.

PLAY: Team A scores a touchdown and elects to attempt a 1 point conversion; then after calling a charged time-out, selects to change and attempt a 2 point conversion.

RULING: Legal. A Team charged time-out only can buy a change on an extra point option.

ARTICLE 3 - CHANGE OF POSSESSION DURING AN EXTRA POINT ATTEMPT: After a score by Team A and during Team A's Extra Point Attempt, if Team B intercepts a pass, blocks a kick and recovers it before it hits the ground, or recovers a fumble in the air before it hits the ground, Team B may advance the ball to Team A's end zone for 2 points.

ARTICLE 4 - FOUL BEFORE A CHANGE OF POSSESSION DURING AN EXTRA POINT ATTEMPT: If the foul is on either Team A or Team B before the change of possession, penalty assessment shall be the same as in regulation play.

ARTICLE 5 - FOUL AFTER A CHANGE OF POSSESSION DURING AN EXTRA POINT ATTEMPT: If a foul occurs after the change of possession, all penalties on Team A will result in the ball being placed on Team A's 10 yard line. Team B shall receive 1 untimed down from the 10 yard line for 2 points. The play must be a running or a passing play. (No kicks allowed). After the attempt, Team A shall still kick-off. If the foul was on Team B, penalty assessment shall be the same as in regulation play.

ARTICLE 6 - INADVERTENT WHISTLE BEFORE A CHANGE OF POSSESSION DURING AN EXTRA POINT ATTEMPT: If an Inadvertent Whistle occurs before a change of possession, penalty assessments shall be the same as in regulation play.

ARTICLE 7 - INADVERTENT WHISTLE AFTER A CHANGE OF POSSESSION DURING AN EXTRA POINT ATTEMPT: An Inadvertent

Whistle after a change of possession shall result in Team B getting the ball on Team A's 10 yard line for 1 untimed down (run or pass) for 2 points, or the result of the play, plus 1 untimed down from the spot of the Inadvertent Whistle.

SECTION 4 - FIELD GOAL:

ARTICLE 1 - WHEN SCORED: A field goal shall be scored for the kicking team, when a place kick in flight, other than a try for a point or a kickoff, passes between the uprights of the receiving team's goal before touching the ground or a member of the kicking team, and no penalty incurred during the down is inflicted. Field Goals are worth 3 points.

ARTICLE 2 - NEXT PLAY: The play following the scoring of a field goal shall be a Free Kick (Kickoff).

SECTION 5 - SAFETY:

ARTICLE 1 - SAFETY (2 POINTS): It is a safety when:

a. A runner carries the ball from the field of play to or across his/her own goal line, and it becomes dead there in his/her team's possession.

EXCEPTION: When a Team B player intercepts a forward pass or catches a scrimmage kick or free kick between his/her 5 yard line and the goal line and his/her original momentum carries him/her into the end zone where the ball is declared dead in his/her team's possession or it goes out-of-bounds in the end zone, the ball belongs to Team B at the spot where the pass was intercepted or the kick was caught. This is known as the momentum rule,

b. A player forces a loose ball from the field of play to or across his/her goal line by his/her kick, pass, fumble, snap, muff, or bat and the ball subsequently becomes dead there in his/her team's possession. This includes when the ball is declared dead on or behind their goal line. However, it does not apply to a legal forward pass which becomes incomplete,

c. A player on offense commits any foul for which the penalty is accepted and measurement is from a spot in his/her end zone; or throws an illegal forward pass from his/her end zone and the penalty is declined in a situation which leaves him/her in possession at the spot of the illegal pass and with the ball having been forced into the end zone by the passing team,

d. Afterwards. When a safety is scored the ball belongs to the defending team at its own 20 yard line and that team shall put the ball in play on the inbounds line by a freekick that may be a punt or place kick.

SECTION 6 - FORCE AND RESPONSIBILITY:

ARTICLE 1 - FORCE: The force imparted by a player who kicks, passes, snaps, or fumbles the ball shall be considered responsible for the ball's progress in any direction even though its course is deflected, or reversed, after striking the ground or after striking a player of either team. However, the initial force is considered expended and a new force is provided if a loose ball is illegally kicked or batted or it is contacted again after coming to rest.

ARTICLE 2 - RESPONSIBILITY: The team responsible for a ball being on, above, or behind a goal line is the team whose player carries the ball to or across that goal line or imparts to the ball an impetus which forces it to or across that line; or incurs a penalty which leaves the ball on or behind the line.

SECTION 7 - MERCY RULE:

ARTICLE 1 - TWO MINUTE WARNING: If a team is 17 or more points ahead when the Referee announces the 2 minute warning for the second half, the game shall be over.

ARTICLE 2 - AFTER THE TWO MINUTE WARNING: If a team scores during the last two minutes of the second half and the score creates a point differential of 17 or more, the game shall end at that point.

SECTION 8 - FORFEITED GAME

ARTICLE 1 - FORFEITED SCORE: The score of a forfeited game shall be: Offended Team - 1, Opponent - 0. If the Offended Team is ahead at the time of the forfeit, the score stands. Game time is forfeited time.

RULE 12 - CONDUCT OF PLAYERS AND OTHERS SUBJECT TO THE RULES

SECTION 1 - UNSPORTSMANLIKE CONDUCT:

ARTICLE 1 - DELIBERATE FLAGRANT FOULS (SUSPENSION FROM THE GAME): Whenever, in the judgment of any game official, the following acts are deliberate or flagrant the players involved shall be disqualified from the game. Examples include, but are not limited to:

  a. Intentionally contacting a game official physically during the game by persons subject to the rules,
  b. Roughing the kicker, center or holder of a kick (S30),
  c. Tackling the ball carrier as in regulation football,
  d. Using fists, kicking or fighting,
  e. Using locked hands, elbows or any part of the forearm or hand, except according to rule,
  f. Any other deliberate or flagrant act.

PENALTY: Unsportsmanlike conduct, 10 yards (S27), and if flagrant, the offender shall be disqualified. (S47).

ARTICLE 2 - PROHIBITED ACTS: There shall be no unsportsmanlike conduct by players, substitutes, coaches or others subject to the rules. Examples include, but are not limited to:

  a. Any acts of unfair play,
  b. Intentionally kicking at the ball, other than during a legal kick,
  c. Using disconcerting acts or words prior to the snap in an attempt to interfere with Team A's signals or movements,
  d. Leaving the field between downs to gain an advantage unless replaced or with permission of the Referee,
  e. Spiking ball, taunting opponent or other similar theatrics before or after a touchdown,
  f. Using profanity, abusive, insulting, or vulgar language or gesture,
  g. Holding an unauthorized conference, or being on the field illegally,
  h. Indicating objections to an official's decision,
  i. Intentionally kick the ball,
  j. Spike the ball into the ground,
  k. Coaches or others on the field of play at any time,

l. Players leaving the field of play other than during the intermission at half time,
m. A substitute or any other person interfering with a player or any play while the ball is alive,
n. The punter delaying the kick, after requesting protection,
o. Using a "hide-out play" by placing a player or players near the side line who were not within 5 yards of the sideline from the time of the ready-for-play signal to the snap,
p. Attempting to substitute a suspended player,
q. Pulling or removing a flag from an offensive player without the ball by a defensive player intentionally.

PENALTY: Unsportsmanlike conduct, 10 yards (S27), and if flagrant, the offender shall be disqualified (S47).

PLAY: Team A substitutes voice their disapproval using abusive language concerning a judgment call by the back judge.

RULING: The Referee should call an "Officials time-out." inform Team A captain that such behavior is unacceptable, and tell the captain to communicate this information to his/her bench. If such behavior is exhibited again during the game, penalize 10 yards for unsportsmanlike conduct. It is imperative that the officials stop such behavior the first time it occurs. Team A and B are present to play the game, not officiate it. When the officials accept the game assignment, they must be strong and ready to take control.

ARTICLE 3 - DEAD BALL PLAYER FOULS: When the ball becomes dead in possession of a player, he/she shall not:

a. Intentionally kick the ball,
b. Spike the ball into the ground,
c. Throw the ball high into the air,
d. Fail to return the ball to the huddle.

PENALTY: Unsportsmanlike conduct 10 yards (S27), and if flagrant, the offender shall be disqualified (S47).

SECTION 2 - UNFAIR ACTS:

ARTICLE 1 - REFUSAL TO PLAY OR HALVING THE DISTANCE:

If a team refuses to play within two minutes after being ordered by the Referee, or if a team repeatedly commits fouls which can be penalized only by halving the distance to its goal line, the Referee may enforce any penalty he/she considers equitable, including the awarding of a score. For refusal to play, or for repeated fouls, the Referee shall, after one warning, forfeit the game to the opponents.

ARTICLE 2 - UNFAIR ACTS: No player, substitute, coach or others subject to the Rules shall use disconcerting words or phrases or commit any act not in accordance with the spirit of fair play for the purposes of confusing the opponent.

PENALTY: Unfair Act, Live Ball Foul, 10 yards (S38).

PLAY: Center A-2 shouts to the Referee "wet ball, wet ball" in an attempt to have Team B relax. A-2 then snaps the ball and play begins.

RULING: Unfair Act. Use of disconcerting words or acts to gain an unfair advantage. Penalize as All-But-One.

PLAY: Center A-2 snaps the ball but only one person leaves the scrimmage line. All other teammates stand up and yell at the person that the snap count was on 3. When Team B relaxes, A-1 throws the ball to the person who left the scrimmage line.

RULING: Unfair Act. Use of disconcerting words or acts to gain an unfair advantage. Penalize as All-But-One.

SECTION 3 - PERSONAL FOULS:

ARTICLE 1 - PLAYER RESTRICTIONS: No player shall commit a personal foul during a period or an intermission. Any act prohibited hereunder or any other act of unnecessary roughness is a personal foul. No player shall:

  a. No player shall block in a manner that would cause his or her feet, knees, or legs to strike an opponent. All blocking shall be done with the feet in contact with the ground (S38 & S40),
  b. There shall be no high-low blocking (S38 & S40),
  c. There shall be no contact to the head, shoulders or below waist (S38 & S40),
  d. There shall be no contact of any nature in screen flag football (S38),
  e. There shall be no contact with an opponent who is on the ground (S38),
  f. The runner shall not be thrown to the ground (S38),
  g. There shall be no hurdling to advance the ball. Hurdling to avoid injury is acceptable (S38),
  h. There shall be no tripping (S46),
  i. There shall be no clipping (S39),
  j. No player shall contact an opponent obviously out of the play either before or after the ball is declared dead (S38),
  k. The ball carrier shall not deliberately drive or run into a defensive player (S38),
  l. There shall be no unnecessary roughness of any nature (S38),
  m. Tackling (S38 & S47),
  n. Using fists (S38),
  o. Knocking out-of-bounds (S38),
  p. Punch, strike, strip, steal, or attempt to steal the ball from a player in possession (S38),
  q. Position himself/herself on the shoulders or body of a teammate or opponent to gain an advantage (S38),
  r. Make any contact with an opponent which is deemed unnecessary of any nature including using fists, locked hands, elbows or any part of the forearm or hand, except according to Rule (S38).

PENALTY: 10 yards (S38), and if flagrant, the offender shall be disqualified (S47).
  s. There shall be no diving to advance the ball.

PLAY #1: B-2, moving toward A-1 who has the ball in his/her possession:
  a) grabs/strips the ball from A-1, or
  b) tries to knock the ball out of A-1's hands.

RULING: In a) and b) this is a personal foul penalty. B must go for the flag belt or the tag.

PLAY #2: A-1, running for a score, dives into the end zone:

a) breaks the plane with the ball without contacting any Team B player; or
b) charges into B-3 at the 1 yard line; or
c) charges into B-4 in the end zone after crossing the goal line.

RULING: In a) and b) a 10 yard penalty is assessed against Team A from the 1 yard line. In c) the score counts and Team A will be assessed a 10 yard penalty on the try-for-point.

ARTICLE 2 - ROUGHING THE PASSER: Defensive players must make a definite effort to avoid charging into a passer after it is clear the ball has been thrown. No defensive player shall contact the passer who is standing still or fading back as he/she is considered out of the play after the pass. Roughing the passer restrictions end if the forward pass is thrown from beyond Team A's scrimmage line.

PENALTY: Roughing the passer, 10 yards, automatic first down, plus gained yardage of reception (S34 & S8). (NOTE: In order to protect the quarterbacks in Flag & Touch Football, arguably the most important player on their team, and definitely the most vulnerable to injury, the U.S.F.T.L. has decided to maximize the penalty for Roughing The Passer: The penalty for Roughing The Passer shall be an automatic 1st down plus 10 yards from the line of scrimmage if the pass attempt was incomplete; if the pass was completed legally, and there was Roughing The Passer, the penalty shall be an automatic 1st down, the gained yardage from the pass completed and then, 10 extra yards added on.) If Roughing the Passer occurs after a legal touchdown pass is thrown, tack on 10 yards to the kick-off.

PLAY: B-3 rushing, jumps to block a pass thrown by A-1 and:
a) blocks the ball and, avoiding unnecessary contact, brushes A-1; or
b) is unsuccessful in blocking the pass and charges into A-1; or
e) blocks the ball and charges into A-1; or
d) contacts passer A-1's arm.

RULING: In a), no call is made, in b), c) and d) roughing the passer, 10 yards and an automatic first down. If the defender contacts the passer's arm, whether or not he/she touches the pass, it is roughing the passer.

SECTION 4 - BLOCKING:

ARTICLE 1 - CONTACT BLOCKING: Contact blocking is legally hindering the progress of an opponent in a fair and safe manner. Blockers must be on their feet before, during and after contact is made with their opponent. You may not dive to block. Two on one blocking is permitted anywhere on the field, at any time. Under no conditions shall a high-low block, cross body block or rolling block be permitted. The blocker is allowed to contact only that portion of the opponent's body between the waist and shoulders. An open hand, straight arm block, within the framework of the blocker's body, is the ideal block to avoid unnecessary rough play. You may not grab the jersey of an opponent while attempting to block. The blocker's hands may not be locked together. The blocker may not swing, throw or flip the elbow or forearm. There shall be no contact of any kind to the head and/or shoulders in the attempt to block an opponent. The main concept to keep contact blocking under control is to stress safe, clean, sportsmanlike contact between opponents. In general, players shall be limited to the following:

a. In all instances, blockers must be on their feet when blocking, accidentally

falling when attempting a block is not an illegal block,
b. The blocker's hands may not be locked,
c. The blocker may not swing, throw, or flip the elbow or forearm,
d. The hands may be closed or cupped and the palms may be facing the opponent being blocked,
e. Blocking below the waist is illegal,
f. Neither the offensive or defensive team may make contact with the other players' head or neck.

PENALTY: Personal Foul, 10 yards (S38). Players of either team may block opponents provided it is neither forward pass interference, fair catch interference, nor a personal foul. Teammates of a ball carrier or passer may interfere by blocking, but there shall be no interlocking interference. This prohibition includes grasping or encircling one another, to any degree with the hand or arm.

PENALTY: Personal Foul, 10 yards (S38).

ARTICLE 2 - SCREEN BLOCKING: Screen blocking is legally obstructing an opponent without initiating contact with him/her with any part of the screen blocker's body. The offensive screen block shall take place without contact. The screen blocker shall have his/her hands and arms at his/her side or behind his/her back. Any use of the arms, elbows, or legs to initiate contact during an offensive player's screen block is illegal. A blocker may use his/her hand or arm to break a fall or to retain his/her balance. A player must be on his/her feet before, during and after screen blocking.

PENALTY: Personal Foul, 10 yards (S38).

PLAY: A-2, a blocking back, extends his/her arms from his/her side while screen blocking, but causes no contact.

RULING: The officials must determine if A-2 gained an advantage. If so, penalize 10 yards; however, if no advantage was gained do not penalize. Once the down has ended, inform A-2 about proper arm position. If A-2 then continues to extend his/her arms, penalize.

SECTION 5 - RUNNER:

ARTICLE 1 - GUARDING THE FLAG: Runners shall not flag guard by using their hands, arms, or the ball to deny the opportunity for an opponent to pull or remove the flag belt. Flag guarding includes:

a. Swing the hand or arm over the flag belt to prevent an opponent from deflagging:
b. Place the ball in possession over the flag belt to prevent an opponent from deflagging.
c. Lower the shoulders in such a manner which places the arm over the flag belt to prevent an opponent from deflagging.

PENALTY: Flag Guarding, 10 yards and loss of down (S24 & S9).

PLAY: A-1 catches the snap from center A-2, fakes a handoff to A-3, then places the ball on his/her hip (bootleg), rolls out, and throws a forward pass. Should A-1 be penalized for guarding the flag?

RULING: If B-1 could not reach the flag belt because A-1 had placed the ball on the belt, then penalize; however, if a B player was not close enough to deflag A-1, then do not penalize. Advantage versus disadvantage is the key.

ARTICLE 2 - HELPING THE RUNNER: The runner shall not grasp a teammate or be grasped, pulled or pushed by a teammate.

PENALTY: Helping Runner, 5 yards (S44).

ARTICLE 3 - STIFF ARM: The runner shall be prohibited from contacting an opponent with extended hand or arm. This includes the use of a "stiff arm" extended to ward off an opponent attempting to deflag/tag.

EXEPTION: Stiff arm is allowed in Ineligible Lineman Flag. Stiff arm may not contact shoulders or head of an opponent or may not guard the flag.

PENALTY: Personal Foul, 10 yards (S38).

ARTICLE 4 - OBSTRUCTION OF RUNNER: The defensive player shall not hold, grasp, or obstruct the forward progress of a runner when in the act of removing the flag or making a legal tag.

PENALTY: Personal Foul, 10 yards (S38).

PLAY: A-1 running toward B-2, who is attempting to deflag A-1:

a) goes around B-2 to avoid being deflagged;
b) deliberately runs through B-2 making no attempt to avoid contact; or
c) ducks his/her head while contacting B-2.

RULING: In a), play is legal. In b) and c), Team A personal foul, 10 yards. If B-2 is stationary, A-1 must go around. The charge/block principles used in basketball apply.

ARTICLE 5 - DIVING TO ADVANCE THE BALL: Diving to advance the ball is an illegal advancement.

PLAY: A-1 running toward B-2, who is attempting to deflag A-1:

a) A-1 goes around B - 2 to avoid being deflagged;
b) A-1 deliberately dives into the end zone to score a touchdown; or
c) A-1 ducks his/her head while contacting B -2.

RULING: In a), play is legal. In b) and c), Team A personal foul, l0 yards (S38). In play C, B-2 is stationary, A-1 must go around. The charge/block principles used in basketball apply.

SECTION 6 - BATTING AND KICKING:

ARTICLE 1 - BATTING A FREE BALL: Players shall not bat a loose ball other than a pass or a fumble in flight. A backward pass in flight shall not be batted forward by the passing team. Player may bat a low scrimmage kick or free kick in flight which he/she is attempting to block or recover in the neutral zone or on the kicking team side of the ball. A ball in player possession shall not be batted forward by a player of the team in possession. You may not bat a loose ball, either forward or backward, to gain an advantage.

EXCEPTION: The kicking team may bat a grounded protected scrimmage kick beyond the Team A scrimmage line toward their own goal line.

PENALTY: Illegal batting, 10 yards (S31).

ARTICLE 2 - ILLEGAL KICKING: No player shall intentionally kick a ball other than as a free kick or a protected scrimmage kick.

PENALTY: Illegal kicking, 10 yards (S31).

SECTION 7 - FLAG REMOVAL:

ARTICLE 1 - LEGAL AND ILLEGAL FLAG REMOVAL: There are basic rules which are established for flag football because of legal or illegal removal of the flag:

a. Players must have possession of the ball before they can legally be deflagged,
b. When a runner loses his/her flag either accidentally, inadvertently (not remove by grabbing or pulling), or on purpose, play continues. The deflagging reverts to a two hand touch of the runner between the shoulders and the knees,
c. In circumstances where a flag is removed illegally, play should continue with the option of the penalty or the play.

PENALTY: Personal Foul, 10 yards (S38),

d. Defensive player intentionally pulling a flag from an offensive player without the ball is illegal.

PENALTY: Personal Foul, 10 yards (S38),

e. Tampering with the flag in any way to gain an advantage including tying, using foreign materials, or other such acts is illegal.

PENALTY: Unsportsmanlike conduct, 10 yards from the previous spot, loss of down and player disqualification (S27, S9 & S47).

PLAY: A-1 tampers with his/her flag belt and scores a touchdown with or without any B player having a chance to deflag A-1.

RULING: The official pulls A-1's flag belt and finds it has been tampered with. Unsportsmanlike Conduct, 10 yard penalty, loss of down from previous spot, A-1 is disqualified and the touchdown is disallowed.

PLAY: B-2 deflags/tags A-4 after the passed ball is touched by A-4 and:
   a.) the ball is muffed then caught by A-4; or
   b.) the ball is muffed then intercepted by B-2, or
   c.) the ball is muffed then touched by B-2 and finally caught by A-4.

RULING: In a.), b.), and c.), the ball is alive and reverts to two hand tag. The ball becomes dead when the runner is tagged/deflagged legally.

PLAY: A-2 carries the ball when B-3 and B-4 attempt to deflag A-2. B-3 and B-4 touch or grasp the flag or flagbelt momentarily. A-2 continue to run a few steps and the flag or flagbelt fall to the ground.

RULING: A-2 is down where the original deflag was attempted. B-3 and B-4 are deemed to have caused the deflag.

SECTION 8 - ILLEGAL PARTICIPATION:

ARTICLE 1 - HINDER AN OPPONENT: No replaced player or substitute shall hinder an opponent, touch the ball, influence the play, or otherwise participate.

ARTICLE 2 - BLOCKED OR PUSHED OUT-OF-BOUNDS: Prior to a change of possession, no player of A or K shall go out-of-bounds and return during the down unless blocked out-of-bounds by an opponent. If a player is blocked out-of-bounds by an opponent and returns inbounds during the down, he/she shall return at the first opportunity. During the down, no player shall intentionally go out-of-bounds and return.

ARTICLE 3 - ILLEGAL PARTICIPATION:

a. To have the following amount of players on the field at the snap or free kick:
3 players in 2 Man, 4 players in 3 Man, 5 players in 4 Man, 6 players in 5 Man, 7 players in 6 Man, 8 players in 7 Man, 9 players in 8 Man,
10 players in 9 Man, 11 players in 10 Man, 12 players in 11 Man,
b. If an injured player is not replaced for at least one down, unless the halftime or overtime intermission occurs,
c. For a disqualified player to reenter the game,
d. To use a replaced player or substitute in a substitution or pretended substitution to deceive opponents at or immediately before the snap or free kick,
e. For a player to be lying on the ground to deceive opponents at or immediately before the snap or free kick.
f. A player who comes off the bench and tackles a ball carrier, who in the Official's estimation would have scored a touchdown, the ball carrier is awarded a touchdown and the player who came off the bench during the live ball play is ejected.

PENALTY: Illegal Participation, 10 yards. (S28).

PLAY: QB A-1 throws a legal forward pass to A-2. A-2 steps on the sideline, returns and touches the pass.

RULING: A-2, Illegal Participation, 10 yards. (S28).

SECTION 9 - EJECTIONS:

ARTICLE 1: A player that is ejected during a tournament shall be suspended from playing the game in which he was ejected and also the following game. That next game cannot be a forfeited game. He must also pay a fine before reinstatement.

PENALTY: Player Disqualification. (S47).

SECTION 10 - LAST MAN RULE:

ARTICLE 1: A player who comes off the bench and tackles a ball carrier, who in the Official's estimation would have scored a touchdown, the ball carrier is awarded a touchdown and the player who came off the bench during the live ball play is ejected.

SECTION 11 - TEAM NOT LEAVING FIELD OF PLAY:

ARTICLE 1: A Team that will not leave the field of play at the end of the game will be subject to a fine and disbarment.

RULE 13 - ENFORCEMENT OF PENALTIES

SECTION 1 - PROCEDURE AFTER A FOUL:

ARTICLE 1 - CAPTAIN'S CHOICE: When a foul occurs during a live ball, the Referee shall, at the end of the down, notify both captains. He/she shall inform the captain of the offended team regarding the rights of penalty acceptance or declination and shall indicate to him/her the number of the ensuing down, distance to be gained, and status of the ball for each available choice. THE DISTANCE PENALTY FOR ANY FOUL MAY BE DECLINED. If the penalty is declined or if there is a double foul, there is no loss of distance. A captain's choice of options may not be revoked.

ARTICLE 2 - DEAD BALL FOUL: When a foul occurs during a dead ball either between downs or prior to a free kick or snap, the officials shall not permit the ball to become alive. The penalty for any foul between downs, any nonplayer foul, or any unsportsmanlike foul, is enforced from the succeeding spot. The succeeding spot is where the ball would next be snapped or free kicked if a foul had not occurred. If a dead ball foul occurs after time expires for any period, the penalty shall be measured from the succeeding spot.

ARTICLE 3 - LIVE BALL/DEAD BALL FOUL: When a live ball foul by one team is followed by a dead ball foul by the opponent, the penalties are administered separately and in the order of occurrence. When the same team commits a live ball foul followed by one or more dead ball fouls, all fouls may be penalized.

ARTICLE 4 - ESTABLISH ZONE LINE-TO-GAIN: On a live ball foul mark off the penalty yardage first, then establish the zone line-to-gain. However, with a dead ball foul, establish the zone line-to-gain first, and then mark off the penalty yardage.

PLAY: Third and 2 on A 18. A-2 runs to the A 26.
   a) A-2 flag guards at the A 25 and is deflagged at the A 35; or
   b) A-2 is deflagged at the A 26. The Referee calls an unsportsmanlike conduct foul on A-2.

RULING: a) Penalize Team A 10 yards for flag guarding and loss of down, A's ball fourth and 5 on A 15. b)Penalize Team A 10 yards for the dead ball foul from the A 26, first and 24 on A 16. The zone line-to-gain has been reached legally since there are no live ball fouls. The Referee will signal first down, establish a new zone line-to-gain, the 40, then penalize the dead ball foul from the succeeding spot, the A 26.

SECTION 2 - TYPES OF PLAY AND BASIC ENFORCEMENT SPOTS:

ARTICLE 1 - LIVE BALL FOULS: Any live ball foul is penalized according to the all-but-one enforcement principle except:

   a. A foul which occurs simultaneously with the snap or free kick, penalize at the previous spot,
   b. Nonplayer foul, unsportsmanlike foul, or dead ball foul, penalize at the succeeding spot.
   c. An invalid fair catch signal is penalized from the succeeding spot.

ARTICLE 2 - TWO TYPES OF PLAYS: Whenever the ball is alive, 1 of 2 types of plays is in progress, either a loose ball play or a running play. The type of play has no significance unless a foul occurs. If a foul does occur, the officials must know whether it was during a loose ball play or during a running play. This determines the basic spot of enforcement.

ARTICLE 3 - LOOSE BALL PLAY:. A loose ball play is action during:

   a. A free kick or protected scrimmage kick,
   b. A legal forward pass,
   c. A backward pass or fumble made by A from on or behind his/her scrimmage line. It includes the run(s) which precede such legal pass, fumble or kick. If a

foul occurs during a loose ball play, the basic enforcement spot is the previous spot, either the spot of the snap or the free kick.

ARTICLE 4 - ALL-BUT-ONE ENFORCEMENT PHILOSOPHY: Enforcement philosophy is based on the fact that a team is given the advantage of the distance which is gained without assistance of a foul. It is assumed that the only foul which would give this aid is a foul by the offense behind the basic spot. Therefore, all fouls but this one, that is a foul by the offense behind the basic spot, are penalized from the basic spot, unless it occurs behind the line of scrimmage. Then it is assessed from the line of scrimmage.

EXCEPTION: Any foul that occurs by the offense in their own end zone shall be ruled a safety.

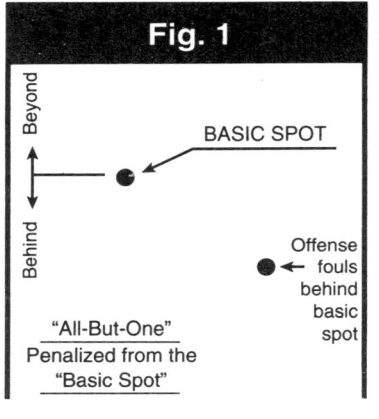
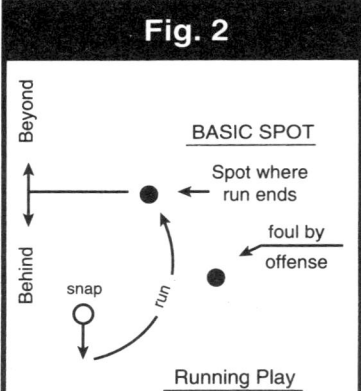
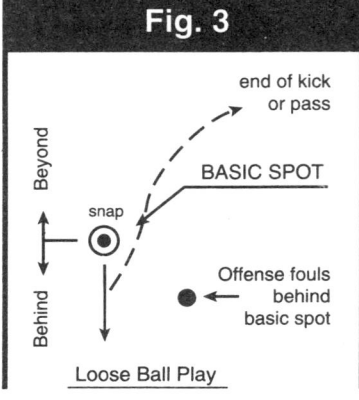
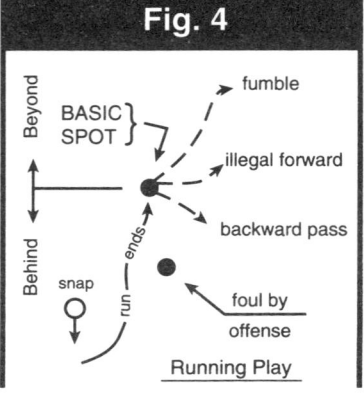

ARTICLE 5 - RUNNING PLAY: A running play is any action which is not a loose ball play:

  a. Behind the line it includes:
    1. A run which is not followed by a loose ball behind the line,
    2. A run which is followed by an illegal pass from behind the line.
  b. Beyond the line it includes any run. A run ends when a runner loses possession, but the related running play continues until the ball becomes dead or some player again gains possession. If a foul occurs during a running play, the basic enforcement spot is the spot where the run ended. If the runner does not lose possession, the ball becomes dead when the run ends.

PLAY: K-1's kickoff is caught by R-1. During the run R-1 guards the flag at his/her 22 yardline. R-1 is then deflagged by K-1 at the 40 yardline.

RULING: Penalize Team R 10 yards from the 22 yard line which is the spot of the foul, R's ball, first and 8 on K's 12-yard line. Once the kickoff is caught the loose ball play has ended. It is now a running play. The foul by the offensive team behind the basic spot, the end of the run, is enforced from the spot of the foul.

PLAY: K-1's protected scrimmage kick is caught by R-1. During the run K-2 illegally contacts R-1 at the K 35 yard line. R-1 is deflagged/tagged at the K 28 yardline.

RULING: Penalize K Team K-10 yards from the K 28 yardline which is the end of the run, R's ball first and 2 on K 38. All fouls, except by the offense behind the end of the run, are penalized from the basic spot, the end of the run.

PLAY: Third and 2 on Team A 38. QB A-1 runs two yards beyond the Team A scrimmage line and throws an illegal forward pass from the 40 yard line.

RULING: Fourth and 5 on Team A 35. All illegal forward passes are treated as running plays. Penalize from the spot of the pass where the run has ended.

PLAY: Third and 5 on Team A 35. QB A-1 thro ws a legal forward pass to receiver A-2 who runs to the Team B 19 yardline and flag guards. A-2 scores an apparent touchdown.

RULING: No touchdown. Penalize Team A-2 10 yards from the Team B 19 yard line, first and 9 on Team B 29 yard line. Once A-2 caught the pass it became a running play. Since there was a foul by the offense behind the end of the run, which is the goal line, penalize from the spot of the foul.

SECTION 3 - SPECIAL ENFORCEMENTS:

ARTICLE 1 - HALF THE DISTANCE: A measurement cannot take the ball more than half the distance from the enforcement spot to the offending team's goal line. If the penalty is greater than this, the ball is placed halfway between the enforcement spot and the goal line.

ARTICLE 2 - FORFEITURE OF THE GAME: A Referee's decision to forfeit a game is final.

ARTICLE 3 - DISQUALIFIED PLAYER: A disqualified player must be removed from the playing field and has 5 minutes to leave the playing field or the game may be forfeited to the disqualified players team's opponent. The disqualified players team coach must be notified of disqualified player.

ARTICLE 4 - FAIR CATCH INTERFERENCE: R may choose a 10 yard penalty from the previous spot with K retaining the football and the down replayed, or they may accept an awarded fair catch at the spot of the foul.

ARTICLE 5 - SAFETY/GOAL LINE: If the offensive team throws an illegal forward pass from its end zone or commits any other foul for which the penalty is accepted and measurement is from on or behind its goal line which is now the basic spot, it is a safety. For a defensive team foul, if the enforcement spot which is now the basic spot, is on or behind the offended team's goal line any measurement is from the goal line.

ARTICLE 6 - FOUL ON A SCORE: If there is a player foul by the offensive team, other than unsportsmanlike, during a down which results in a successful touchdown or extra point, the acceptance of the penalty nullifies the score. If there is a player foul by the defensive team, other than unsportsmanlike, during a down which results in a successful touchdown or extra point, the offensive team must decline the penalty and accept the score.

PLAY: QB A-1 runs for a touchdown. Cornerback B-1 illegally holds A-1 during the run.

RULING: Team A must decline the holding foul to score the touchdown. The same ruling applies on an extra point.

ARTICLE 7 - FOUL PRIOR TO AN EXTRA POINT: When a foul occurs after a touchdown and before the ball is ready for play for the extra point, the enforcement is at the succeeding spot where the ball will be next snapped for the extra point, usually the 3 or 10 yard line.

PLAY: QB A-1 scores a touchdown and then spikes the ball.

RULING: The touchdown counts. The Referee will ask the Team A captain whether they wish to go for a 1 or 2 extra points. Once the Team A captain makes a decision, penalize Team A 10 yards on the extra point from the 3 or 10 yard line.

ARTICLE 8 - DOUBLE FOUL: It is a double foul if both teams commit fouls, other than unsportsmanlike, during the same live ball period in which:

a. There is no change of team possession;
b. There is a change of team possession, and the team in possession at the end of the down fouls prior to final change of possession;
c. There is a change of possession and the team in final possession accepts the penalty for its opponent's foul.

In a, b and c the penalties cancel and the down is replayed.

EXCEPTION: If each team fouls during a down in which there is a change of team possession, the team last gaining possession may retain the ball, provided its foul is not prior to the final change of possession and it declined the penalty for its opponents foul(s), other than unsportsmanlike. This exception is continuously referred to as the principle of "clean hands."

PLAY: K-1 kicks off, R-1 catches the ball and throws an illegal forward pass from his/her 26 yard line. R-2 catches the pass and K-2 holds R-2 prior to the tag/deflag.

RULING: The Referee will present the following options to the R captain:

1) If you accept the holding foul by K-2, it is a double foul, and the ball will be rekicked;

2) If you want to keep the ball, you must decline the holding foul by K-2. The Referee would then mark off 5 yards to R's 21 yard line, R's ball, first and 19.

ARTICLE 9 - MULTIPLE LIVE BALL FOULS: When two or more live ball fouls are committed by the same team, only one penalty may be chosen except when a foul(s) for unsportsmanlike conduct occurs. In such cases, the penalty/penalties for the unsportsmanlike conduct is administered from the succeeding spot as a dead ball foul.

ARTICLE 10 - MULTIPLE DEAD BALL FOULS: Penalties for dead ball fouls are administered separately and in the order of occurrence. Dead ball fouls are not coupled with live ball fouls or other dead ball fouls to create double or multiple fouls. Penalize all unsportsmanlike fouls separately.

ARTICLE 11 - LOSS OF DOWN FOULS: Fouls which include loss of down are those where Team A loses its right to repeat the down as:
a. Illegally handing the ball forward.
b. Illegal forward pass by Team A.
c. Forward pass interference by Team A.
d. Illegally secured flag belt.
e. Flag Guarding.

ARTICLE 12 - AUTOMATIC FIRST DOWN FOULS: Fouls by Team B which give Team A an automatic first down are:
a. Forward Pass interference by Team B.
b. Roughing the Passer who has thrown from behind the Team A scrimmage line.
c. Roughing the Kicker or Holder who was behind the team A scrimmage line.
d. Illegally Secured Flag Belt.

ARTICLE 13 - FOUL ON PASS ATTEMPT PLAYS IN OFFENSIVE BACKFIELD BY THE OFFENSE: The penalty enforcement on fouls on passing attempt in the offensive backfield shall be administered from the line of scrimmage. The concept behind this penalty enforcement has been instituted because flag and touch football is primarily a passing game, so this rule has been created to address this issue.

ARTICLE 14 - FOULS ON PASSING PLAYS CAUGHT PAST THE LINE OF SCRIMMAGE: The penalty enforcement on fouls on passing plays caught past the line of scrimmage shall be administered from the spot of the foul.

PLAY: A pass is completed 25 yards down the field, a clip is made by an offensive player during the run after the reception.

RULING: Administer a 10 yard penalty for clipping from the spot of the foul.

SECTION 4 - PENALTY ENFORCEMENT PHILOSOPHY:

ARTICLE 1 - BASIC INTERPRETATION: Whenever the ball is alive one of two types of plays is in progress. It is either a running play or a loose ball play. The type of play has no significance unless a foul occurs. When a foul occurs, in order to determine the basic spot of enforcement, the official must know

1) which team committed the foul and where it occurred in relation to where the play started;
2) whether the foul was during a running play; or

3) whether it was during a loose ball play. If a foul occurs during a running play, the basic enforcement spot is the spot where the run ends.

PLAY: A-1 runs to Team B's 20 where he/she is touched or his/her flag is removed. During the run there is a foul by Team A. The run ended at Team B's 20, therefore, that is the spot of enforcement. All fouls on this play would be penalized from Team B's 20 except a foul by Team A behind Team B's 20, which would be penalized from the spot of the foul. A running play which is followed by a loose ball such as a backward pass, fumble, or illegal pass by Team A during which a foul occurs, either during the run or the loose ball, is also enforced from the spot where the run ended, unless it is by the offense behind where the run ends, in which case it would be enforced from the spot of the foul. If a foul occurs during a loose ball play, the basic penalty enforcement spot is the previous spot, which is either the spot of the snap or the spot of the free kick.

PLAY: K-1 punts and between the time of the snap and the time the kick ends there is a foul by Team A or Team B.

RULING: The foul occurred during a loose ball play, therefore, the previous spot (same as the spot of the snap) is the basic enforcement spot. The only exception would be a foul by the offense behind the basic spot, which would be enforced from the spot of the foul.

RULE 14 - FORMULA FOR IDENTICAL RECORDS
SECTION 1 - GENERAL GUIDELINES:

ARTICLE 1 - FORMULA: In all U.S.F.T.L. League and Tournament competition, teams that end up with identical records shall use the following formula to determine the exact order of finish:

    a. Head to Head competition, or
    b. Total point differential between tied teams (total point differential is found by adding up the offensive and defensive points in games played between the 2 tied teams), or
    c. If 2 teams have the same point differential, point differential for the entire season or tournament is used, or
    d. If 3 teams have the same point differential, total points scored between the tied teams is used, or
    e. If 2 teams have scored the same number of points, head to head competition between the 2 tied teams is used, or
    f. If 3 teams have scored the same number of points, then the fewest points allowed between the 3 teams is used, or
    g. If 2 teams have allowed the same number of points, then head to head com petition between the 2 tied teams is used, or
    h. If 3 teams have allowed the same number of points, a regular overtime procedure shall be used. See Rule 5, Section 5, Article 1, 2 and 3 for this procedure.
    i. A team may not forfeit to gain an advantage. The penalty for this action shall be automatic elimination from the tournament or league. The team that forfeits to gain an advantage shall finish last in the final standings.

RULE 15 - PROTESTS

SECTION 1 - GENERAL GUIDELINES:

ARTICLE 1 - PROTEST PROCEDURE: In all U.S.F.T.L. Tournament or League competition, the following procedure must be followed to file a legitimate protest:

  a. Protests will not be received or considered if they are based solely on a decision involving the accuracy of judgment on the part of an Official:
    1. As to whether a player made a legal reception.
    2. As to whether a player was in or out-of-bounds.
    3. As to whether a field goal or extra kick was good or not, etc.
  b. Protests that shall be received and considered concern matters of the following types:
    1. Misinterpretation of a playing rule;
    2. Failure of an Official to apply the correct rule to a given situation;
    3. Failure of an Official to impose the correct penalty for a given violation.
  c. The notification of intent to protest must be made immediately before the next legal or illegal snap.

EXCEPTION: Player eligibility.

    1. The coach or acting coach or the protesting team shall immediately notify the Referee that the game is being played under protest. The Referee shall in turn notify the opposing coach.
    2. All interested parties shall take notice of the conditions surrounding the making of the decision, which will aid in the correct determination of the issue.
    3. Once the game is completed and both teams have left the field, no protest can be filed.

EXCEPTION: Player eligibility.

  d. The official written protest must be filed within a reasonable time:
    1. A protest should be considered filed within a reasonable time, depending upon the nature of the case and the difficulty of obtaining the information on which to base the protest.
    2. Within 48 hours after the scheduled time of the contest is generally considered a reasonable time.
  e. The formal written protest should contain the following information:
    1. The date, time, and place of the game,
    2. The names of the Officials, teams, and team coaches,
    3. The rule and section of the official rules or local rules under which the protest is made,
    4. The decision and conditions surrounding the making of the decision, and
    5. All essential facts involved in the matter protested.
  f. The decision rendered on a protested game must result in one of the following:
    1. The protest is found invalid, and the game score stands as played.
    2. When a protest is allowed for misinterpretation of a playing rule, the game is replayed from the point at which the incorrect decision was made with the decision coffected.
    3. When a protest for ineligibility is allowed, the offending team shall forfeit the game being played, or the game last played, to the offended team.

g. A protest fee must accompany any official written protest to the proper authority. The proper authority, being the local league director or the tournament director. The protest fee will be returned if the protest is upheld.

h. Tournament protests do not need to be in writing, a verbal protest to the Tournament Director shall suffice.

RULE 16 - NATIONAL RANKING SYSTEM

SECTION 1 - GENERAL GUIDELINES:

ARTICLE 1 - FORMULA: The formula that shall be used to create the U.S.F.T.L. National Ranking System shall be as follows:

a. Points will ONLY be awarded in sanctioned U.S.F.T.L. events.
b. All teams MUST be U.S.F.T.L. registered to receive points.
c. The point breakdown is as follows:

    1. National Championships:
- SUPER DIVISION = 150 Points per place
- "A" DIVISION = 120 Points per place
- "B" DIVISION = 90 Points per place
- "C" DIVISION = 60 Points per place
- "D" DIVISION = 30 Points per place

    2. Major N.I.T.'S, State Tournaments, Regional Tournaments:
- SUPER DIVISION = 100 Points per place
- "A" DIVISION = 80 Points per place
- "B" DIVISION = 60 Points per place
- "C" DIVISION = 40 Points per place
- "D" DIVISION = 20 Points per place

    3. Local Tournaments, N.I.T.'s, Sectional Tournaments:
- SUPER DIVISION = 50 Points per place
- "A" DIVISION = 40 Points per place
- "B" DIVISION = 30 Points per place
- "C" DIVISION = 20 Points per place
- "D" DIVISION = 10 Points per place

EXAMPLE:
National Championships - SUPER DIVISION (4 teams) = 1st Place = 600 Points
2nd Place = 450 Points
3rd Place = 300 Points
4th Place = 150 Points

N.I.T. - "C" DIVISION (4 teams) = 1st Place = 80 Points
2nd Place = 60 Points
3rd Place = 40 Points
4th Place = 20 Points

d. National Ranking Points can be accumulated.

e. Participation - The U.S.F.T.L. National Ranking System rewards participants in U.S.F.T.L. sanctioned events - the more tournament or league participation, the more points accumulated.

f. Number of Teams - The U.S.F.T.L. National Ranking System rewards teams that participate in U.S.F.T.L. sanctioned events that have a larger number of teams entered in the tournament;

    1. Awarding of points by place of finish - higher finish, more points;

    2. The more teams participating, the more points are available.

g. U.S.F.T.L. National Ranking System Points are used to determine all U.S.F.T.L. sanctioned tournament seedings - (State Tournaments, N.I.T.'s, Sectional Tournaments, Regional Tournaments or National Tournaments).
h. World Tournament seedings are found in the U.S.F.T.L. Constitution - Article 26- Section 23- (g).
i. U.S.F.T.L. Sanctioned Leagues are awarded National Ranking Points.

SECTION 2 - RANKING POINTS:
ARTICLE 1 - EXPLANATION:

1. Number of teams in a tournament/league multiplied by a specific number of points per division: Super division = 50 points, A division = 40 points, B division = 30 points, C division = 20 points, D division = 10 points.

2. For combined division tournaments/leagues, points are given based on highest division ranked team in event.

Example: 10 teams in a tournament, 1 of the teams are A division, the rest are B & C division teams, multiply 10 teams x 40 points per place = 400 points, 2nd place = 360 points, 3rd place = 320 points, 4th place = 280 points, etc.

3. For USFTL "MAJOR NIT'S", State Tournaments and Regional Tournaments, teams are awarded double ranking points for these events: Super division = 100 points, A division = 80 points, B division = 60 points, C division = 40 points, D division = 20 points.

4. For the USFTL National Championships, teams are awarded triple ranking points: Super division = 150 points, A division = 120 points, B = 90 points, C division = 60 points, D division = 30 points.

SECTION 3- TOURNAMENT SEEDING:
ARTICLE 1 - EXPLANATION:

1. National Ranking points are used to seed all USFTL Tournaments, except at USFTL State Championships, where USFTL State Ranking points are used to seed USFTL State Championship Tournaments. Teams cannot use ranking points from one Game to seed them into another Game:

Example: If a 4 on 4 team plays in a 5 on 5 tournament, the 4 on 4 team cannot use their 4 on 4 points to seed them in the 5 on 5 tournament.

Note: Teams cannot transfer ranking points from one Game to another.

Example: A 9-man Ineligible Lineman flag team plays in an 8-man eligible tournament - the 9-man team will earn points from that tournament but they must be used for 8-man eligible only.

SECTION 4- PROCEDURE FOR CHANGING DIVISION RANKING:
ARTICLE 1 - EXPLANATION:

1. If a team wants to classify up a division, example: going from C division to B division, they may classify up a division at anytime.

2. If a team wants to classify down a division, example: going from B division to C division, they must contact their Local Director and/or the USFTL National Office for reclassification and this must be done at least **6 weeks** before a USFTL sanctioned event (excluding USFTL National Championships).

3. All teams must be classified no later than October 1st for the USFTL National Championships. **NO EXCEPTIONS!**

4. A team can always check their current National or State ranking from the USFTL website at www.usftl.com.

RULE 17 - COMMUNICABLE DISEASE PROCEDURES

SECTION 1 - GENERAL GUIDELINES:

ARTICLE 1 - PROCEDURES: While risk of one athlete infecting another with HIV/AIDS during competition is close to non-existent, there is a remote risk that other blood home infectious diseases can be transmitted. For example, Hepatitis B can be present in blood as well as in other body fluids. Procedures for reducing the potential for transmission of these infectious agents should include, but not limited to, the following:

1. The bleeding must be stopped, the open wound covered and if there is an excessive amount of blood on the uniform it must be changed before the athlete may participate.

2. Routine use of gloves or other precautions to prevent skin and mucous-membrane exposure when contact with blood or other body fluids is anticipated.

3. Immediately wash hands and other skin surfaces if contaminated (in contact) with blood or other body fluids. Wash hands immediately after removing gloves.

4. Clean all blood contaminated surfaces and equipment with a solution made from proper dilution of household bleach (CDC recommends 1-100) or other disinfectants before competition resumes.

5. Practice proper disposal procedures to prevent injuries caused by needles, scalpels and other sharp instruments or devices.

6. Although saliva has not been implicated in HIV transmission, to minimize the need for emergency mouth-to-mouth resuscitation, mouthpieces, resuscitation bags, or other ventilation devices should be available for use.

7. Athletic trainers/coaches with bleeding or oozing skin conditions should refrain from all direct athletic care until the condition resolves.

8. Contaminated towels should be properly disposed of/disinfected.

9. Follow acceptable guidelines in the immediate control of bleeding and when handling bloody dressings, mouthguards and other articles containing body fluids.

RULES 18 - MEN'S PROGRAM

SECTION 1 - GENERAL GUIDELINES:

ARTICLE 1 - THE MEN'S PROGRAM: The Men's Program shall be offered to adult players of the male sex.

ARTICLE 2 - THE GAMES: The Games offered in the Men's Program shall be Touch Football, Contact Flag Football, Screen Flag Football and Ineligible Lineman Flag Football.

ARTICLE 3 - DIVISIONS OF PLAY: There shall be 5 divisions of play offered in the Men's Program: Super, A, B, C and D.

ARTICLE 4 - AGE CLASSIFICATION: The Age Classification in the Men's Program shall be 18 & Over and 35 & Over. Players must be the particular age offered in that particular age classification during that calendar year.

ARTICLE 5 - NUMBER OF PLAYERS ON THE FIELD: The number of players on the field in the Men's Program shall be dictated by the Game being played or the Program being offered:

   a. Touch = 7 players.
   b. Screen Flag = 7 players.
   c. Contact Flag = 8 players
   d. Ineligible Lineman Flag = 9 players
   e. 4 on 4 = 4 players
   f. 5 on 5 = 5 players

ARTICLE 6 - THE BALL: The ball that is used in the Men's Program shall be a regular size football. An Officially Licensed Football of the U.S.F.T.L. must be used.

ARTICLE 7 - THE FLAGS: The Flags that shall be used in the Men's Program shall be an Officially Licensed Flag of the U.S.F.T.L.

ARTICLE 8 - PLAYING FIELD SIZE: The playing field size that is used in the Men's Program shall be the regulation field size (100 yd X 53 1/3 yd), the abbreviated field size (80 yd X 40 yd) or the 4on4/5on5 field size (40 yd X 25 yd).

ARTICLE 9 - SCORING: The scoring system used in the Men's Program shall be the same as found in Rule 11 of this book.

ARTICLE 10 - TYPE OF BLOCKING: The type of blocking offered in the Men's Program shall be dictated by the Game being played.

   a. Touch = Contact blocking.
   b. Contact Flag = Contact Blocking.
   c. Ineligible Lineman Flag = Contact blocking.
   d. Screen Flag = Screen blocking.

ARTICLE 11 - RECEIVING = ELIGIBLE OR INELIGIBLE: The type of receiving offered in the Men's Program shall be dictated by the Game being played:

   a. Touch = Everyone eligible.
   b. Contact Flag = Everyone eligible.
   c. Screen Flag = Everyone eligible.
   d. Ineligible Lineman Flag = Lineman ineligible (Center and 2 lineman).

ARTICLE 12 - PLAYING RULES CAN BE MODIFIED: All playing rules not specifically covered in Rule 18 (Men's Program) of this book shall be governed by the other Rules as outlined in Rules I through 17 of this book. Any rule found in this book may be altered to suit the needs of the Local Men's Program. The U.S.F.T.L. recommends using the Official U.S.F.T.L. Rule Book as closely as possible for the following reasons:

   a. For a better understanding of all the rules of Flag and Touch Football.
   b. For uniformity in playing rules, so that different areas of the United States can compete against one another in a safe and fair manner.

RULE 19 - WOMENS PROGRAM

SECTION 1 - GENERAL GUIDELINES:

ARTICLE 1 - THE WOMEN'S PROGRAM: The Women's Program shall be offered to Adult players of the female sex.

ARTICLE 2 - THE GAMES: The Games offered in the Women's Program shall be Touch Football, Contact Flag Football, Screen Flag Football and Ineligible Lineman Flag Football.

ARTICLE 3 - DIVISIONS OF PLAY: There shall be 5 divisions of play offered in the Women's Program: SUPER, A, B, C, & D

ARTICLE 4 - AGE CLASSIFICATION: The Age Classification in the Women's Program shall be 18 & Over and 35 & Over. Players must be the particular age offered in that particular age classification during that calendar year.

ARTICLE 5 - NUMBER OF PLAYERS ON THE FIELD: The number of players on the field in the Women's Program shall be dictated by the Game being played or the Program being offered:

a. Touch = 7 players
b. Screen Flag = 7 players
c. Contact Flag = 8 players.
d. Ineligible Lineman Flag = 9 players.
e. 4 on 4 = 4 players.
f. 5 on 5 = 5 players.

ARTICLE 6 - THE BALL: The ball that is used in the Women's Program shall be a regular, intermediate, junior or youth size football. An Officially Licensed Football of the U.S.F.T.L. must be used.

ARTICLE 7 - THE FLAGS: The flags that shall be used in the Women's Program shall be an Officially Licensed Flag of the U.S.F.T.L.

ARTICLE 8 - PLAYING FIELD SIZE: The playing field size that is used in the Women's Program shall be the regulation field size (100 yd X 53 1/3 yd), the abbreviated field size (80 yd X 40 yd) or the 4on4/5on5 field size (40 yd X 25 yd).

ARTICLE 9 - SCORING: The scoring system used in the Women's Program shall be the same as found in Rule 11 of this book.

ARTICLE 10 - TYPE OF BLOCKING: The type of blocking offered in the Women's Program shall be dictated by the Game being played.

a. Touch = Contact blocking.
b. Contact Flag = Contact blocking.
c. Ineligible Lineman Flag = Contact blocking.
d. Screen Flag = Screen blocking.

ARTICLE 11 - RECEIVING = ELIGIBLE OR INELIGIBLE: The type of receiving offered in the Women's Program shall be dictated by the Game being played:

a. Touch = Everyone eligible.
b. Contact Flag = Everyone eligible.
c. Screen Flag = Everyone eligible.

d. Ineligible Lineman Flag = Lineman Ineligible (Center and 2 lineman).

ARTICLE 12 - PLAYING RULES CAN BE MODIFIED: All playing rules not specifically covered in Rule 19 (Women's Program) of this book shall be governed by the other Rules as outlined in Rules I through 17 of this book. Any rule found in this book may be altered to suit the needs of the Local Women's Program. The U.S.F.T.L. recommends using the Official U.S.F.T.L.. Rule Book as closely as possible for the following reasons:

a. For a better understanding of all the rules of Flag and Touch Football.
b. For uniformity in playing rules, so that different areas of the United States can compete against one another in a safe and fair manner.

RULE 20 - CO-RECREATION (CO-REC) PROGRAM

SECTION 1 - GENERAL GUIDELINES:

ARTICLE 1 - THE CO-REC PROGRAM: The Co-Rec Program shall be offered to adult players of the female and male sex.

ARTICLE 2 - THE GAMES: The Games offered in the Co-Rec Program shall be Touch Football, Contact Flag Football, Screen Flag Football and Ineligible Lineman Flag Football.

ARTICLE 3 - DIVISIONS OF PLAY: There shall be 5 divisions of play offered in the Co-Rec Program: SUPER, A, B, C and D.

ARTICLE 4 - AGE CLASSIFICATION: The age classification in the Co-Rec Program shall be 18 & Over and 35 & Over. Players must be the particular age offered in that particular age classification during that calendar year.

ARTICLE 5 - NUMBER OF PLAYERS ON THE FIELD: The number of players on the field in the Co-Rec Program shall be dictated by the Game being played or the Program being offered:

a. Touch = 7 players (4 men & 3 women) or (3 men & 4 women) (5 players are required to avoid a forfeit -2 men & 3 women or 3 men & 2 women)
b. Screen Flag = 8 players (4 men & 4 women) or (3 men & 5 women) or (5 men & 3 women) (6 players are required to avoid forfeit - 3 men & 3 women, 4 men & 2 women, or 2 men & 4 women).
c. Contact Flag = 8 players (4 men & 4 women) or (3 men & 5 women) or (5 men & 3 women) (6 players are required to avoid forfeit - 3 men & 3 women, 4 men & 2 women, or 2 men & 4 women).
d. Ineligible Lineman Flag = 9 players (5 men & 4 women) or (4 men & 5 women) (7 players are required to avoid forfeit - 3 men & 4 women or 4 men & 3 women).
e. 4 on 4 = 4 players (2 men & 2 women) or (3 men & 1 woman) or (3 women & 1 man). (2 players are required to avoid forfeit - 1 man & 1 woman).
f. 5 on 5 = 5 players (3 men & 2 women) or (2 men & 3 women) (3 players are required to avoid forfeit - 2 men & 1 woman or 1 man & 2 women).

ARTICLE 6 - THE BALL: The ball that is used in the Co-Rec program shall be a regular, intermediate, junior or youth size football. Male players must use the regular size football and females may use a regular, intermediate, junior or youth size football. An Officially Licensed Football of the U.S.F.T.L. must be used.

ARTICLE 7 - THE FLAGS: The flags that shall be used in the Co-Rec Program shall be an Officially Licensed Hag of the U.S.F.T.L.

ARTICLE 8 - PLAYING FIELD SIZE: The playing field size that is used in the Co-Rec Program shall be the regulation field size (100yd X 53 1/3 yd), the abbreviation field size (80yd X 40yd) or the 4on4/5on5 field size (40 yd X 25 yd).

ARTICLE 9 - SCORING: The scoring system used in the Co-Rec Program shall be the same as found in Rule 11 of this book. (NOTE.- A Touchdown scored or a Touchdown pass thrown by a female player shall be worth 9 points; an Extra Point scored or an Extra Point pass thrown by female player shall be worth 2 or 3 points).

ARTICLE 10 - TYPE OF BLOCKING: The type of blocking offered in the Co-rec Program shall be dictated by the Game being played: Page 82

a. Touch = Contact blocking.
b. Contact Flag = Contact blocking.
c. Ineligible Lineman Flag = Contact blocking.
d. Screen Flag = Screen blocking.

Contact Blocking in the Co-Rec Game shall follow these particular guidelines:

a. All contact blocks must use the straight arm, open handed style of blocking,
b. You may not leave your feet to block,
c. You may only contact your opponent between the shoulders and the waist,
d. There shall be no downfield blocking allowed past the line of scrimmage,
e. Male players cannot block female players,
f. Female players may block anyone,
g. All other contact blocking rules shall be found in Rule 1, Section 2, Article 1 of this book.

Screen Blocking in the Co-Rec Game shall follow the particular guidelines as set forth in Rule 1, Section 2, Article 2 of this book.

ARTICLE 11 - RECEIVING = ELIGIBLE OR INELIGIBLE: The type of receiving offered in the Co-Rec Program shall be dictated by the Game being played:

a. Touch = Everyone eligible.
b. Contact Flag = Everyone eligible.
c. Screen Flag = Everyone eligible.
d. Ineligible Lineman Flag = Lineman Ineligible (Center and 2 lineman).

ARTICLE 12 - RUSHING THE PASSER: The Co-Rec Program shall allow the rushing of the passer in the following procedure:

a. Any player and/or any amount of players may rush the passer on a scrimmage play.
b. A male player on the defensive line of scrimmage may not line up across from a female player who is on the line of scrimmage next to the center. The offensive male player must line up at least 2 yards away from the female player.
c. Male players must rush at least 5 yards wide of the center.
d. Male players shall not rush up the middle.

ARTICLE 13 - THE KICKING GAME: The Co-Rec Program shall use these particular kicking rules:

   a. Kickoff & Punt Returns:

      1. Only female players may return kickoffs and punts,

      2. There shall only be Screen Blocking allowed on kickoff and punt returns, no matter what Game is being played,

      3. A male player may receive a kickoff or punt but may only carry the ball backward or parallel,

      4. After the kickoff or punt has been caught by the receiving team, and then there is a change of possession, either a male or female player may advance the ball,

   b. Extra Points and Field Goals:

      1. On extra points and field goal attempts, a female player must be the kicker or holder, or both,

      2. The offensive team must declare it's intention to attempt a field goal or extra point by kick,

      3. The defense shall not be allowed to rush the kicker on a declared field goal or extra point by kick,

      4. The defense may jump at the line of scrimmage to attempt to block a field goal, extra point by kick or protected scrimmage kick (punt),

      5. The defense may not climb onto each other in the attempt to block a field goal, extra point by kick or a protected scrimmage kick (punt).

ARTICLE 14 - QUARTERBACK RUNS: The Co-Rec Program shall allow a male or female quarterback to advance the ball by a running attempt across the line of scrimmage.

ARTICLE 15 - INTERCEPTION: The Co-rec program shall allow a male or female player to return an interception.

ARTICLE 16 - MALE TO MALE COMPLETION: During the offensive team's possession, there may not be 2 consecutive legal forward pass completions from a male passer to a male receiver. This rule applies to the try. If a male passer completes a legal forward pass to a male receiver, the next legal forward pass completion must involve either a female passer or a female receiver for positive yards. The spot where the ball becomes dead by rule must be beyond the Team A scrimmage line. There are no other restrictions concerning a male passer completing legal forward passes to a female receiver, or female to female, or female to male.

PENALTY: Illegal Forward Pass, 5 yards from the spot where the second consecutive male to male completed legal forward pass is released, and a loss of down. (S35 and S9)

ARTICLE 17 - PLAYING RULES CAN BE MODIFIED: All playing rules not specifically covered in Rule 20 (Co-Rec Program) of this book shall be governed by the other rules as outlined in Rules 1 through 16 of this book. Any rule found in this book may be altered to suit the needs of the Local Co-Rec Program. The U.S.F.T.L. recommends using the Official U.S.F.T.L. Rule Book as closely as possible for the following reasons:

   a. For a better understanding of all the rules of Flag & Touch Football.

   b. For uniformity in playing rules, so that different areas of the United States can compete against one another in a safe and fair manner.

RULE 21 - YOUTH PROGRAM

SECTION 1 - GENERAL GUIDELINES:

ARTICLE 1 - THE YOUTH PROGRAM: The Youth Program shall be offered to both boys and girls, however, the boys program should be entirely separate from the girls program. Co-Rec Youth Programs are acceptable also. The rules for the Co-Rec Youth program shall be the same as the Co-Rec Program for adults found in Rule 20 of this book.

ARTICLE 2 - THE GAMES: The games offered in the Youth Program shall be Touch Football, Contact Flag Football, Screen Flag Football and Ineligible Lineman Flag Football.

ARTICLE 3 - DIVISIONS OF PLAY: There shall be no competitive Divisions Play offered in the Youth Program. There shall only be Age Classification offered.

ARTICLE 4 - AGE CLASSIFICATION: The Age Classification in the Youth Programs shall be:
- a. 6 years old and under.
- b. 8 years old and under.
- c. 10 years old and under.
- d. 12 years old and under.
- e. 14 years old and under.
- f. 16 years old and under.
- g. 18 years old and under.

Players must be the particular age offered in that particular age classification during that calendar year. Any player may play in an older age classification, but may not play in a younger age classification.

ARTICLE 5 - NUMBER OF PLAYERS ON THE FIELD: The number of players on the field in the Youth Program shall be dictated by the Game being played or the Program being offered:
- a. Touch = 7 players.
- b. Screen Flag = 7 players.
- c. Contact Flag = 8 players.
- d. Ineligible Lineman Flag = 9 players.
- e. 4 on 4 = 4 players.
- f. 5 on 5 = 5 players.

ARTICLE 6 - THE BALL: The ball that is used in the Youth Program shall be a regulation, intermediate, junior or youth size football. An Officially Licensed Football of the U.S.F.T.L. must be used.

ARTICLE 7 - THE FLAGS: The flags that shall be used in the Youth Program shall be an Officially Licensed Flag of the U.S.F.T.L.

ARTICLE 8 - PLAYING FIELD SIZE: The playing field size that is used in the Youth Program shall be the regulation field size (100 yard X 53 1/3 yards), the abbreviated field size (80 yard X 40 yard) or the 4on4/5on5 field size (40 yd X 25 yd).

ARTICLE 9 - SCORING: The scoring system used in the Youth Program shall be the same as found in Rule 11 of this book.

ARTICLE 10 - TYPE OF BLOCKING: The type of blocking offered in the

Youth Program shall be dictated by the Game being played:

   a. Touch = Contact blocking
   b. Contact Flag = Contact blocking
   c. Ineligible Lineman Flag = Contact blocking
   d. Screen flag = Screen blocking

ARTICLE 11 RECEIVING = ELIGIBLE OR INELIGIBLE: The type of receiving offered in the Youth Program shall be dictated by the Game being played:

   a. Touch = Everyone eligible.
   b. Contact Flag = Everyone eligible.
   c. Screen Flag = Everyone eligible.
   d. Ineligible Lineman Flag = Lineman Ineligible (Center and 2 lineman).

ARTICLE 12 - PLAYING RULES CAN BE MODIFIED: All playing rules not specifically covered in Rule 21 (Youth Program) of this book shall be governed by the other rules as outlined in rules 1 through 17 of this book. Any rule found in this book may be altered to suit the needs of the Local Youth Program. The U.S.F.T.L. recommends using the Official U.S.F.T.L. Rule Book as closely as possible for the following reasons:

   a. For a better understanding of all the rules of Flag & Touch Football.
   b. For uniformity in playing rules, so that different areas of the United States can compete against one another in a safe and fair manner.
   c. For an easier progression from the Youth Programs to the Adult Programs.

RULE 22 - MASTERS PROGRAM

SECTION 1 - GENERAL GUIDELINES:

ARTICLE 1 - THE MASTERS PROGRAM: The Masters Program shall be offered to male and female adult players who are 35 years of age or older. All players are required to have picture identification and age verification and must produce it upon request.

ARTICLE 2 - THE GAMES: The Games offered in the Masters Program shall be Touch Football, Contact Flag Football, Screen Flag Football and Ineligible Lineman Flag Football.

ARTICLE 3 - DIVISIONS OF PLAY: There shall be 5 divisions of play offered in the Masters Program: SUPER, Al B, C & D.

ARTICLE 4 - AGE CLASSIFICATION: The Age Classification in the Masters Program shall be 35 years of age or older. Players must be 35 years of age or older during that calendar year to participate in the Masters Program.

ARTICLE 5 - NUMBER OF PLAYERS ON THE FIELD: The number of players on the field in the Masters Program shall be dictated by the Game being played or the Program being offered:

   a. Touch = 7 players.
   b. Screen Flag = 7 players.
   c. Contact Flag = 8 players.
   d. Ineligible Lineman Flag = 9 players.
   e. 4 on 4 = 4 players.

f. 5 on 5 = 5 players.

ARTICLE 6 - THE BALL: The ball that is used in the Masters Program shall be a regular, intermediate, junior or youth size football. Male players must use the regular size football. Female players may use a regular, intermediate, junior or youth size football. An Officially Licensed Football of the U.S.F.T.L. must be used.

ARTICLE 7 - THE FLAGS: The flag that shall be used in the Master's Program shall be an Officially Licensed Flag of the U.S.F.T.L.

ARTICLE 8 - PLAYING FIELD SIZE: The playing field size that is used in the Masters Program shall be the regulation field size (100 yd X 53 1/3 yd), the abbreviated field size (80 yd X 40 yd) or the 4on4/5on5 field size (40 yd X 25 yd).

ARTICLE 9 - SCORING: The scoring system used in the Masters Program shall be the same as found in Rule 11 of this book.

ARTICLE 10 - TYPE OF BLOCKING: The type of blocking offered in the Masters Program shall be dictated by the Game being played:
a. Touch = Contact blocking.
b. Contact Flag = Contact blocking.
c. Ineligible Lineman Flag = Contact blocking.
d. Screen Flag = Screen blocking.

ARTICLE 11 - RECEIVING = ELIGIBLE OR INELIGIBLE: The type of receiving offered in the Masters Program shall be dictated by the game being played:
a. Touch = Everyone eligible.
b. ContactFlag = Everyone eligible.
c. Screen Flag = Everyone eligible.
d. Ineligible Lineman Flag = Lineman Ineligible (Center and 2 lineman).

ARTICLE 12 - PLAYING RULES CAN BE MODIFIED: All playing rules not specifically covered in Rule 22 (Masters's Program) of this book shall be governed by the other rules as outlined in Rules I through 17 of this book. Any rule found in this book may be altered to suit the needs of the Local Masters Program. The U.S.F.T.L. recommends using the Official U.S.F.T.L. Rule Book as closely as possible for the following reasons:
a. For a better understanding of all the rules of Flag & Touch Football.
b. For uniformity in playing rules, so that different areas of the United States can compete against one another in a safe and fair manner.

RULE 23 - 4 ON 4 PROGRAM

SECTION 1 - GENERAL GUIDELINES:

ARTICLE 1 - THE 4 ON 4 PROGRAM: The 4 on 4 Program shall be offered to youth and adult players of the male and female sex.

ARTICLE 2 - THE GAMES: The Games offered in the 4 on 4 Program shall be Touch Football and Flag Football.

ARTICLE 3 - DIVISIONS OF PLAY: There shall be 5 divisions of play offered in the 4 on 4 Program: SUPER, A, B, C, & D.

ARTICLE 4 - AGE CLASSIFICATION: The Age Classification in the 4 on 4

Program shall be:

YOUTH	- 6 and under
	- 8 and under
	- 10 and under
	- 12 and under
	- 14 and under
	- 16 and under
	- 18 and under
ADULT	- 18 and over
MASTERS	- 35 and over

Players must be the particular age offered in that particular Age Classification during that calendar year.

ARTICLE 5 - NUMBER OF PLAYERS ON THE FIELD: The number of players on the field in the 4 on 4 Program shall be four (4). 2 players are required to avoid forfeit. The number of players on the field in the Co-Rec 4 on 4 Program shall be (2 men & 2 women) or (3 men & 1 woman) or (3 women & 1 man). In the Co-Rec 4 on 4 Program, 2 players are required to avoid a forfeit (1 man & 1 woman).

ARTICLE 6 - THE BALL: The ball that is used in the 4 on 4 Program shall be the regular, intermediate, junior or youth size football. Male players must use the regular size football. Female and Youth players may use the regular, intermediate, junior or youth size football. An Officially Licensed Football of the U.S.F.T.L. must be used.

ARTICLE 7 - THE FLAGS: The flags that shall be used in the 4 on 4 Program shall be an Officially Licensed Flag of the U.S.F.T.L.

ARTICLE 8 - PLAYING FIELD SIZE: The playing field size that is used in the 4 on 4 Program shall be the 4 on 4 field size (46 yd X 25 yd).

ARTICLE 9 - SCORING: The scoring system that is used in the 4 on 4 Program shall be: .

A. Mercy Rule: If a team is ahead by 17 or more points at the 1 minute warning of the second half, the game shall be over. If a team scores after the 1 minute warning of the second half to create a 17 point lead, the game shall be over.
B. Touchdown = 6 points
C. Touchdown (female) = 9 points (Co-Rec Only)
D. Safety = 2 points
E. Forfeited Game = 1 point
F. Extra Points:
   1. By running or passing only (no kicking allowed) from 5 yards = 1 point. (2 points - female, Co-Rec only).
   2. By running or passing only (no kicking allowed) from 10 yards = 2 points.(3 points - female, Co-Rec only).
(NOTE: A team is given one choice which cannot be changed even if a penalty should occur. If you declare you are going for 2 points, the ball is placed at the 10 yard line and even if a penalty shall occur, the team will only be able to run or Pass and if successful, no matter from what distance, the value of the try is 2 points).
G. The return of Extra Point attempt = 2 points.

ARTICLE 10 - TYPE OF BLOCKING: The type of blocking offered in the 4 on 4 Program shall be Screen Blocking only.

ARTICLE 11 - RECEIVING = ELIGIBLE OR INELIGIBLE: The type of receiving offered in the 4 on 4 Program shall be everyone eligible.

ARTICLE 12 - PLAYING RULES CAN BE MODIFIED: All playing rules not specifically covered in Rule 23 (4 on 4 Program) of this book shall be governed by other rules outlined in Rules 1 through 17 of this book. Any rule found in this book may be altered to suit the needs of the Local 4 on 4 Program. The U.S.F.T.L. recommends using the Official U. S.F.T.L. Rule Book as closely as possible for the following reasons:

    a. For better understanding of all the rules of Flag & Touch Football.
    b. For uniformity in playing rules, so that different areas of the United States can compete against one another in a safe and fair manner.
    c. For an easier progression from the Youth Programs to the Adult Programs.

SECTION 2 - RULES & REGULATIONS:
ARTICLE 1 - BASIC RULES OF 4 ON 4:

A. A coin toss shall begin each game. The captain winning the toss shall choose one of the following options:
    1. Offense
    2. Defense
    3. Designate which goal his/her team will defend.
    4. Defer choice to the second half.

B. Loser of the coin toss shall make a choice of the remaining options.
C. Before the start of the second half, the choice of options shall be reversed.
D. The offensive team takes possession of the ball at their 5-yard line and has three (3) plays to cross mid-field. Once a team crosses mid-field, they will have three (3) plays to score a touchdown. If the offense fails to score, the ball changes possession and the new offensive team takes over on their 5-yard line.
E. If the offensive team fails to cross mid-field, possession of the ball changes and the opposite team starts their drive from their 5-yard line.
F. All drives and possession changes except interceptions, start on the 5-yard line of the offense.
G. Teams will switch ends after the first 12 minutes (Halftime).
H. Ball must be snapped between the legs, not off to one side, to start play. Direct snaps are legal.
I. The Ball is ruled dead when:

    1. A snap to a Quarterback hits the ground
    2. A fumble hits the ground (no fumble recoveries allowed).
    3. A ball carrier's knee touches the ground.
    4. A ball carrier's steps out of bounds.
    5. A ball carrier's flags are legally removed, (<u>NOTE:</u> if a ball carrier's flags fall off inadvertently, play shall revert to a 2 hand touch between the shoulders and the knees).

J. 25 Second Clock - Each time the ball is spotted, a team has 25 seconds to snap the ball.
K. Blocking - NO BLOCKING and NO CONTACT ALLOWED - anywhere, anytime. <u>NOTE:</u> Screen Blocking Only!

L. Interceptions may be returned.
M. 24 Minute Game - two (2) -12 minute halves with a running clock.
N. One (1) Minute Warning - When there is 1 minute left in the game, the game clock shall stop for incomplete passes, out-of-bounds, change of possessions, first downs and time-outs and starts and re-starts on the snap.

ARTICLE 2 - THE FIELD:

A. Field Size - 46 yards in length; 25 yards in width
B. End Zones - (2) 7 yard endzones

ARTICLE 3 - THE PLAYERS:

A. Roster size - Teams consist of a total of 8 players on the roster.
B. Number of players on field - 4 players on the field at one time.
C. Forfeits - to avoid a forfeit, you must have at least 2 players to begin the game.
D. Co-Rec team must have (2 male & 2 female) or (3 male & 1 female) or (1 male & 3 female) players on the field at one time.
E. Forfeits in the 4 on 4 Co-Rec Program - to avoid a forfeit, Co-Rec teams must have 1 man and 1 woman to begin the game.

ARTICLE 4 - SCORING & OVERTIME:

A. Touchdowns = 6 points
   Extra Points = 1 point (5 yards) - (run or pass - No kicks allowed).
      (2 points - female, Co-Rec only).
             = 2 points (10 yards) - (run or pass - No kicks allowed).
      (3 points - female, Co-Rec only).
   Safety - 2 points
   Forfeited game = 1 point
B. Overtime = All overtime rules in the 4 on 4 Program are the same as found in Rule 5, Section 5 - Overtime, Articles 1-5 with the following expections: Each team gets 3 downs from 10 yard line to score. Scoring is same as in regular game. A coin toss determines possession in each overtime period.
C. U.S.F.T.L. Sudden Death Overtime = In U.S.F.T.L. Championship Games (League & Tournament Championship Games only), a Sudden Death Overtime is used. Same procedure as start of game - coin toss followed by regular game conditions with each team having 1 series of downs to score. All other rules apply as found in Rule 5, Section 5, Article 4 - U.S.F.T.L. Sudden Death.

ARTICLE 5 - RUNNING PLAYS:

A. The Quarterback ("QB") CANNOT run the ball at any time.
B. Handoffs are allowed.
C. Laterals and pitches are NOT allowed anywhere on the field.
D. The player who takes a handoff can throw the ball as long as he does not cross the line of scrimmage.
E. Once the ball has been handed off, all defensive players are eligible to rush.
F. The player who takes a hand off may run with the ball.
G. The "No Running Zone" is designed to avoid short yardage power running situations. (No Run Zones are located 5 yards from each end zone and 5 yards on either side of mid-field). No player is allowed to run inside of the No Run Zones.

ARTICLE 6 - PASSING:
A. Backward passes and laterals are not allowed.
B. Quarterback has a 7 second Pass Clock. If a pass is not thrown within the 7 seconds, play is dead, loss of down. The ball is spotted at the line of scrimmage. The Referee shall count 7 seconds.
C. Interceptions change the possession of the ball at the point of interception. Interceptions are the only change of possession that do not start on the 5-yard line. Interception may be returned.
D. Only 1 forward pass per down.
E. If a passer crosses the line of scrimmage, and comes back behind the line of scrimmage and throws a pass, it is an illegal forward pass.

ARTICLE 7 - RECEIVING:
A. Eligible Receivers - All players are eligible to receive passes (including the Quarterback after the ball has been handed off behind the line of scrimmage).
B. A player must have at least one foot in bounds to make a legal reception.

ARTICLE 8 - RUSHING THE QUARTERBACK:
A. Defensive players that rush the passer must be a minimum of 7 yards from the line of scrimmage when the ball is snapped. Any number of players can rush the Quarterback.
B. 1. Ball spotter - A ball spotter shall be used to mark the line of scrimmage
2. Rush spotter - A rush spotter shall be used to mark the rushers starting point.
C. Rushers must go for the Quarterback's flag and are not allowed to make contact. (NOTE: You cannot hit the Quarterback's arm to block a pass. You must go for the flag).

ARTICLE 9 - EQUIPMENT:
A. The Ball - Male players shall use a regulation size football. Female and youth players may use a regular, intermediate, junior or youth size football. An Officially Licensed Football by the U.S.F.T.L. must be used.
B. The Flags - All flags used in the 4 on 4 Program shall be an Officially Licensed Flag of the U.S.F.T.L.
C. Shoes - Cleats are allowed, but they must be rubber. No metal spikes are allowed. Screw-in cleats are allowed, if the screw is part of the cleat. Inspections will be made.
D. Jerseys - All jerseys shall be tucked in the pants and shorts. No shimmel length, waist length or half jerseys allowed.
E. Mouthpiece - All players must wear a protective mouthpiece. If you do not have a mouthpiece, there will be one available on-site for a fee.

ARTICLE 10 - TIME OUTS:
A. Each team has one 30 second time out per game.
B. Each team has one 30 second time out per overtime period.

ARTICLE 11 - PENALTY ENFORCEMENT:
A. Offensive Penalties:
1. Illegal Motion - (More than 1 person moving at the snap, false start, illegal shift, illegal motion) = 5 yards from line of scrimmage and loss of down.
2. Illegal Forward Pass - (Pass thrown beyond the line of scrimmage) = 5 yards

from line of scrimmage and loss of down.
3. Offensive Pass Interference - (Illegal pick play, pushing off or away from the defender) = 10 yards from line of scrimmage and loss of down,
4. Flag Guarding = 10 yards from line of scrimmage and loss of down.
5. Delay of Game = 5 yards from line of scrimmage, loss of down and clock will be automatically stopped until the next legal snap.
6. Encroachment = 5 yards from line of scrimmage and loss of down.
7. Illegal Contact (Holding, Blocking, etc.) = 10 yards from line of scrimmage and loss of down.
8. Batting the ball to gain an advantage = 10 yards from line of scrimmage and loss of down.

B. Defensive Penalties:
   1. Offsides = 5 yards from line of scrimmage and automatic 1st Down.
   2. Defensive Pass Interference = Spot of Foul and automatic 1st Down.
   3. Illegal Contact - (Holding, blocking, etc.) = 10 yards from line of scrimmage and automatic 1st Down.
   4. Illegal Flag Pull - (Pulling of runner's flags before he has the ball) = 10 yards from line of scrimmage and automatic 1st Down, unless it was a touch down then offense has option of the yardage or the score.
   5. Illegal Rushing - (Starting to rush the Quarterback from inside 7 yard rush marker) = 10 yards from line of scrimmage and automatic 1st Down.

C. Flagrant Fouls: Any flagrant contact whatsoever (tackling, elbowing, cheap shots, blocking, taunting or similar unsportsmanlike acts shall not be tolerated). The Official shall stop the game, eject the player from the game, administer a 10 yard penalty from the line of scrimmage with an automatic 1st Down if it was on the defense or a loss of down if it was on the offense and give the coach a verbal warning - FOUL PLAY WILL NOT BE TOLERATED!!!

D. Games cannot end upon a defensive penalty, unless the offense declines it.

RULE 24 - CORPORATE PROGRAM

SECTION 1 - GENERAL GUIDELINES:

ARTICLE 1 - THE CORPORATE PROGRAM: The Corporate Program shall be offered to male and female adult players who are bonafide full time employees of the team sponsor. All bonafide full time employees with less than 60 days continuous service with a team sponsor will not be eligible to play in the Corporate Program. Employees who might be on military duty shall be considered eligible to compete. Corporate sponsors, such as corporations, industries base, government agencies, etc., that operate in more than one location within a state may be considered as one sponsor. Such sponsor cannot combine with an out of state location. All players of a local union team must be bonafide union members from the same local with a minimum of 60 days membership. Union local players or teams may be eligible to participate in the Corporate Program only if they meet the guidelines for industrial participation and eligibility. Trade union local teams may participate in the Corporate Program if they meet the following criteria:

   a. All team members are bonafide members of the trade union they represent,
   b. All team members are covered under a negotiated trade union contract providing wages and benefits,
   c. All players that compete in the Corporate Program must have 60 days continuous service with the trade union local they represent, prior to participating in any Corporate Program.

ARTICLE 2 - THE GAMES: The Games offered in the Corporate Program shall be Touch Football, Contact Flag Football, Screen Flag Football and Ineligible Lineman Flag Football.

ARTICLE 3 - DIVISIONS OF PLAY: There shall be 5 divisions of play offered in the Corporate Program: SUPER, A, B, C and D.

ARTICLE 4 - AGE CLASSIFICATION: The Age Classification in the Corporate Program shall be 18 & Over and 35 & Over. Players must be the particular age offered in that particular age classification during that calendar year.

ARTICLE 5 - NUMBER OF PLAYERS ON THE FIELD: The number of players on the field in the Corporate Program shall be dictated by the Game being played or the Program being offered:

a. Touch = 7 players.
b. Screen Flag = 7 players.
c. Contact Flag = 8 players.
d. Ineligible Lineman Flag = 9 players.
e. 4 on 4 = 4 players.
f. 5 on 5 = 5 players.

ARTICLE 6 - THE BALL: The ball that is used in the Corporate Program shall be the regular, intermediate, junior or youth size football. Male players must use the regular size football. Female players may use the regular, junior or youth size football. An Officially Licensed Football of the U.S.F.T.L. must be used.

ARTICLE 7 - THE FLAGS: The Flags that shall be used in the Corporate Program shall be an Officially Licensed Flag of the U.S.F.T.L.

ARTICLE 8 - PLAYING FIELD SIZE: The playing field size that is used in the Corporate Program shall be the regulation field size (100yd X 53 1/3yd), the abbreviated field size (80yd X 40yd) or the 4on4/5on5 field size (40 yd X 25).

ARTICLE 9 - SCORING: The scoring system used in the Corporate Program shall be the same as found in Rule II of this book.

ARTICLE 10 - TYPE OF BLOCKING: The type of blocking offered in the Corporate Program shall be dictated by the Game being played:

a. Touch = Contact blocking
b. Contact Flag = Contact blocking
c. Ineligible Lineman Flag = Contact blocking
d. Screen Flag = Screen blocking.

ARTICLE 11 - RECEIVER = ELIGIBLE OR INELIGIBLE: The type of receiving offered in the Corporate Program shall be dictated by the Game being played:

a. Touch = Everyone eligible.
b. Contact Flag = Everyone eligible,
c. Screen Flag = Everyone eligible.
d. Ineligible Lineman Flag = Lineman Ineligible (Center and 2 linemen).

ARTICLE 12 - PLAYING RULES CAN BE MODIFIED: All playing rules not specifically covered in Rule 24 (Corporate Program) of this book shall be governed by the other rules as outlined in Rules 1 through 17 of this book. Any rule found in this book may be altered to suit the needs of the Local Corporate Program. The U.S.F.T.L. recommends using the Official U.S.F.T.L. Rule Book as closely as possible for the following reasons:

a. For a better understanding of all the rules of Flag & Touch Football,
b. For uniformity in playing rules, so that different areas of the United States can compete against one another in a safe and fair manner.

RULE 25 - CHURCH PROGRAM

SECTION 1 - GENERAL GUIDELINES:

ARTICLE 1 - THE CHURCH PROGRAM: The Church Program shall be offered to male and female adult players that are active participants in the worship services of the church for which they are playing during the current calendar year. State directors shall contact the church pastor or church official who signs the roster to certify that the roster is in compliance with the U.S.F.T.L. Constitution prior to allowing players and/or teams to participate in the Church Program.

ARTICLE 2 - THE GAMES: The Games offered in the Church Program shall be Touch Football, Contact Flag Football, Screen Flag Football and Ineligible Lineman Flag Football.

ARTICLE 3 - DIVISIONS OF PLAY: There shall be 5 divisions of play offered in the Church Program: SUPER, A, B, C & D.

ARTICLE 4 - AGE CLASSIFICATION: The Age Classification in the Church Program shall be 18 & Over and 35 & Over. Players must be the particular age offered in that particular age classification during that calendar year.

ARTICLE 5 - NUMBER OF PLAYERS ON THE FIELD: The number of players on the field in the Church Program shall be dictated by the Game being played or the Program being offered:

a. Touch = 7 players.
b. Screen Flag = 7 players.
c. Contact Flag = 8 players.
d. Ineligible lineman flag = 9 players.
e. 4 on 4 = 4 players.
f. 5 on 5 = 5 players.

ARTICLE 6 - THE BALL: The ball that is used in the Church Program shall be the regular, intermediate, junior or youth size football. Male players must use the regular size football. Female players may use the regular, intermediate, junior or youth size football. An Officially Licensed Football of the U.S.F.T.L. must be used.

ARTICLE 7 - THE FLAGS: The flags that shall be used in the Church Program shall be an Officially Licensed Flag of the U.S.F.T.L.

ARTICLE 8 - PLAYING FIELD SIZE: The playing field size that is used in the Church Program shall be the regulation field size (100yd X 53 1/3 yd), the abbreviated field size (80yd X 40yd) or the 4on4/5on5 field size (40 yd X 25 yd).

ARTICLE 9 - SCORING: The scoring system used in the Church Program shall be the same as found in Rule 11 of this book.

ARTICLE 10 - TYPE OF BLOCKING: The type of blocking offered in the Church Program shall be dictated by the Game being played:

a. Touch = Contact blocking.
b. Contact Flag = Contact blocking.
c. Ineligible Lineman Flag = Contact blocking.
d. Screen Flag = Screen blocking.

ARTICLE 11 - RECEIVING = ELIGIBLE OR INELIGIBLE: The type of receiving offered in the Church Program shall be dictated by the Game being played:

a. Touch = Everyone eligible.
b. Contact Flag = Everyone eligible.
c. Screen Flag = Everyone eligible.
d. Ineligible Lineman Flag = Lineman Ineligible (Center and 2 linemen).

ARTICLE 12 - PLAYING RULES CAN BE MODIFIED: All playing rules not specifically covered in Rule 25 (Church Program) of this book shall be governed by the other rules as outlined in Rules 1 through 17 of this book. Any rule found in this book may be altered to suit the needs of the Local Church Program. The U.S.F.T.L. recommends using the Official U.S.F.T.L. Rule Book as closely as possible for the following reasons:

a. For a better understanding of all the rules of Flag & Touch Football,
b. For uniformity in playing rules, so that different areas of the United States can compete against one another in a safe and fair manner.

RULE 26 - ARMED FORCES PROGRAM

SECTION 1 - GENERAL GUIDELINES:

ARTICLE 1 - THE ARMED FORCES PROGRAM: The Armed Forces Program shall be offered to male and female adult players who are bonafide employees in a branch of the Armed Forces, which shall include the following:

a. Air Force
b. Army
c. Marines
d. Navy

State Directors shall contact the Armed Forces base commander who signs the roster to certify that the roster is in compliance with the U.S.F.T.L. Constitution prior to allowing players and or teams to participate in the Armed Forces Program.

ARTICLE 2 - THE GAMES: The Games offered in the Armed Forces Program shall be Touch Football, Contact Flag Football, Screen Flag Football, and Ineligible Lineman Flag Football.

ARTICLE 3 - DIVISIONS OF PLAY: There shall be 5 divisions of play offered in the Armed Forces Program: SUPER, A, B, C & D.

ARTICLE 4 - AGE CLASSIFICATION: The Age Classification in the Armed Forces Program shall be 18 & Over and 35 & Over. Players must be the particular age offered in that particular age classification during that calendar year.

ARTICLE 5 - NUMBER OF PLAYERS ON THE FIELD: The number of players on the field in the Armed Forces Program shall be dictated by the Game being played or the Program being offered:

a. Touch = 7 players.
b. Screen Flag = 7 players.
c. Contact Flag = 8 players.
d. Ineligible Lineman Flag = 9 players.
e. 4 on 4 = 4 players.
f. 5 on 5 = 5 players.

ARTICLE 6 - THE BALL: The ball that is used in the Armed Forces Program shall be the regular, intermediate, junior or youth size football. Male players must use the regular size football. Female players may use the regular, intermediate, junior or youth size football. An Officially Licensed Football of the U.S.F.T.L. must be used.

ARTICLE 7 - THE FLAGS: The flags that shall be used in the Armed Forces Program shall be an Officially Licensed Flag of the U.S.F.T..L.

ARTICLE 8 - PLAYING FIELD SIZE: The playing field size that is used in the Armed Forces Program shall be the regulation field size (100 yd X 53 1/3 yd), the abbreviated field size (80 yd X 40 yd) or the 4on4/5on5 field size (40 yd X 25 yd).

ARTICLE 9 - SCORING: The scoring system used in the Armed Forces Program shall be the same as found in Rule 11 of this book.

ARTICLE 10 - TYPE OF BLOCKING: The type of blocking offered in the Armed Forces Program shall be dictated by the Game being played:

a. Touch = Contact blocking.
b. Contact Flag = Contact blocking.
c. Ineligible Lineman Flag = Contact blocking.
d. Screen Flag = Screen blocking.

ARTICLE 11 - RECEIVING = ELIGIBLE OR INELIGIBLE: The type of receiving offered in the Armed Forces Program shall be dictated by the Game being played:

a. Touch = Everyone eligible.
b. Contact Flag = Everyone eligible.
c. Screen Flag = Everyone eligible.
d. Ineligible Lineman Flag = Lineman Ineligible (Center and 2 linemen).

ARTICLE 12 - PLAYING RULES CAN BE MODIFIED: All playing rules not specifically covered in Rule 26 (Armed Forces Program) of this book shall be governed by the other rules as outlined in Rules I through 17 of this book. Any rule found in this book may. be altered to suit the needs of the Local Armed Forces Program. The U.S.F.T.L. recommends using the Official U.S.F.T.L. Rule Book as closely as possible for the following reasons:

a. For a better understanding of all the rules of Flag & Touch Football.
b. For uniformity in playing rules, so that different areas of the United States can compete against one another in a safe and fair manner.

RULE 27 - LAW ENFORCEMENT PROGRAM

SECTION 1 - GENERAL GUIDELINES:

ARTICLE 1 - THE LAW ENFORCEMENT PROGRAM: The Law Enforcement Program shall be offered to male and female adult players who must be certified Law Enforcement Officers with full powers of arrest within their jurisdiction. They must also be bonafide full time Law Enforcement Officers, with at least 30 hours per week and with 60 days continuous Law Enforcement service, prior to participating in the Law Enforcement Program. They may be retired Law Enforcement Officers with full arrest authority. All players must play in a state where they are employed. All players are required to have picture identification from their Department of Employment and must produce it on request. The same requirement shall be required for the Firefighters Division of the Law Enforcement Program.

ARTICLE 2 - THE GAMES: The games offered in the Law Enforcement Program shall be Touch Football, Contact Flag Football, Screen Flag Football and Ineligible Lineman Flag Football.

ARTICLE 3 - DIVISIONS OF PLAY: There shall be 5 divisions of play offered in the Law Enforcement Program: SUPER, A, B, C & D.

ARTICLE 4 - AGE CLASSIFICATION: The Age Classification in the Law Enforcement Program shall be 18 & Over and 35 & Over. Players must be the particular age offered in that particular age classification during that calendar year.

ARTICLE 5 - NUMBER OF PLAYERS ON THE FIELD: The number of players on the field in the Law Enforcement Program shall be dictated by the Game being played or the game being offered:

a. Touch = 7 players.
b. Screen Flag = 7 players.
c. Contact Flag = 8 players.
d. Ineligible Lineman Flag = 9 players.
e. 4 on 4 = 4 players.
f. 5 on 5 = 5 players.

ARTICLE 6 - THE BALL: The ball that is used in the Law Enforcement Program shall be the regular, intermediate, junior or youth size football. Male players must use the regular size football. Female players may use the regular, intermediate, junior or youth size football. An Officially Licensed Football of the U.S.F.T.L. must be used.

ARTICLE 7 - THE FLAGS: The flags that shall be used in the Law Enforcement Program shall be an Officially Licensed Flag of the U.S.F.T.L.

ARTICLE 8 - PLAYING FIELD SIZE: The playing field size that is used in the Law Enforcement Program shall be the regulation field size (100yd X 53 1/3yd), the abbreviated field size (80yd X 40yd) or the 4on4/5on5 field size (40 yd X 25 yd).

ARTICLE 9 - SCORING: The scoring system used in the Law Enforcement Program shall be the same as found in Rule 11 of this book.

ARTICLE 10 - TYPE OF BLOCKING: The type of blocking offered in the

Law Enforcement Program shall be dictated by the Game being played:
   a. Touch = Contact blocking.
   b. Contact Flag = Contact blocking.
   c. Ineligible Lineman Flag = Contact blocking.
   d. Screen Flag = Screen blocking.

ARTICLE 11 - RECEIVING = ELIGIBLE OR INELIGIBLE: The type of receiving offered in the Law Enforcement Program shall be dictated by the game being played:
   a. Touch = Everyone eligible.
   b. Contact Flag = Everyone eligible.
   c. Screen Flag = Everyone eligible.
   d. Ineligible Lineman Flag = Lineman Ineligible (Center and 2 linemen).

ARTICLE 12 - PLAYING RULES CAN BE MODIFIED: All playing rules not specifically covered in Rule 27 (Law Enforcement Program) of this book shall be governed by the other rules as outlined in Rules 1 through 17 of this book. Any rule found in this book may be altered to suit the needs of the Local Law Enforcement Program. The U.S.F.T.L. recommends using the Official U.S.F.T.L. Rule Book as closely as possible for the following reasons:

   a. For a better understanding of all the rules of Flag & Touch Football.
   b. For uniformity in playing rules, so that different areas of the United States can compete against one another in a safe and fair manner.

RULE 28 - INDOOR RULES

SECTION 1 - GENERAL GUIDELINES:

ARTICLE 1 - INDOOR PLAYING RULES: The Indoor Playing Rules are the same as the rules as outlined in Rules 1 though 17 of this book. All games, division of play, age classification, number of players on the field, the ball, the flags, scoring, type of blocking and eligibility of receivers are the same as in the other programs (Rules 18 through 29) in this book.

ARTICLE 2 - PLAYING FIELD SIZE: The playing field size may be altered to fit the different sized indoor facilities.

ARTICLE 3 - PLAYING RULES CAN BE MODIFIED: All playing rules not specifically covered in Rule 28 (Indoor Rules) of this book shall be governed by the other rules as outlined in Rules 1 through 17 of this book. Any rule found in this book may be altered to suit the needs of the Local Indoor Program. The U.S.F.T.L. recommends using the Official U.S.F.T.L. Rule book as closely as possible for the following reasons:

   a. For a better understanding of all rules of Flag & Touch Football.
   b. For uniformity in playing rules, so that different areas of the United States can compete against one another in a safe and fair manner.

RULE 29 - 5 ON 5 PROGRAM

SECTION 1 - GENERAL GUIDELINES:

ARTICLE 1 - THE 5 ON 5 PROGRAM: The 5 on 5 Program shall be offered to youth and adult players of the male and female sex.

ARTICLE 2 - THE GAMES: The Games offered in the 5 on 5 Program shall be Touch Football and Flag Football.

ARTICLE 3 - DIVISIONS OF PLAY: There shall be 5 divisions of play offered in the 5 on 5 Program: SUPER, A, B, C, & D.

ARTICLE 4 - AGE CLASSIFICATION: The Age Classification in the 5 on 5 Program shall be:

YOUTH	- 6 and under
	- 8 and under
	- 10 and under
	- 12 and under
	- 14 and under
	- 16 and under
	- 18 and under
ADULT	- 18 and over
MASTERS	- 35 and over

Players must be the particular age offered in that particular Age Classification during that calendar year.

ARTICLE 5 - NUMBER OF PLAYERS ON THE FIELD: The number of players on the field in the 5 on 5 Program shall be five (5). 3 players are required to avoid forfeit. The number of players on the field in the Co-Rec 5 on 5 Program shall be (3 men & 2 women) or (2 men & 3 women). In the Co-Rec 5 on 5 Program, 3 players are required to avoid a forfeit (2 men & 1 woman) or (1 man & 2 women).

ARTICLE 6 - THE BALL: The ball that is used in the 5 on 5 Program shall be the regular, intermediate, junior or youth size football. Male players must use the regular size football. Female and Youth players may use the regular, intermediate, junior or youth size football. An Officially Licensed Football of the U.S.F.T.L. must be used.

ARTICLE 7 - THE FLAGS: The flags that shall be used in the 5 on 5 Program shall be an Officially Licensed Flag of the U.S.F.T.L.

ARTICLE 8 - PLAYING FIELD SIZE: The playing field size that is used in the 5 on 5 Program shall be the 5 on 5 field size (46 yd X 25 yd).

ARTICLE 9 - SCORING: The scoring system that is used in the 5 on 5 Program shall be: .

A. Mercy Rule: If a team is ahead by 17 or more points at the 1 minute warning of the second half, the game shall be over. If a team scores after the 1 minute warning of the second half to create a 17 point lead, the game shall be over.
B. Touchdown = 6 points
C. Touchdown (female) = 9 points (Co-Rec Only)
D. Safety = 2 points
E. Forfeited Game = 1 point
F. Extra Points:

1. By running or passing only (no kicking allowed) from 5 yards = 1 point. (2 points - female, Co-Rec only).
  2. By running or passing only (no kicking allowed) from 10 yards = 2 points. (3 points - female, Co-Rec only).

(NOTE: A team is given one choice which cannot be changed even if a penalty should occur. If you declare you are going for 2 points, the ball is placed at the 10 yard line and even if a penalty shall occur, the team will only be able to run or Pass and if successful, no matter from what distance, the value of the try is 2 points).

G. The return of Extra Point attempt = 2 points.

ARTICLE 10 - TYPE OF BLOCKING: The type of blocking offered in the 5 on 5 Program shall be Contact Blocking.

ARTICLE 11 - RECEIVING = ELIGIBLE OR INELIGIBLE: The type of receiving offered in the 5 on 5 Program shall be everyone eligible.

ARTICLE 12 - PLAYING RULES CAN BE MODIFIED: All playing rules not specifically covered in Rule 29 (5 on 5 Program) of this book shall be governed by other rules outlined in Rules 1 through 17 of this book. Any rule found in this book may be altered to suit the needs of the Local 5 on 5 Program. The U.S.F.T.L. recommends using the Official U. S.F.T.L. Rule Book as closely as possible for the following reasons:

a. For better understanding of all the rules of Flag & Touch Football.
b. For uniformity in playing rules, so that different areas of the United States can compete against one another in a safe and fair manner.
c. For an easier progression from the Youth Programs to the Adult Programs.

SECTION 2 - RULES & REGULATIONS:

ARTICLE 1 - BASIC RULES OF 5 ON 5:

A. A coin toss shall begin each game. The captain winning the toss shall choose one of the following options:
  1. Offense
  2. Defense
  3. Designate which goal his/her team will defend
  4. Defer choice to the second half

B. Loser of the coin toss shall make a choice of the remaining options.
C. Before the start of the second half, the choice of options shall be reversed.
D. The offensive team takes possession of the ball at their 5-yard line and has three (3) plays to cross mid-field. Once a team crosses mid-field, they will have three (3) plays to score a touchdown. If the offense fails to score, the ball changes possession and the new offensive team takes over on their 5-yard line.
E. If the offensive team fails to cross mid-field, possession of the ball changes and the opposite team starts their drive from their 5-yard line.
F. The offensive team has three (3) plays to cross mid-field. Once a team crosses mid-field, they will have three (3) plays to score a touchdown.
G. All drives and possession changes except interceptions, start on 5 yard line of offense.
H. Teams will switch ends after the first 12 minutes (Halftime).
I. Ball must be snapped between the legs, not off to one side, to start play. Direct snaps are legal.
J. The Ball is ruled dead when:

1. A snap to a Quarterback hits the ground
2. A fumble hits the ground (no fumble recoveries allowed).
3. A ball carrier's knee touches the ground.
4. A ball carrier's steps out of bounds.
5. A ball carrier's flags are legally removed, (NOTE: if a ball carrier's flags fall off inadvertently, play shall revert to a 2 hand touch between the shoulders and the knees).

K. 25 Second Clock - Each time the ball is spotted, a team has 25 seconds to snap the ball.
L. Blocking - CONTACT BLOCKING IS ALLOWED. Contact between shoulders and waist only.
M. Receivers may be bumped one time within 5 yards of line of scrimmage.
N. Interceptions may be returned.
O. 24 Minute Game - two (2) -12 minute halves with a running clock.
P. One (1) Minute Warning - When there is 1 minute left in the game, the game clock shall stop for incomplete passes, out-of-bounds, change of possessions, first downs and time-outs and starts and re-starts on the snap.

ARTICLE 2 - THE FIELD:

A. Field Size - 46 yards in length; 25 yards in width
B. End Zones - (2) 7 yard endzones

ARTICLE 3 - THE PLAYERS:

A. Roster size - Teams consist of a total of 10 players on the roster.
B. Number of players on field - 5 players on the field at one time.
C. Forfeits - to avoid a forfeit, you must have at least 3 players to begin the game.
D. Co-Rec team must have (3 male & 2 female) or (2 male & 3 female) players on the field at one time.
E. Forfeits in the 5 on 5 Co-Rec Program - to avoid a forfeit, Co-Rec teams must have 2 men and 1 woman or 1 man & 2 women to begin the game.

ARTICLE 4 - SCORING & OVERTIME:

A. Touchdowns = 6 points
   Extra Points = <u>1 point</u> (5 yards) - (run or pass - no kicks allowed).
        (2 points - female, Co-Rec only).
       = <u>2 points</u> (10 yards) - (run or pass - no kicks allowed).
        (3 points - female, Co-Rec only).
  Safety - 2 points

  Forfeited game = 1 point

B. Overtime = All overtime rules in the 5 on 5 Program are the same as found in Rule 5, Section 5 - Overtime, Articles 1-5 with the following expections: Each team gets 1 down from 10 yard line to score. Scoring is same as in regular game. A coin toss determines possession in each overtime period.
C. U.S.F.T.L. Sudden Death Overtime = In U.S.F.T.L. Championship Games (League & Tournament Championship Games only), a Sudden Death Overtime is used. Same procedure as start of game - coin toss followed by regular game conditions with each team having 1 series of downs to score. All other rules apply as found in Rule 5, Section 5, Article 4 - U.S.F.T.L. Sudden Death.

ARTICLE 5 - RUNNING PLAYS:
A. The Quarterback ("QB") MAY run the ball at any time.
B. Handoffs are allowed.
C. Laterals and pitches are NOT allowed anywhere on the field.
D. The player who takes a handoff can throw the ball as long as he does not cross the line of scrimmage.
E. The player who takes a hand off may run with the ball.
F. The "No Running Zone" is designed to avoid short yardage power running situations. (No Run Zones are located 5 yards from each end zone and 5 yards on either side of mid-field). No player is allowed to run inside of the No Run Zones.

ARTICLE 6 - PASSING:
A. Backward passes, laterals and shovel passes are NOT allowed.
B. Interception may be returned.
C. Only 1 forward pass per down.
D. If a passer crosses the line of scrimmage, and comes back behind the line of scrimmage and throws a pass, it is an illegal forward pass.
E. Quarterback has unlimited time to throw the ball.

ARTICLE 7 - RECEIVING:
A. Eligible Receivers - All players are eligible to receive passes (including the Quarterback after the ball has been handed off or lateraled behind the line of scrimmage).
B. A player must have at least one foot in bounds to make a legal reception.

ARTICLE 8 - RUSHING THE QUARTERBACK:
A. Defensive players may rush the passer immediately from the line of scrimmage. Any number of players can rush the Quarterback.
B. Ball spotter - A ball spotter shall be used to mark the line of scrimmage
C. Rushers must go for the Quarterback's flag and are not allowed to make contact. (NOTE: You cannot hit the Quarterback's arm to block a pass. You must go for the flag).

ARTICLE 9 - EQUIPMENT:
A. The Ball - Male players shall use a regulation size football. Female and youth players may use a regular, intermediate, junior or youth size football. An Officially Licensed Football by the U.S.F.T.L. must be used.
B. The Flags - All flags used in the 5 on 5 Program shall be an Officially Licensed Flag of the U.S.F.T.L.
C. Shoes - Cleats are allowed, but they must be rubber. No metal spikes are allowed. Screw-in cleats are allowed, if the screw is part of the cleat. Inspections will be made.
D. Jerseys - All jerseys shall be tucked in the pants and shorts. No shimmel length, waist length or half jerseys allowed.
E. Mouthpiece - All players must wear a protective mouthpiece. If you do not have a mouthpiece, there will be one available on-site for a fee.

ARTICLE 10 - TIME OUTS:
A. Each team has one 30 second time out per game.
B. Each team has one 30 second time out per overtime period.

ARTICLE 11 - PENALTY ENFORCEMENT:

A. Offensive Penalties:
   1. Illegal Motion - (More than 1 person moving at the snap, false start, illegal shift, illegal motion) = 5 yards from line of scrimmage and loss of down.
   2. Illegal Forward Pass - (Pass thrown beyond the line of scrimmage) = 5 yards from line of scrimmage and loss of down.
   3. Offensive Pass Interference - (Illegal pick play, pushing off or away from the defender) = 10 yards from line of scrimmage and loss of down.
   4. Flag Guarding = 10 yards from line of scrimmage and loss of down.
   5. Delay of Game = 5 yards from line of scrimmage, loss of down and clock will be automatically stopped until the next legal snap.
   6. Encroachment = 5 yards from line of scrimmage and loss of down.
   7. Illegal Contact (Holding, Contact to Head, etc.) = 10 yards from line of scrimmage and loss of down.
   8. Batting the ball to gain an advantage = 10 yards from line of scrimmage and loss of down.

B. Defensive Penalties:
   1. Offsides = 5 yards from line of scrimmage and automatic 1st Down.
   2. Defensive Pass Interference = Spot of Foul and automatic 1st Down.
   3. Illegal Contact - (Holding, Contact to Head, etc.) = 10 yards from line of scrimmage and automatic 1st Down.
   4. Illegal Flag Pull - (Pulling of runner's flags before he has the ball) = 10 yards from line of scrimmage and automatic 1st Down, unless it was a touchdown, then offense has option of the yardage or the score.
   5. Roughing Quarterback or Center - 10 yard penalty from line of scrimmage and automatic 1st Down.

C. Flagrant Fouls: Any flagrant contact whatsoever (tackling, elbowing, cheap shots, illegal contact, taunting or similar unsportsmanlike acts shall not be tolerated). The Official shall stop the game, eject the player from the game, administer a 10 yard penalty from the line of scrimmage with an automatic 1st Down if it was on the defense or a loss of down if it was on the offense and give the coach a verbal warning - FOUL PLAY WILL NOT BE TOLERATED!!!

D. Games cannot end upon a defensive penalty, unless the offense declines it.

RULE 30 - PAID BIDS

SECTION 1 - PAID BID EXPLANATION FOR COMBINED DIVISION TOURNAMENTS:

ARTICLE 1 - PAID BID CHART: Refer to the following chart explaining the USFTL National Tournament Paid Bid pay outs for a combined division tournament that has Super, A, B, C, and D teams competing against each other in the event:

Example 1:
1st Place - A Team = 1/2 paid bid
*2nd Place - B team = 1/4 paid bid
*3rd Place - C team - 1/4 paid bid

Example 2:
1st Place - A Team = 1/2 paid bid
*2nd Place - C Team = 1/2 paid bid
3rd Place - B Team= None

Example 3:
1st Place - B Team = 1/2 paid bid
2nd Place - A Team = None
*3rd Place - C Team= 1/2 paid bid

Example 4:
1st Place - B Team = 1/2 paid bid
*2nd Place - C Team = 1/2 paid bid
3rd Place - A Team= None

Example 5: 1st Place - C Team = Full paid bid
2nd Place - A Team = None
3rd Place - B Team = None

Example 6: 1st Place - C Team = Full paid bid
2nd Place - B Team = None
3rd Place - A Team = None

*These paid bids will NOT be awarded to teams that already have full paid bids. The bid would then go to the next appropriate team without a full paid bid.

*Also, if there are 8 or more teams per division, there is a FULL PAID BID awarded. If there are 7 teams or less, a 1/2 PAID BID is awarded.

SECTION 2 - TRAVEL EXPENSE EXPLANATION:

Article 1: TRAVEL EXPENSE DISTRIBUTION: Travel Expense monies are awarded to tournament/league winners ONLY. Travel Expense monies will be paid to teams from USFTL tournaments/leagues after paid bids have been earned. **Example:** If a team has already won a full paid bid, then wins another tournament/league offering a paid bid, that winning team will receive 1/2 of the paid bid money paid to them as travel expense money, because they have already previously won their full paid bid. Teams that continue to win tournaments/leagues can accumulate numerous travel expense monies to defray their cost to the USFTL Nationals. If a team has a partial paid bid and wins another bid, they will receive monies to cover their full paid bid and all monies left over will be given to them as travel expense money.

All travel expense monies must be picked up at the USFTL National Championship coaches meeting.

*Also, if there are 8 or more teams per division, there is a FULL PAID BID awarded. If there are 7 teams or less, a 1/2 PAID BID is awarded.

PLAY RULINGS

A play ruling is an official decision on a given statement of fact. It illustrates the spirit and application of the rules.

RULE 5 - PERIODS, TIME FACTORS AND OVERTIME:

a. After a one-minute intermission one of the teams is not ready to play.

RULING: Penalize the offending team for illegal delay.

b. A shoelace, jersey, or other equipment breaks or tears. Should repair or replacement be made on the Referee's time?

RULING: No-unless the Referee considers such equipment dangerous to other players.

c. Neither team has been charged with a time-out when a field captain requests a time-out and designates an injured player who is replaced.

RULING: Charge the Referee with a time out.

RULE 7 - BALL IN PLAY, DEAD BALL, OUT-OF-BOUNDS:

a. A ball carrier inbounds bumps into or is touched by a player on the side line.

RULING: The ball is not out-of-bounds.

RULE 8 - SERIES OF DOWNS, NUMBER OF DOWNS, ZONE LINE-TO-GAIN AND TEAM POSSESSION AFTER PENALTY:

a. Team A ball carrier attempts a backward pass which is ruled forward and illegal. The pass strikes the ground.

RULING: Penalize Team A 5 yards at the spot from where the pass was thrown and, unless the current series is broken, the down counts.

b. Team A's scrimmage kick goes out-of-bounds at Team B's 29 yard line after which a Team B player commits illegal use of the hands.

RULING: 1st and two zones to go. This is a dead ball foul.

c. Team B runs back Team A's kick or intercepted pass. During the run a Team B player holds.

RULING: Team B is penalized 15 yards utilizing the three and one application. It is Team B's ball, 1st and zone in advance of the succeeding spot.

RULE 9 - THE SCRIMMAGE, SNAPPING, HANDING AND PASSING THE BALL:

a. After a huddle or shift all offensive players come to a legal stop and remain stationary for a full second. Then, before the snap, two or more of them simultaneously change their positions.

RULING: A second shift. All offensive players must remain stationary for one full second before the snap. Otherwise it is an illegal shift.

b. Following a huddle or shift offensive players take preliminary positions, then advance or drop into final positions.

RULING: Such movements constitute a shift; players must hold their final positions for one second before a snap.

c. A defensive player charges into the neutral zone, but gets back into legal position before the snap.

RULING: Encroachment—5 yards. Dead ball foul.

d. A Team B player, defending against a legal forward pass, with back to the ball and waving his or her arms in the face of an eligible receiver of Team A, who is attempting to catch the pass, bumps into the Team B player.

RULING: Defensive pass interference by the Team B player. A bonafide attempt to catch or bat the pass was not being made. Automatic first down at the spot of the interference.

e. An opponent snatches ("steals") the ball from the ball carrier.

RULING: Fumble. The ball continues in play.

f. Team A's legal forward pass is first touched by one of its receivers, then caught by another.

RULING: Completed pass. On such a play the passer also becomes an eligible receiver.

g. A player of the receiving team catches a kick, then fumbles the ball. A player of the kicking team catches the fumbled ball before it strikes the ground.

RULING: The ball continues in play and may be advanced.

RULE 10 - THE KICKING GAME:

a. A player of Team A recovers a rolling free kick beyond Team B's restraining line and makes a backward pass which goes out-of-bounds.

RULING: The ball is dead and belongs to Team B where the Team A player recovered it.

b. Team A player touches a rolling free kick before it reaches the opponents' restraining line.

RULING: Team B can either take the ball at the spot of "first touching" or the result of the play. If the kick hits the ground after being touched by Team A player, the ball is dead once it strikes the ground after being muffed by K.

c. Team B player about to catch a scrimmage kick is touched or deflagged before the ball arrives but catches the kick.

RULING: Fair catch interference 10 yards from the previous spot or an awarded fair catch at the spot of the interference.

d. A player of the receiving team attempting to catch a free or scrimmage kick, touches the ball which is then caught by an opponent before striking the ground.

RULING: Not interference. Protection against fair catch interference to catch a kick ceases when any player of the receiving team touches it. Ball is dead where caught and belongs to kicking team. 1st and zone line-to-gain.

e. Team A player catches a free kick, thus preventing a nearby opponent from making the catch.

RULING: Fair catch interference 10 yards from previous spot or awarded fair catch at the spot of the interference.

RULE 11 - SCORING:

a. A Team B player intercepts a legal forward pass in Team B's end zone, attempts to run it out, but is touched or has the flag removed behind his/her goal line.

RULING: Touchback.

b. The ball is snapped to a Team A player who punts from Team A's end zone, the ball going out-of-bounds behind the kicker's goal line. RULING: Safety.

c. A Team B player catches a scrimmage/free kick in Team B's end zone: then fumbles and the ball goes out-of-bounds behind the goal line.

RULING: Touchback. The kick was dead once it was fumbled.

d. The ball carrier, after receiving the snap in the end zone, is touched or the flag is removed with the ball resting inside the end zone.

RULING: Safety.

CONSTITUTION

of the
United States
Flag & Touch
Football League

(Important U.S.F.T.L. Constitution Articles
pertaining to Team and Player Eligibility).

Approved by the voting delegates at the
National Meeting of the U.S.F.T.L.

ARTICLE 1 - ORGANIZATION

SECTION 1 - NAME: This organization shall be known as the "United States Flag & Touch Football League", also referred to as U.S.F.T.L. It is a 501(C)-(3), non-profit membership based organization.

SECTION 2 - MISSION STATEMENT:

a) The Mission Statement of the U.S.F.T.L. shall be to promote the games of Flag & Touch Football to all people regardless of race, religion, sex, nationality or age.
b) To establish uniformity in Flag & Touch Football rules and regulations making the game safe and enjoyable for everyone.
c) To encourage sportsmanship and fair play at all levels.
d) To educate and teach the proper skills of Flag & Touch Football through the creation of rules, promoting, organizing, conducting clinics, seminars and training courses.

SECTION 3 - VISION STATEMENT: "IT'S TIME TO GIVE THE GAME TO THE PLAYERS."

SECTION 4 - FISCAL YEAR: The league shall operate on an established fiscal year commencing September 1 and ending on August 31.

ARTICLE 2 - MEMBERSHIP

SECTION 1 - DEFINITION: Any qualified person and or team may apply for membership in this league with an application accompanied by the established membership fee.

SECTION 2 - TYPES: There shall be different types of membership in the U.S.F.T.L. They are as follows:

a) TEAM MEMBERSHIP: Any amateur team which competes and plays Flag & Touch Football is eligible for team membership. In order to become a U.S.F.T.L. adult or youth team member, a team must pay a registration fee. (Any fees beyond the National Registration Fee shall be at the Regional President's and State Director's discretion.)

The portion of fees due to the U.S.F.T.L. National Headquarters must be forwarded to the U.S.F.T.L. National Headquarters with a properly executed team registration form by the State Director. A team can register directly with the U.S.F.T.L. National Headquarters only in a state that has no program or appointed directors. Team registration fees are paid annually and expire August 31 of each year. A team may register in only one state. Under no circumstances shall a team be required to pay any regional or sectional registration fees. This membership entitles a team to compete and enter any U.S.F.T.L. sanctioned league or tournament. Each team will be eligible to purchase insurance if offered by the U.S.F.T.L. Each team manager will receive a membership card, rule book and a one year subscription to the U.S.F.T.L. National Newspaper. Each team will be assured of proper administration of the U.S.F.T.L. as set forth in this Constitution. Any team that changes its name during the season must re-register with the U.S.F.T.L.

b) OFFICIAL'S MEMBERSHIP: Any person who is considered as a qualified official may apply for official membership. In order to become a U.S.F.T.L. official, the official must take a certification test, attend two clinics yearly, and pay a registration fee to the State Director. (Any fees beyond the national registration fee shall be at the Regional President's, and State Director's discretion.) The fee due to the U.S.F.T.L. National Headquarters must be forwarded to the U.S.F.T.L. National Headquarters with a properly executed officials registration form by the State Director. An official can register directly with the U.S.F.T.L. National Director of Officials only in a state that has no program or appointed directors. State officials fees shall be used to offset expenses of the State Officials Program. Under no circumstances shall an official be required to pay any Regional or Sectional registration fees. This membership entitles an official the right to be considered for assignment in U.S.F.T.L. sanctioned leagues or tournaments. Each official will be eligible to purchase insurance if provided by the U.S.F.T.L. All registered officials will receive a membership card, rule book and patch. All officials, upon presentation of membership card, will be permitted free admission to any U.S.F.T.L. sanctioned tournament. Each official will receive a one year subscription to the U.S.F.T.L. National Newspaper. Official registration fees are paid annually and expire August 31 of each year.

c) **ALLIED MEMBERSHIP:** An Allied Membership may be awarded to any professional association or organization involved in the administration of an athletic or recreational program. The granting of an Allied Membership shall be awarded by the U.S.F.T.L. Executive Board of Directors by a majority vote and shall be reviewed for renewal yearly. An Allied Member shall be presented a rule book, a patch, an Allied Membership plaque and a membership card-which shall permit free admittance to any U.S.F.T.L. sanctioned tournament. An Allied Member shall receive a subscription to the U.S.F.T.L. National Newspaper and will be extended an invitation to attend the U.S.F.T.L.'s Annual National Meeting, without voting privileges. Allied Members are not required to pay any membership fees. Allied Members shall appear in the U.S.F.T.L. Rule Book and Constitution.

d) **DIRECTORS MEMBERSHIP:** All Local Directors, State Directors, Sectional Vice Presidents, Regional Presidents, Executive Committee Members, Executive Board of Director Members, Board of Trustees Members, National Officers of the U.S.F.T.L., National Program Directors, Local Directors of Officials, State Directors of Officials, Sectional Directors of Officials and Regional Directors of Officials will be awarded this type of membership. Appointments and elections of such members will be in accordance with procedures as set forth in the U.S.F.T.L. Constitution. Duties, responsibilities and voting rights will be in accordance with guidelines as set forth in the U.S.F.T.L. Constitution. All such members will receive a rule book, a membership card, a patch and a subscription to the U.S.F.T.L. National Newspaper. All such members, upon presentation of membership card, will be permitted free admission to any U.S.F.T.L. sanctioned tournament. Director's membership fees paid directly to the U.S.F.T..L. National Headquarters. Director registration fees are paid annually and expires August 31 of each year.

e) **STATE MEMBERSHIP:** Each state in the U.S.F.T.L. shall pay a fee annually, on or before September 1. The State Director is responsible for this payment and shall receive a rule book, membership card, a patch, a subscription to the U.S.F.T.L. National Newspaper and a membership plaque which will be issued in his honor. State registration fees are paid annually and expire August

31 of each year.

f) ASSOCIATE MEMBERSHIP: An Associate Membership may be awarded to any individual, business or company interested in the advancement of Flag & Touch Football and the U.S.F.T.L. Associate Membership is awarded on an individual basis with requests being made through the U.S.F.T.L. National Headquarters. Approval of such requests shall be made by the U.S.F.T.L. Executive Board of Directors by a majority vote. Associate Membership fees are paid directly to the U.S.F.T.L. National Headquarters. Associate Members shall receive a subscription to the U.S.F.T.L. National Newspaper, a rule book, a membership card, a patch and a membership plaque. Any Associated Member, upon presentation of membership card will be permitted free admission to any U.S.F.T.L. sanctioned tournament. Associate registration fees are paid annually and expire August 31 of each year.

g) LIFE MEMBERSHIP: A Life Membership is issued to those individuals who desire to aid in the promotion of the games of Flag & Touch Football. Life Membership fees are paid directly to the U.S.F.T.L. National Headquarters. Life Members shall receive a rule book, a patch, a membership card, a subscription to the U.S.F.T.L. National Newspaper and a membership plaque. Any Life Member, upon presentation of membership card, will be permitted free admission to any U.S.F.T.L. sanctioned tournament. Life Membership registration fees are paid one time only. Life Members shall appear in the U.S.F.T.L. Rule Book and Official's Manual.

ARTICLE 11 - TEAM ELIGIBILITY

<u>SECTION 1:</u> The U.S.F.T.L. shall be for amateur Flag & Touch Football players to compete as a team under an adopted set of administrative rules and playing rules.

<u>SECTION 2:</u> No team shall be allowed to compete in U.S.F.T.L. sanctioned leagues or tournaments without paying their National and State team registration fees to the U.S.F.T.L.

<u>SECTION 3:</u> A team shall be composed of not more than thirty (30) eligible players in Flag Football, Touch Football & Ineligible Lineman Flag Football, and eight (8) eligible players in 4 on 4, and ten (10) eligible players in 5 on 5. Coaches must be included on the roster in order to be eligible to play.

<u>SECTION 4:</u> When a member of a team is called into the Armed Forces, he may be replaced by any other eligible player. Players returning from active military service may be added to a team's eligible roster, provided that the number of eligible players on the team's roster does not exceed the total number allowed at any one time.

<u>SECTION 5:</u> The cut-off date for adding players to a team roster shall be in accordance with rules set forth in the U.S.FT.L. Constitution.

<u>SECTION 6:</u> A team winning a U.S.F.T.L. Tournament and advancing to a higher U.S.F.T.L. Tournament may be allowed expense money in accordance with advance rules governing the tournament, which rules shall be promulgated by the National Headquarters of the U.S.F.T.L. and are consistent with the Constitution of the U.S.F.T.L. Such expense monies shall be presented to the team and not tne individual players and must be used by the team to offset team expenses. This same rule shall apply to any such rule governing league winners advancing to U.S.F.T.L.

Tournaments.

SECTION 7: Teams properly registered with the U.S.F.T.L. may be given permission to compete against, or on the same program with teams, when it has been publicized that other team's members will be eligible to receive a portion of the gross receipts. Such approval may be granted by State or Local Directors.

SECTION 8:
a) An official U.S.F.T.L. team registration receipt must be obtained by all teams that wish to compete in out-of-state tournaments sanctioned by the U.S.F.T.L. The team registration receipt form must be approved by the traveling team's Local Director, State Director or Regional President. The form must be shown to the Tournament Director before the team competes in the out-of-state tournament. This registration receipt will be good for the entire current season as long as the team is in good standing with the U.S.F.T.L.
b) The team registration receipt form will consist of three copies as follows:
1.) Original (white copy) - This copy must be forwarded to the U.S.F.T.L. National Headquarters.
2.) Duplicate (yellow copy) - This copy must be forwarded to the State Director.
3.) Duplicate (pink copy) - This copy must be retained by the Local Director and made available to the team coach. This copy must be shown to the Tournament Director.
c) State Directors, Sectional Vice Presidents or Regional Presidents, who issue Team Registration Receipt Forms, shall be responsible for collection and payment of Team Registration fees. The registration of teams is the responsibility of the state or local area in which the team first participates.
d) A Tournament Director shall not accept an out-of-state team without a team registration receipt, unless: He contacts the team's State Director to establish proper team classification. He collects the proper team registration fee if the team cannot show proof of prior registration. A team registration form should then be filled out. He issues a team registration receipt showing the proper team classification. He submits the proper paperwork and fees to the U.S.F.T.L. National Headquarters with copies of the paperwork sent to the team's State Director. Tournament Directors in violation of this rule shall be subject to sanction by the U.S.F.T.L. and the Tournament which violated this rule may not be considered sanctioned by the U.S.F.T.L. and the awarding of any advancement berth may not be honored.
e) A U.S.F.T.L. Registration card will also be issued upon payment of registration fees and must be shown at all U.S.F.T.L. events.

ARTICLE 12 - INDIVIDUAL PLAYER ELIGIBILITY

SECTION I - DEFINITION: A player is eligible to compete in the U.S.F.T.L. Program as long as he abides by the U.S.F.T.L. Constitution, By-Laws, and Playing Rules, when listed as a member of an eligible team.

SECTION 2 - TRAVEL EXPENSE GUIDELINES:
a) Per Diem per day meal allowance.
b) Payment of up to federal limits per mile auto allowance to travel to and from home to playing destination.
c) Exact reimbursement for rail, airfare and ground transportation.

d) Exact reimbursement for lodging expenses. The above player expense limits are established for all programs. Any player receiving compensation greater than the above travel expense guidelines must have a registered personal services contract.

SECTION 3 - PERSONAL SERVICE CONTRACT: A personal services contract is a contract between an individual sponsor, sporting goods manufacturer, or other sponsor and a player, which provides for the player to receive compensation, including bonuses, promotional fees and the like, which are paid in addition to those set forth in the U.S.F.T.L. travel expense guidelines as set forth in Article 12; Section 2. All sponsors, manufacturers, and players who have business understandings which fall within the definition of a personal services contract are required to memorialize such understandings in written form on contracts which substantially conform to those provided by the U.S.F.T.L. National Headquarters. Such contracts must be filed and approved with the U.S.F.T.L. National Headquarters prior to participation in the U.S.F.T.L. Program.

SECTION 4 - AWARDS: A player shall not be permitted to accept an award other than a watch, charm, trophy, jacket, ball or other like award. No cash awards.

SECTION 5 - CLASSIFICATION:
a) The method to be used to classify a team in the Super, A, B, C and D program will be governed by the U.S.F.T.L. Constitution and whatever system the State Director has created for his state.

SECTION 6 - PARTICIPATION: A player shall not compete in any sanctioned tournament of the U.S.F.T.L. with more than one team during the same tournament per division.

SECTION 7 - ROSTERS:
a) When a team qualifies for a Local, State, Sectional, Regional, National or World Tournament, the team roster will be frozen. Players will be bound to this qualified team, up to and including, the team's respective Local, State, Sectional, Regional, National or World Tournament. A team coach may release and add up to three players from his team's qualified frozen roster.
b) Any player that is released from a qualifying teams roster cannot return to that team during the current season.
c) Thirty (30) player roster limit in Flag Football, Touch Football and Ineligible Lineman Flag Football, eight (8) player roster limit in 4 on 4, and ten (10) player roster limit in 5 on5.
d) All rosters must be submitted to the Local Director by October 1st! (NO EXCEPTIONS)
e) No players may be added to a roster after October 1st.
f) A player may change teams only if his current team coach gives a written release to the Local Director.
g) A player may only change teams one time per year.

SECTION 8 - PROFESSIONAL PLAYERS; (TACKLE, FLAG OR TOUCH) :
Any player who either plays or is under contract to play professional football will not be allowed to participate in the U.S.F.T.L. program as a player. Players who have been released as a professional football player, may apply for reinstatement as an amateur player with the U.S.F.T.L. as follows:
a) Any former professional football player who has been released contractually may apply in writing to the U.S.F.T.L. National Headquarters for amateur

status at any time. If reinstatement is approved, then the player will be eligible to participate in the U.S.F.T.L. program.
b) A fee shall be charged for reinstatement.
c) A player who tries out for a professional football team and does not play in any scheduled games shall not be considered a professional.
d) If a player participates in an event that gives away cash as prizes, they are considered "Professional." Travel Expense Monies and Paid Bids are not considered "Cash Prizes."

SECTION 9 - ILLEGAL PLAYER: A player who is in violation of the U.S.F.T.L. Constitution and or official playing rules and regulations shall be considered an illegal player.

SECTION 10 - SCOPE OF AUTHORITY:
a) Anytime during a game or after, it the Tournament Director discovers an illegal player, he has the authority to apply penalties as described in the U.S.F.T.L. Rule Book and Constitution.
b) If an illegal player is discovered anytime during or after a tournament game or after the completion of an entire tournaments (up to one year from the tournament date), penalties may be applied as described in the U.S.F.T.L. Rule Book and Constitution.

SECTION 11 - CORPORATE PROGRAM:
a) All players of Corporate teams that compete in Local, State, Sectional, Regional, National or World Tournaments that are considered Corporate Tournaments must be bonafide full time employees of the team sponsor at the time the tournament is played. All bonafide full time employees with less than sixty (60) days continuous service with a team sponsor will not be eligible to play in the Corporate Tournament. Employees who might be on military duty shall be considered eligible to compete. Corporate sponsors, such as Corporations, Businesses, Government Agencies, etc., that operate in more than one location, within a State, may be considered as one sponsor. Such sponsors cannot combine with an out-of-state location.
b) All players of Local Union teams that compete in Local, State, Sectional, Regional, National or World Tournaments that are considered Union Local Tournaments must be bonafide Union members from the same local with a minimum of sixty (60) days membership.
c) Union Local players or teams may be eligible to participate in the Corporate Program only if they meet the guidelines for Corporate participation and eligibility.
d) Trade Union Local teams may participate in the Corporate Program if they meet the following criteria:

> **1.)** All team members are bonafide members of the Trade Union they represent.
> **2.)** All team members are covered under a negotiated Trade Union contract providing wages and benefits.
> **3.)** All players of Trade Union Local teams that compete in Local, State, Sectional, Regional, National or World Tournaments that are considered Corporate Tournaments must have sixty (60) days, continuous service with the Trade Union Local they represent, prior to participating in any Corporate Tournaments.

SECTION 12 - CHURCH PROGRAM:
a) Any player of a Church Team that is competing in a Local, State, Sectional, Regional, National or World Tournament that are considered exclusive Church tournaments must be active participants in the worship services of the Church for which he is playing the current year.
b) State Directors shall contact the church pastor or church official who signs the roster to certify roster is in compliance with the U.S.F.T.L. Constitution prior to advancing teams to Local, State, Sectional, Regional, National or World Tournaments.

SECTION 13 - LAW ENFORCEMENT PROGRAM: All players of Law Enforcement teams must be certified Law Enforcement Officers with full powers of arrest within their jurisdiction. They must also be bonafide full time Law Enforcement Officers, with at least 30 hours per week and with 60 days' continuous Law Enforcement service, prior to participating in Law Enforcement Tournament play or be retired Law Enforcement Officers with full arrest authority. All players must play on a team within the State where they are employed. All players are required to have picture identification from Department of Employment and must produce it on request.

SECTION 14 - MEN'S PROGRAM: Teams participating in the U.S.F.T.L. Men's Program will be allowed to have only Male players on its roster. region.

SECTION 15 - WOMEN'S PROGRAM: Teams participating in the U.S.F.T.L. Women's Program will be allowed to have only Female players on its roster.

SECTION 16 - CO-REC PROGRAM: Teams participating in the U.S.F.T.L. Co-Rec's Program will be allowed to have both Male and Female players on its roster.

SECTION 17 - YOUTH PROGRAM: If players in the Youth Program are the particular age of that division during the calendar year, then they would be eligible to participate in that division. There shall be a Boys, Girls and Co-Rec Youth Division offered.
   1.) 6 & Under
   2.) 8 & Under
   3.) 10 & Under
   4.) 12 & Under
   5.) 14 & Under
   6.) 16 & Under
   7.) 18 & Under

SECTION 18 - MASTERS PROGRAM: Players participating in the U.S.F.T.L. Masters Program must be 35 years or older in that calendar year to be eligible to compete in the Masters Program. There shall be Men, Women and Co-Rec divisions offered. All players are required to have picture identification and age verification and must produce it upon request.

SECTION 19 - ARMED FORCES PROGRAM: Players participating in the U.S.F.T.L. Armed Forces Program shall be active or retired members of the Armed Forces. There shall be Men, Women and Co-Rec divisions offered.

SECTION 20 - 4 ON 4 PROGRAM: Rosters are limited to eight (8) players and must abide by all of the rules as set forth in the U.S.F.T.L. Rule Book and Constitution. There shall be Men, Women, Co-Rec and Youth divisions offered.

SECTION 21 - 5 ON 5 PROGRAM: Rosters are limited to ten (10) players and must abide by all of the rules as set forth in the U.S.F.T.L. Rule Book and Constitution. There shall be Men, Women, Co-Rec and Youth divisions offered.

ARTICLE 13 - WORLD CHAMPIONSHIP

SECTION 1 - RULES AND PROCEDURES: In the event the U.S.F.T.L. holds a World Championship Play-off to determine a true World Champion then it shall be the duty of the Executive Board of Directors to establish all rules and procedures to govern such an event. Finalizing and announcing plans to hold such an event should be made at the National Meeting of the U.S.F.T.L.

ARTICLE 15 - ACTS OF DISBARMENT

SECTION 1 - ACTS OF DISBARMENT:
a) Physical attack on an Official, Tournament Director, or U.S.F.T.L. Directors, or U.S.F.T.L Officers during a game or immediately following a game, played under the administration of the U.S.F.T.L.
b) Player, coach or sponsor threatening an Official, Tournament Director, U.S.F.T.L. Director or U.S.F.T.L. Officer.
c) Player, coach, or sponsor fighting, using unsportsmanlike conduct or abusive tactics, or derogatory or unbecoming acts that are detrimental and not in the best interest of the U.S.F.T.L. and U.S.F.T.L. league and tournament play.
d) Destruction of property or abuse of hotel property, or failure to pay hotel or motel bills.
e) Participating in a tournament in which cash prizes are offered. In referring to cash prizes, the following shall define a cash prize. "Cash prize" shall mean prizes in cash that is awarded to players or teams based on the final standings of a tournament or other competition. A player or team may receive reimbursement for actual travel expenses incurred as long as the expense goes to a team advancing in U.S.F.T.L. Tournament Competition.
f) By knowingly competing with or against illegal or suspended players.
g) By participating in or permitting a fraud to be perpetrated.
h) Any director of the U.S.F.T.L. who refuses to submit funds to the U.S.F.T.L. that are due to the U.S.F.T.L.
i) Competing under an assumed name.
j) Submitting a bad check to the U.S.F.T.L.
k) Failure to show up after entering a Local, State, NIT, Sectional, Regional, National or World Tournament unless reasonable advance notice is given.
l) Purposely using false information to hurt the U.S.F.T.L.
m) Violating the contract rights granted to any individual by the U.S.F.T.L. under its Constitution. The penalty for violation of this paragraph shall be immediate suspension from any activities of the U.S.F.T.L.

SECTION 2 - DIRECTOR DISBARMENT:
a) Any U.S.F.T.L. Officer or Director that violates any Articles of the Constitution or U.S.F.T.L. policies may be suspended.

b) Any U.S.F.T.L. Officer or Director that fails to submit fees and/or information due the U.S.F.T.L. in a timely manner may be suspended.

c) Any U.S.F.T.L. Officer, Director, Official or participant that is suspended for any reason, shall not be allowed to participate in any capacity within the U.S.F.T.L., until such suspension has been lifted.

SECTION 3 - AUTHORITY OF DISBARMENT:

Only State Directors, Sectional Vice Presidents, the Regional Presidents and the Executive Director have the authority to issue disbarments for a period of one year from the time of the incident. Any disbarment beyond the one year suspension shall be ruled upon by the Executive Board of Directors. In order for such action to be effective, reasonable notice (at least 30 days) shall be given to the offending person before the convening of the Executive Board of Directors. Such notice shall be deemed sufficient if sent by registered mail to the address of the offending party last on file with the U.S.F.T.L. National Headquarters or the U.S.F.T.L. State Director's Headquarters; and contains a written statement of the offense and the length and terms of the requested additional disbarment beyond the one year suspension. The offending party may appear at the convening of the Executive Board of Directors and give evidence on its behalf as to why the additional suspension or disbarment should not be imposed. The decision of the Executive Board of Directors shall be final and binding and not be the subject of an appealable issue.

SECTION 4 - APPEALS:

a) Players or other announced participants, who have been disbarred or declared illegal, may use the appeal process procedure as set forth in the U.S.F.T.L. Constitution, except as limited by the provision of Article 15; Section 3 of the U.S.F.T.L. Constitution.

b) Any person so disbarred or suspended shall have the right to apply for reinstatement to membership in the U.S.F.T.L., on an annual basis, provided he gives the National Headquarters 30 days written notice of his intention to so reapply. The Executive Board of Directors shall act on such applications at the National Meeting of the U.S.F.T.L.

SECTION 5 - STATE FINANCIAL DISBARMENT: State Officers and Directors have the authority to issue indefinite suspensions for players or other announced participants who fail to meet financial responsibilities to that State.

SECTION 6 - SUSPENSION REPORTS: All reports of suspension must be in writing and submitted to the U.S.F.T.L. National Headquarters within five (5) days of the suspension. Copies of such suspensions shall be sent to the party against whom it is directed, the suspended party's Local Director and also to the suspended party's State Director and Regional President.

ARTICLE 23 - COPYRIGHTS, TELECAST & BROADCAST RIGHTS

SECTION 1 - OWNERSHIP: The U.S.F.T.L. shall own all copyrights, telecast and broadcast rights, (including all rights to telecast or broadcast by television, cable, radio or other visual or audio media) and similar rights, to all U.S.F.T.L. sponsored or sanctioned sporting events, including but not limited to games, tournaments, championships, award ceremonies and related events (collectively, the "Games"), together with the right to record, tape, videotape, broadcast, reproduce, copy, display or distribute any game (collectively, the "Rights").

SECTION 2 - PARTICIPATION: By participating in any U.S.F.T.L. sponsored or sanctioned game, a participant shall be deemed to have acknowledged and agreed that, as a condition to his membership in the U.S.F.T.L.

a) The participant has transferred and granted to the U.S.F.T.L. any and all rights he or she may have in any Game

b) The participant consents to the recording, taping, videotaping, use, broadcasting, telecasting, reproduction, copying, display and/or distribution of his name, voice, photograph, image or description in connection with the U.S.F.T.L.'s marketing, licensing, transfer or other disposition of the rights in the Games;

c) The U.S.F.T.L. shall have the exclusive right to market, license, transfer or otherwise dispose of with any of the rights in any of the Games;

d) The participant shall not assert any claim to any rights in any Games, whether against the U.S.F.T.L. or any third party.

SECTION 3 - PROCEEDS: The proceeds of the U.S.F.T.L. from any license transfer or other disposition of any rights in the Games shall belong solely to the U.S.F.T.L. and shall be used for such purposes as shall be designated by the Executive Board of Directors of the U.S.F.T.L. consistent with the charitable purposes of the U.S.F.T.L.

ARTICLE 26 - TOURNAMENT PROCEDURES, BY-LAWS AND GUIDELINES

SECTION I - TYPES OF TOURNAMENTS:

a) Local
b) N.I.T. (National Invitational Tournament)
c) State
d) Sectional
e) Regional
f) National
g) World

SECTION 2 - TOURNAMENT DIRECTORS:

a) Local Tournament - Local Tournament Director (Chosen by State Director)
b) State Tournament - State Tournament Director (Chosen by State Director)
c) N.I.T. Tournament - N.I.T. Tournament Director (Chosen by National Headquarters)
d) Sectional Tournament - Sectional Tournament Director (Chosen by National Headquarters)
e) Regional Tournament - Regional Tournament Director (Chosen by National Headquarters)
f) National Tournament - National Tournament Director (Chosen by National Headquarters)
g) World Tournament - World Tournament Director (Chosen by National Headquarters)

SECTION 3 - SANCTIONING: All teams and officials must be registered with the U.S.F.T.L. to participate.

SECTION 4 - ENTRANCE FEES: Entrance fees for U.S.F.T.L. tournaments shall be left up to the discretion of the U.S.F.T.L. and its Directors.

SECTION 5 - AWARDS: It shall be mandatory that the following awards be presented at all U.S.F.T.L. Tournaments.

a) 1st through 4th Place Sponsor Awards at all Local, NIT, State, Sectional and Regional U.S.F.T.L. Tournaments.

b) All other awards, (individual, all tournament, M.V.P.'s, etc.) shall be distributed at the discretion of the Tournament Director.

c) National Tournaments Only:

1.) 1ST THROUGH 4TH PLACE SPONSOR AWARDS

2.) INDIVIDUAL AWARDS: Individual Awards are given to each player on the Championship Team. Total not to exceed thirty (30) for Flag Football, Touch Football and Ineligible Lineman Flag Football, eight (8) for 4 on 4 and ten (10) for 5 on 5.

3.) ALL AMERICAN TEAM: An All American Team will be chosen at all National Tournaments. In Contact Flag Football eight (8) players, in Touch Football seven (7) players, in Screen Flag Football seven (7) players, in Ineligible Lineman Flag Football nine (9) players, in Co-Rec Flag Football eight (8), in 4 on 4 four (4) players, and in 5 on 5 (5) players shall be chosen on both offense and defense to make up the All American Team. All American Teams are picked by the coaches of the top four (4) teams by order of finish.

4.) MOST VALUABLE PLAYER AWARDS: A total of three (3) M.V.P. Awards shall be presented. The procedure for M.V.P. distribution shall be as follows:

M.V.P. OFFENSE: This award is given to the most valuable player on Offense. The 1st place coach has the option of picking a player on his team's Offense first. If, for some reason, he fails to choose one of his own players, then the choice goes to the 2nd place coach. If the 2nd place coach fails to choose one of his players, then the choice goes to the 3rd place coach, and so on, until an Offensive M.V.P.. has been chosen.

M.V.P. DEFENSE: Follow the same procedures as previously described for M.V.P. Offense.

M.V.P. SPECIAL TEAMS: Follow the same procedures as previously described for M.V.P. Offense. This award can be given to a Kicker (Place Kicker or Punter) or to an unsung member of a team who epitomizes team play.

5.) CO-REC ALL AMERICAN AND M.V.P. AWARDS: All American and M.V.P. awards at Co-Rec Tournaments are awarded as previously described in Article 26, Section 5, C-3 & 4.

6.) ALL AMERICAN OFFENSE AND DEFENSE: A player can be selected as All American Offense and Defense if he is judged worthy by his coach.

7.) ALL AMERICAN AND M.V.P.: A player that is selected M.V.P. is also an All American.

8.) EXTRA AWARDS: A Team Sportsmanship Award shall be given to a team at the National Tournament. Any extra awards, such as Best Uniform,

Championship Game M.V.P., Best Official, Scoring Leader, etc., may also be given out at the discretion of the U.S.F.T.L. Executive Board of Directors. The National Tournament Director shall make all final decisions regarding the distribution of awards.

d) WORLD TOURNAMENTS ONLY:
1.) 1ST THROUGH 4TH PLACE SPONSOR AWARDS

2.) INDIVIDUAL AWARDS: Individual Awards are given to each player on the Championship Team.

3.) ALL WORLD TEAM: An All World team will be chosen at All World Tournaments.

4.) MOST VALUABLE PLAYER AWARDS: A total of three (3) M.V.P. awards shall be presented. The procedure for M.V.P. distribution shall be as follows.

M.V.P. OFFENSE: This award is given to the most valuable player on Offense. The 1st place coach has the option of picking a player on his team's Offense fast. If, for some reason he fails to choose one of his own players, then the choice goes to the 2nd place coach. If the 2nd place coach fails to choose one of his players, then the choice goes to the 3rd place coach, and so on, until an Offensive M.V.P. has been chosen.

M.V.P. DEFENSE: Follow the same procedures as previously described for M.V.P. Offense.

M.V.P. SPECIAL TEAMS: Follow the same procedures as previously described for M.V.P. Offense. This award can be given to a Kicker (Place Kicker or Punter) or to an unsung member of a team who epitomizes team play.

5.) CO-REC ALL WORLD AND M.V.P. AWARDS: All World and M.V.P. awards at Co-Rec Tournaments shall be distributed as previously described in Article 26, Section 5, C - 3 & 4.

6.) ALL WORLD OFFENSE AND DEFENSE: A player can be selected as All World Offense and Defense if he is judged worthy by his coach.

7.) ALL WORLD AND M.V.P.: A player can be selected M.V.P. and All World if he is judged worthy by his coach.

8.) EXTRA AWARDS: A team Sportsmanship Award shall be given to a team at the World Tournament. Any extra awards such as Best Uniform, Championship Game M.V.P., Best Official, Scoring Leader, etc., may also be given out at the discretion of the U.S.F.T.L. Executive Board of Directors. The World Tournament Director shall make all final decisions regarding the distribution of awards.

SECTION 6 - TRAVEL EXPENSE MONEY:
a.) Team sponsor travel expense monies may be awarded in qualifying U.S.F.T.L. Tournaments that lead to advancement to U.S.F.T.L. State or National Tournaments. The money can only be distributed to the qualifying team, when that particular team shows up at the U.S.F.T.L. State or National Tournament. Any qualified team failing to participate in their respective, qualified (State or National) Tournament would become ineligible to receive the Travel Expense

Money. The Travel Expense Money would then be given to the next highest placing team from that particular, qualifying tournament, that proceeds to participate in the U.S.F.T.L. State or National Tournament. If no team advances, the Travel Money shall be the property of that particular qualifying Tournament Director. The Travel Expense Money can only be picked up by the coach of the qualified team, from the U.S.F.T.L. Tournament Director, at the site of the State or National Tournament. The qualifying Tournament Director will forward all Travel Expense Money for qualifying teams, to the State Tournament Director or National Tournament Director, whichever is applicable. The amount of the Travel Expense Money is left up to the discretion of the qualifying Tournament Director.
b.) Travel Expense Money goes toward the State or National Tournament entrance fees. Any money won beyond the entrance fee is paid to the qualifying teams coach, by check, at the State or National Tournament Registration site for general Travel Expenses.
c.) Travel Expense Money for State Tournament qualifiers is held by the State Director or Regional President.
d.) Travel Expense Money for National Tournament qualifiers is held by the U.S.F.T.L. National Headquarters.
e.) Teams may accumulate Travel Expense Money, above and beyond the amount needed for State or National Tournament entrance fees, to help defray the cost of travel.

SECTION 7 - ROSTERS AND ADDING PLAYERS:
a.) Maximum roster limit is thirty (30) players for Flag Football, Touch Football and Ineligible Lineman Flag Football, eight (8) players for 4 on 4 and ten (10) players for 5 on 5.
b.) All rosters must be forwarded to the National Headquarters.
c.) When a team qualifies for a Local, State, Sectional, Regional, National or World Tournament, the team rosters will be frozen. Players will be bound to this qualified team, up to and including the team's respective Local, State, Sectional, Regional, National or World Tournament. A team coach may release and add up to three (3) players from his team's qualified frozen roster, as long as the total does not exceed the maximum amount. If the maximum amount is exceeded, then any player over that amount must be dropped.
d.) Any player that is released from a qualifying teams roster cannot return to that team during the current season.
e.) All rosters must be submitted to the Local Director by October 1st, in Local League Play only. (NO EXCEPTIONS.)
f.) NO players may be added to a roster after October 1st, in Local League Play only.
g.) A player may change teams only if his team coach gives a written release to the Local Director.
h.) A player may only change teams one time per year.

SECTION 8 - CLASSIFICATION OF TEAMS:
a.) The State Director, with the help of the local Director, has the final say on a team's classification.
b.) The main criteria for classifying teams is the overall strength of the team's offense, defense and kicking game.
c.) Teams have the right to be re-classified by notifying their State or Local Director of their intentions.

d.) At all U.S.F.T.L. Tournaments, a classification board of five individuals, chosen by the Tournament Director, shall be on hand to handle emergency classification problems. This board will have final say on all emergency classification issues at a U.S.F.T.L. Tournament site.

SECTION 9 - QUALIFYING TEAMS:

a.) Local Leagues or Local Tournaments that qualify teams to State Tournaments may use the following procedures:

8 teams or less = 1 unpaid berth to State Tournament.
9-12 teams = 2 unpaid berths to State Tournament.
13-15 teams = 3 unpaid berths to State Tournament.
16 teams and above = 4 unpaid berths to State Tournament.

b.) N.I.T.'s, State, Sectional and Regional Tournaments that qualify teams to the National Tournament, may use the following procedures:

8 teams or less = 1 unpaid berth to National Tournament
9-12 teams = 2 unpaid berths to National Tournament.
13-15 teams = 3 unpaid berths to National Tournament.
16 teams and above = 4 unpaid berths to National Tournament.

c.) Substitution of a qualified team - When a qualified team, for some legitimate reason, cannot compete in their respective qualified tournament, the next highest placing team replaces the original team. This procedure applies to paid and unpaid berths.

d.) It is the option of the Tournament Director to provide a paid berth at a particular Qualifying Tournament.

SECTION 10 - TOURNAMENT DATES:

a.) Local Tournament date shall be played before the State Tournament date provided reasonable time is given for a local qualifier to travel to the State Tournament.

b.) N.I.T., State, Sectional and Regional Tournament dates shall be played before the National Tournament date provided reasonable time, is given for each qualifier to travel to the National Tournament.

c.) National Tournament dates and World Tournament dates shall be decided upon at the U.S.F.T.L. National Meeting by a majority vote of the Executive Board of Directors.

SECTION 11 - LICENSED FOOTBALLS: U.S.F.T.L. Licensed Footballs displaying the U.S.F.T.L. approval and logo must be used in all U.S.F.T.L. Tournaments. Approval of footballs to be used as Officially Required Footballs in the U.S.F.T.L. program must be made by executing an Official Licensing and Royalties Agreement, prepared by the U.S.F.T.L.'s Legal Counsel, and signed by the U.S.F.T.L.'s Executive Director. All Licensed Footballs shall be voted upon by a majority vote of the Executive Board of Directors at the National Meeting. The description and dimensions shall appear in the U.S.F.T.L. Rule Book.

SECTION 12 - LICENSED FLAG BELTS: U.S.F.T.L. Licensed Flag Belts displaying the U.S.F.T.L. approval and logo must be used in all U.S.F.T.L. Tournaments. Approval of Flag Belts to be used as Officially Licensed Flag Belts in the U.S.F.T..L. program must be made by executing an Official Licensing and Royalties Agreement, prepared by the U.S.F.T.L.'s Legal Counsel, and signed by the U.S.F.T.L.'s Executive Director. All Licensed Flag Belts shall be voted upon by a majority vote of the Executive Board of Directors at the National Meeting. The description and dimensions shall appear in the U.S.F.T.L. Rule Book.

SECTION 13 - GUARANTEED NUMBER OF GAMES:
a.) In all Local Tournaments, it is up to the discretion of the Local Director for specified tournament format.
b.) N.I.T., State, Sectional, Regional, National and World Tournaments - The double elimination format, ensuring all teams of two (2) games, will be used.

SECTION 14 - REFUND OF TOURNAMENT ENTRY FEES:
Refund of Tournament Entry Fees for any U.S.F.T..L. Sanctioned Tournament will be made only under the following conditions:

a.) Request for refund must be made in writing prior to the published tournament cut-off date for acceptance of entries. Such request must be sent by certified mail, Return Receipt Requested to the Tournament Director. U.S. Postal Mark will be considered as date of refund request.
b.) Immediately upon receipt of such request, the Tournament Director will forward a check to cover the fee previously paid.
c.) Tournament Directors shall not be compelled to make refunds after the published Tournament cut-off date regardless of circumstances.

SECTION 15 - PLAYING FIELD:
The Official U.S.F.T.L. Playing Field dimensions shall be found in the Official U.S.F.T.L. Rule Book. Two field sizes are offered, 40 yd width X 80 yd length, or 53 1/3 yd wide X 100 yds length. Field dimension abbreviations, because of facility limitation, may sometimes occur, especially in indoor facilities. Tournament Directors make all final judgments on field usage. (NOTE: 4 on 4 and 5 on 5 field dimensions are 25 yards wide x 46 yards long, with two (2), 7 yard end zones.)

SECTION 16 - UNIFORMS:
a.) Local, N.I.T., State, Sectional and Regional Tournaments – The official playing uniform shall consist of: alike colored jerseys with the number on the front and back.
b.) National and World Tournaments – The complete uniform must be worn. This consists of alike colored jerseys, pants, hats, socks, etc.. The number shall be shown on the front and back of the jersey.
c.) Protests on uniforms are not allowed.
d.) The Tournament Director has final authority on uniform legality.
e.) Violation of the uniform rule will result in the violator being allowed to conform or be removed from the game.

SECTION 17 - DEADLINE FOR ENTRY FEES:
All U.S.F.T.L. Tournament entrance fees are due one week before the scheduled starting date of the U.S.F.T.L. Tournament. Failure to comply may result in a team not being able to participate.

SECTION 18 - LICENSED SOUVENIRS:
The U.S.F.T.L. shall reserve the right to operate a souvenir booth at any U.S.F.T.L. Tournament. All profits realized from operation of such a booth shall go to the U.S.F.T.L. The U.S.F.T.L. Director may sell TShirts, Hats, Souvenirs, etc., or purchase a souvenir package from the U.S.F.T.L. National Headquarters at a predetermined cost and re-sell these items for a profit if he desires. Details and costs of U.S.F.T.L. Tournament Souvenir Packages may be obtained from the U.S.F.T.L. National Headquarters.

SECTION 19 - ORDER OF FINISH:
An Order of Finish will be determined

by the following procedure:
- **a.)** Top 4 teams based on actual finish.
- **b.)** Remaining teams listed by descending order of finish according to their bracket position when eliminated (Example. 5th place will show 2 teams tied for that position, the next 2 teams tied for 7th, the next 4 teams tied for 9th, etc.)
- **c.)** Teams with an identical records in Hight Tournaments or Leagues will be determined by the following procedures:
    - **1.)** Won-loss records overall in tournament or league.
    - **2.)** Head-to-Head competition.
    - **3.)** Point differential-points scored vs. points against between tied teams.
    - **4.)** Coin toss.
- **d.)** Forfeits or disqualification. If a team forfeits or is disqualified, that team will finish last in the official order of finish. Also, if a team forfeits to gain any type of advantage, that team will also finish last. A team that forfeits or is disqualified will not be eligible for any awards, sponsor travel expense money, national ranking points or berths intended to be given in that particular tournament.

SECTION 20 - GATE ADMISSION: Players, coaches and officials, participating in U.S.F.T.L. Tournaments cannot be charged any gate fees to the playing site.

SECTION 21 - NUMBER OF OFFICIALS: The number of officials for U.S.F.T.L. Tournament competition shall be three (3) officials on all games until the Championship Game, where four (4) officials then shall be used where applicable. (The U.S.F.T.L. Tournament Director has the option of using a two (2) man crew at his discretion).

SECTION 22 - PARTICIPATION:
- **a.)** In Local, State, Sectional and Regional Tournaments, teams from outside a particular local area, state, section or region may not participate in that particular tournament, without the consent of the U.S.F.T.L. National Headquarters.
- **b.)** In N.I.T. and National Tournaments, teams from anywhere in the United States may participate.
- **c.)** In World Tournaments, teams from any local, state, section, region or country may participate.

SECTION 23 - SEEDINGS AND DRAW PROCEDURES:
- **a.)** The Official U.S.F.T.L. Championship Brackets are to be used in all U.S.F.T.L. Tournaments.
- **b.)** Draws are to be public with all teams being invited to send a representative to the bracketing party.
- **c.)** Each team must be represented at the draw and pre-tournament meeting.
- **d.)** Top Local teams will be assigned times by the Tournament Director to ensure the best possible gate.
- **e.)** Times of games for teams having to travel great distances will be taken into account.
- **f.)** The Official Seeding Procedure for all Local, N.I.T., State, Sectional, Regional and National Tournaments is as follows: The current total points a team has accumulated in the U.S.F.T.L. National Ranking System shall determine their place in the tournaments. If there are teams in the tournament with no points, then these teams will be placed in the tournament in the following manner: Blind Draw, with team from the same area being protected, where possible, from playing each other in the fust round of the winner's bracket.

g.) World Tournaments Only: The official seeding procedure is as follows. All United States teams are placed in a 16 team double elimination bracket. The 16 teams consist of the top 4 finishers in each of the following men's "Super/A" class National Championship Tournament.
    1st through 4th - FLAG
    1st through 4th - TOUCH
    1st through 4th - SCREEN FLAG
    <u>1st through 4th</u> - INELIGIBLE LINEMAN FLAG
    16 Total Teams

    The 4 - 1st place teams are placed on lines 1, 8, 9 & 16.
    The 4 - 2nd place teams are placed on lines 3, 6, 11 & 14.
    The 4 - 3rd place teams are placed on lines 4, 5, 12 & 13.
    The 4 - 4th place teams are placed on lines 2, 7, 10 & 15.

Then, the 4 Sports of FLAG, TOUCH, SCREEN FLAG and INELIGIBLE LINEMAN FLAG are placed, by BLIND DRAW, into the bracket. (EXAMPLE: If Touch is pulled first, then the I st, 2nd, 3 rd and 4th place National Finishers in TOUCH would be placed into the bracket as follows:

    1st Place = line 1   2nd Place = line 14
    3rd Place = line 12   4th Place = line 7

If Flag is pulled second, then the I st, 2nd, 3rd and 4th place National Finishers in FLAG would be placed into the bracket as follows:

    1st Place = line 8   2nd Place = line 11
    3rd Place = line 13   4th Place = line 2

If SCREEN FLAG is pulled third, then the 1st, 2nd, 3rd and 4th place National Finishers in SCREEN FLAG would be placed into the bracket as follows:

    1st Place = line 9   2nd Place = line 6
    3rd Place = line 4   4th Place = line 15

If INELIGIBLE LINEMAN FLAG is pulled last, then the I st, 2nd, 3rd and 4th place National Finishers in INELIGIBLE LINEMAN FLAG would be placed into the bracket as follows:

    1st Place = line 16   2nd Place = line 3
    3rd Place = line 5   4th Place = line 10

After United States teams are placed into the double elimination bracket, then all other countries are drawn into another double elimination tournament bracket by blind draw. The winners of the two (2) double elimination tournaments then play each other in one World Championship Game, the "WORLD FLAG BOWL".

SECTION 24 - OFFICIALS: The Officials of a U.S.F.T.L. Tournament will be directed by a Tournament Director of Officials who reports directly to the Tournament Director. Officials shall receive a pre-determined fee per game and there will be two (2) or three (3) man crews working all games with a four (4) man crew in the final, where applicable. Payment, housing (three (3) officials per room) and feeding the officials shall be the responsibility of the Tournament Director. It is suggested that there be one group of officials from an outside area brought into all tournaments. Travel expense to bring in the outside officials, shall be the responsibility of the Traveling Officials Local Association.

SECTION 25 - TOURNAMENT REPORTS: Each U.S.F.T.L. Tournament Director shall be responsible to send to the U.S.F.T.L. National Headquarters the following post-tournament report within one (1) week of completion of a U.S.F.T.L. Tournament:
  a.) Rosters of teams and officials.
  b.) Brackets - Results, game scores and final standings.
  c.) Registration Fees - All applicable U.S.F.T.L. Registration Fees are to be sent in with the results of the Tournament within one (1) week of the completion of the Tournament.
  d.) All Tournament Team, M.V.P.'s and all award winners
  e.) Re-cap of entire Tournament, plus pictures for possible inclusion in the U.S.F.T.L. National Newspaper, the "First & Twenty."

SECTION 26 - SUSPENSIONS, DISQUALIFICATIONS AND EJECTIONS:
a.) A player that is ejected during a tournament or league game shall be suspended for the next game also.
b.) The game that the suspended players sits out cannot be a forfeited game.
c.) The offending player shall pay an ejection fee before being reinstated into the U.S.F.T.L..
d.) If the act is deemed flagrant enough, the U.S.F.T.L. Tournament Director has the authority to recommend further action be taken by the U.S.F.T.L. National Headquarters.

OFFICIAL'S MANUAL & GUIDE

of the
United States
Flag & Touch
Football League

U.S.F.T.L. FOOTBALL OFFICIAL'S MANUAL

MANUAL PURPOSE: This football official's manual has been designed to give every official detailed information regarding officiating mechanics. Through evaluation and study, the techniques presented are recognized and accepted as officiating standards wherever flag and touch football games are played.

The following position titles are used:

- 2 Person Crew - Referee and Back Judge
- 3 Person Crew - Referee, Line Judge and Back Judge
- 4 Person Crew - Referee, Line Judge, Field Judge and Back Judge

Due to the wide open style of flag and touch football, the umpire position is not needed. Approximately 90 per cent of the plays are passes. Thus, the Back Judge is positioned 15 to 25 yards deep in the secondary behind the deepest defensive back.

Similarly, the Field Judge position is needed for 4 Person Mechanics. He/she is intentionally located off the scrimmage line and downfield due to the exciting style of play. The mechanics are similar to 6 Person N.C.A.A. Mechanics placement of the Field Judge. Their game, like ours, places emphasis downfield on the passing game.

Please write, call, fax or e-mail the USFTL National Headquarters and/or the USFTL National Director of Officials for interpretations of rules or play situations:

U.S.F.T.L.
7709 Ohio Street
Mentor, Ohio 44060
PHONE:(440-974-8735)
Fax:(440-974-8441)
E-Mail: usftl@usftl.com
Website: www.usftl.com

UNITED STATES FLAG & TOUCH FOOTBALL LEAGUE
OFFICIAL'S CODE OF ETHICS

1. Honor all contracts regardless of possible inconvenience or financial loss.

2. Study the rules of the game diligently, observe the work of other officals and attempt to improve at all times.

3. Remember that while your work as an official is important, you must conduct yourself in such a way that spectator attention is directed to those playing the game and not on you.

4. Dress and maintain your appearance in a manner befitting the dignity and importance of the game.

5. Conduct yourself so as to be a worthy example of those playing in the game and to the fans.

6. Be fair, but not companionable; calm, but ever alert.

7. Be prepared both physically and mentally to administer the game.

8. Do not smoke on or in the vicinity of the playing field nor drink any alcoholic beverages on the day of the game.

9. Keep in mind that the game is more important than the wishes of any individual player or coach or the ambitions of any individual official.

PART I - USFTL DUTIES, PRINCIPLES & PROCEDURES FOR GOOD OFFICIATING

SECTION 1 - KNOWLEDGE OF THE RULES

ARTICLE 1: ALL OFFICIALS:
Knowledge of the rules must be perfect and supplemented by ability to interpret them correctly. These abilities are acquired only through devotion of much time and study. All rules should be enforced fairly and consistently.

SECTION 2 - PHYSICAL CONDITION

ARTICLE 1: ALL OFFICIALS:
Football officiating is difficult and exhausting and requires 100 percent efficiency of the mind and the body.

SECTION 3 - JUDGMENT

ARTICLE 1: ALL OFFICIALS:
Decisions must be instantaneous, correct and a ruling announced without delay. Ensure improved instinctive reactions to play situations by reviewing all possible combinations of circumstances before each season.
LET YOUR MIND DIGEST WHAT YOUR EYES HAVE SEEN.

ARTICLE 2: ALL OFFICIALS:
Do not look for fouls. They come on their own. Always be sure of a foul. Never guess, as there are no phantom fouls. Pick up your flag if you realize the foul was not there. Do not try to run a bad call. If you think it is a foul, it is not!

SECTION 4 - DUTIES AND RESPONSIBILITIES

ARTICLE 1: ALL OFFICIALS:
Each official must have a thorough knowledge of duties of his/her position and be fully informed concerning the duties of each of the other officials. Be prepared to assume the other positions whenever circumstances require it. He/she must:

A. Know the down and yardage prior to each snap.

B. Be ready to assist any official who is temporarily out of position.

C. Observe incorrect rulings by other officials and attempt prevention and correction whenever possible.

D. Know the prescribed signals and when and how they should be used.

E. Be alert to happenings away from the ball when play has left the immediate area.

REMEMBER: YOUR CREW IS ONLY AS STRONG AS YOUR WEAKEST OFFICIAL.

SECTION 5 - SIGNALS

ARTICLE 1: ALL OFFICIALS:

All signals should be given promptly and distinctly. The preliminary signal on fouls and the regular signal after enforcement of declination of a penalty shall be given by the Referee. Remember, the only part of officiating to over emphasize is the signaling. See Code of Official Football Signals in the back of this manual.

SECTION 6 - HUSTLE
ARTICLE 1: ALL OFFICIALS:
Keep the game moving smoothly from start to finish. Do not permit haste to interfere with duties. Hustle but do not hurry! Never stand still in one spot during an entire down. Do not move too fast. Sometimes it is better to let the play come to you.

SECTION 7 - COOPERATION & COMMUNICATION
ARTICLE 1: ALL OFFICIALS:
Team work is essential among the officials. Continuous communication between all officials during the game is essential for effective game administration.

SECTION 8 - DO NOT DISCUSS
ARTICLE 1: ALL OFFICIALS:
Do not discuss with a team the play or players of his/her opponents in a game which you will officiate or are officiating. Do not get mad and do not get even with coaches or players who disagree verbally with your calls.

ARTICLE 2: ALL OFFICIALS:
Do not fraternize with the coaches or players before, during or after the game when officiating.

SECTION 9 - PRE-GAME DUTIES & PROCEDURES
ARTICLE 1: ALL OFFICIALS:
A. Attendance at the pre-game conference at the time and place designated in advance is mandatory. It is recommended that a period of at least fifteen minutes prior to game time be allocated for this purpose. If the Referee is detained, he/she must notify the Line Judge and request him/her to conduct the meeting. This manual can be used as a basic outline for material to be covered during the pre-game conference.

B. Coordinate watches, review rule changes, and check officiating equipment: whistles, bean bags, game cards, penalty flags, ball markers, pencils, and down indicators. Also check the playing field and player equipment thoroughly.

ARTICLE 2: THE REFEREE SHALL DISCUSS THE FOLLOWING WITH THE CAPTAINS:
A. Game Time.
B. Halftime intermission.
C. Two-minute notification (halftime).
D. Unusual plays.
E. Arrange for the down marker operator, where applicable.
F. Captains report to midfield for the toss approximately 3 minutes prior to game time.

G. Toss.
H. Sportsmanship - Profanity Rule, Blood Rule.
I. Screen blocking fundamentals or contact blocking fundamentals - (whatever game your are officiating).
J. Have correct time of day and extra stopwatch. Time game and intermission.

SECTION 10 - TOSS OF COIN

ARTICLE 1: REFEREE:
  A. About 2 minutes prior to game time, have team captains report to center of field with backs to their respective sidelines.
  B. Introduce captains to each other.
  C. Ask visiting captain to call the toss in the air.
  D. Catch the toss and without flipping over, show both captains.
  E. Line Judge will repeat the visiting captain's call while coin is in air.
  F. Indicate winner of the toss by placing hand on that captain's shoulder.
  G. Obtain winning captain's option of either kickoff, receive, defend a goal or defer.
  H. Obtain loser's option.
  I. If winning captain defers:
     1. Indicate winner of toss again by putting hand on shoulder.
     2. Turn to press box and signal "choice deferred" (S10).
     3. Request first choice from opposing captain.
     4. Place the captains with their backs to the goal they will defend.
     5. Place hand on captain who chose to receive and give receiving signal,
     6. Place hand on captain who is kicking and give kicking signal.
     7. Have captains shake hands.

ARTICLE 2: ALL OFFICIALS:
  A. Meet and record winner of toss and options elected.
  B. Record which team has second half choice.
  C. Keep team players and personnel behind their respective sidelines.
  D. Hustle to your position for the kickoff.

SECTION 11 - SOUNDING YOUR WHISTLE

ARTICLE 1: OFFICIAL COVERING RUNNER:
  A. Find ball before sounding whistle.
  B. Sound whistle when ball becomes dead:
     1. Quickly and loudly.
     2. Stops action - prevents rough play.
  C. Move in quickly to be certain all action stops on whistle.

ARTICLE 2: ALL OFFICIALS:
  A. Player safety is first responsibility.
  B. When sounding whistle, do it quickly and loudly.
  C. Find ball before sounding whistle.

D. Actually see ball in possession of runner who is down. This prevents early whistle.
E. Ball can be kept in view when officials are positioned properly and working alertly.
F. Be ready to assist covering official after whistle has sounded.
G. Use bean bag or ball marker to mark spot of ball if whistle is sounded inadvertently.

ARTICLE 3: INADVERTENT WHISTLE - (ALL OFFICIALS):
A. Ball becomes dead immediately.
B. Location at which spot ball will be put in play and number of next down determined by location and status of ball when whistle was sounded.

SECTION 12 - STOPPING & STARTING THE CLOCK

ARTICLE 1: BEFORE TWO MINUTES AT END OF GAME - (REFEREE):
A. Stop clock on:
  1. A charged team time-out.
  2. Officials time-out:
     a. Injury.
     b. TV/Radio.
     c. Any other reasons deemed necessary by Referee as provided by rule.
B. Start clock on:
  1. First touching of opening kickoff; if touchback - on snap.
  2. On snap if teams choose to start game from scrimmage.
  3. Team time-out - at snap.
  4. Officials time-out - at Ready-For-Playwhistle.

ARTICLE 2: INSIDE TWO MINUTES OF GAME - (REFEREE):
A. Stop clock on:
  1. Same as before two minutes.
  2. 1st downs.
  3. Out-of-bounds.
  4. Penalties.
  5. Incompletions.
  6. Change of possession.
  7. Fair catch.
B. Start clock on:
  1. Same as before 2 minutes.
  2. 1st Down:
     a. Inbounds - ready for play.
     b. Out-of-bounds - at snap.
  3. Out-of-bounds - at snap.
  4. Penalties - previous play on offense, at snap on defense.
  5. Incompletions - at snap.
  6. Change of possession:
     a. Inbounds - Ready-For-Playwhistle.
     b. Out-of-bounds - snap.
  7. Fair catch - at snap.

ARTICLE 3: HURRY-UP OFFENSE - (REFEREE):
    A. Maintain same tempo throughout game:
        1. Make sure all officials are in position before blowing ready-for-play whistle.
        2. Warn quarterback and center that snapping ball before ready-for-play whistle will result in a delay of game penalty:
            a. 5 yard penalty.
            b. Clock starts on "ready" whistle.

SECTION 13 - DECLARING BALL READY-FOR-PLAY
ARTICLE 1: REFEREE:
    A. After Ball Marker is spotted:
        1. Check that other officials are in position and ready.
        2. First offensive series of game, warn each team's center and quarterback to wait for ready whistle - (dead ball-delay of game).
        3. Give ready-for-play signal accompanied by short blast on whistle and move quickly to position.
        4. Five (5) seconds should be maximum time consumed in spotting and marking ball ready-for-play.
    B. Quick Snap:
        1. When Team A moves quickly, position to observe snap and make sure that all other officials are in position before giving ready-for-play whistle.

ARTICLE 2: ALL OFFICIALS:
    A. Hustle to proper positions.
    B. Team work is essential to prevent delay.

SECTION 14 - OPERATING DOWN MARKER
ARTICLE 1: REFEREE:
The down marker is on the Referee's side of the field using 2 Person Mechanics.

ARTICLE 2: LINE JUDGE:
The down marker is on the Line Judge's side of the field using 3 and 4 Person Mechanics, opposite the announcers box.

ARTICLE 3: ALL OFFICIALS:
Know the down and yardage to be gained on each down. Be cognizant of live ball fouls, which carry loss of down or automatic first downs, and dead ball fouls. Verify the preceding down before changing the down marker.

ARTICLE 4: REFEREE:
Verify each down prior to declaring ball ready for play. Give signal to move marker on first downs and protected scrimmage kicks.

ARTICLE 5: REFEREE/LINE JUDGE:
Instruct down marker operator to anticipate the play. If there is any chance of the play coming near him/her, move the down marker back quickly. Remember: The safety of players and officials is important. Do not drop the down box. Locate the down box a minimum of 6 feet off the sideline.

SECTION 15 - MEASURING FOR 1ST DOWNS
ARTICLE 1: REFEREE:
- A. Give time-out signal if under two (2) minutes.
- B. Notify Line Judge to check for 1st down.
- C. Stand over ball marker.
- D. Motion players away from 1st down line.
- E. When Line Judge gives signal:
  1. Signal number of next down.
  2. Give ready-for-play whistle.
  3. Move into position.

ARTICLE 2: LINE JUDGE:
- A. When notified by Referee to check for 1st down:
  1. Move behind 1st down marker on your sideline.
  2. Motion players away from 1st down line.
  3. Look to opposite 1st down marker on other sideline.
  4. Give appropriate signal if 1st down or not.

ARTICLE 3: ALL OTHER OFFICIALS:
- A. Be alert for illegal substitutions.
- B. Do not permit any team attendants or coaches on field during a measurement.
- C. Follow procedures outlined under run/pass play.

SECTION 16 - TIME-OUT PROCEDURE
ARTICLE 1: REFEREE:
- A. Sound whistle and signal time-out.
- B. If time-out is requested:
  1. Indicate by moving both arms horizontally towards requesting team three (3) times.
  2. If official's time-out, indicate by tapping chest with both hands.
- C. Record number of time-outs charged to team. Record time on clock, half when each time-out is taken and announce to other officials so they can also record on their card.
- D. Notify coach and captain number of time-outs remaining.
- E. Keep time with own watch - (thirty (30) seconds after time-out request is granted).
- F. With 15 seconds left, notify coaches to leave field.
- G. Announce down and distance to both teams.
- H. Blow ready-for-play whistle.
- I. Start 25 second clock.

ARTICLE 2: ALL OTHER OFFICIALS:
- A. Give time-out signal:
  1. Hold respective positions.
  2. Be alert for substitution or attempt to use substitutes for purpose of deception.
- B. Record time-out, which half and time left on clock.
- C. During time-out:
  1. Do not huddle or visit with other officials.
  2. Stand alertly.

3. Do not visit with players.
4. Restrict discussion to captain.
D. Line Judge counts team A players.
E. Back Judge counts team B players.
F. Back Judge makes sure no more than 3 attendants and one coach are on the field, both teams.

ARTICLE 3: INJURY TIME-OUT - (ALL OFFICIALS):
A. Same as charged time-out:
1. Permit as much time is necessary.
2. Safety of injured player is most important.
3. Injured player must leave playing field for at least one play.
4. Don't stop clock immediately if in doubt about nature of injury.
5. Ask player if they are able to continue; wait for a response then assess the situation.

SECTION 17 - ENFORCEMENT OF FOULS

ARTICLE 1: ALL OFFICIALS:
A. Signal time-out when ball is declared dead during the last two minutes of the game.
B. official calling foul reports it to the Referee using the four W's as follows:
1. What-Type of foul. Dead ball or live ball. Describe foul when necessary.
2. Who - Offense or Defense - except in kicking situation. Then report kicking team or receiving team. Give the number and position of player who fouled.
3. When-Status of ball - loose, in possession or after change of team possession.
4. Where-spot where the run ends or spot of foul.
C. Throwing the flag: Spot fouls - drop the flag on corresponding yard line. Fouls that have no spot throw flag high into air to give Referee and Down Marker Operator a chance to see it.
D. Do not place a hand on or point to the offending player. Official calling foul should stand by and double check the Referee's options: If you disagree, ask the Referee to repeat the options.

CALLING FOULS					
1. Stop clock for foul	2. Give preliminary signal	3. Indicate offending team	4. Give offended Captain options	5. Referee-Enforcement Penalty	
6. Repeat penalty signal	7. Indicate offending team	8. Indicate down	9. When ball is ready give "ready for play" or ...	10. Wind clock	

Assist each other in holding the dead ball spot and spot of foul. Cover foul markers whenever possible for each other.
- E. Be sure the down marker is not moved. Be responsible for knowing that the proper yardage has been stepped off. Correct any mistakes immediately.
- F. Alert Referee on penalties enforced half-distance to goal line.

SECTION 18 - COACH-REFEREE CONFERENCE

ARTICLE 1: PURPOSE:
- A. Allows review of possible misapplication or misinterpretation of rules by officials.
- B. Allows corrections when error has been made.

ARTICLE 2: PROCEDURES - (ALL OFFICIALS):
- A. Request for conference must be made prior to ball becoming alive following the play which is to be reviewed.
- B. Coach directs player to request time-out to confer with referee regarding application of a rule.
- C. Time-out granted-charged to requesting team.
- D. Referee (accompanied by Line Judge and/or calling Official) and coach confer at sideline directly in front of team bench.
- E. Rule determined to have been applied correctly:
  1. Time-out remains charged to team.
  2. Ten (10) yard penalty if permissible time-outs have been used.
- F. Rule determined to have been applied incorrectly:
  1. Correction made immediately.
  2. Time-out previously charged to team becomes an officials time-out.
  3. Referee will review and explain situation to opposing coach before continuing game.

SECTION 19 - AFTER A TOUCHBACK, SAFETY, TRY-FOR-POINT OR FIELD GOAL

ARTICLE 1: REFEREE:
- A. Give proper signal including time-out signal if clock has been running.
- B. Count Team A players.
- C. Take ball marker to center of proper yard line unless captain requests it be placed at some other spot.
- D. If ball will be put in play by snap:
  1. Spot ball marker.
  2. Give ready-for-play signal and sound whistle while moving away from ball and start 25 second clock.
- E. If ball will be put in play by free kick - have Back Judge hand ball to kicker.
- F. After safety or touchback, ball placed with foremost point on 20 yard line.

ARTICLE 2: LINE JUDGE/FIELD JUDGE:
- A. Be alert for substitutions and any irregularities as to number of players.
- B. Move to proper position.

ARTICLE 3: BACK JUDGE:

A. Take proper position:
   1. Check ball to make sure it is legal.
   2. Take ball to spot of next snap or free kick.
   3. Count Team B players and be alert for substitutions.
B. If ball is to be put in play by free kick:
   1. Instruct kicker to wait for referee's signal.
   2. Hand ball to kicker.
   3. Move to sideline opposite Line Judge.
   4. Raise arm above head and wait for Referee's ready for play whistle.

ARTICLE 4: ALL OFFICIALS:
A. Do not permit any team attendants or coaches on field following a touchback.
B. Reminder - On a free kick following a safety:
   1. Each official assumes same relative position and has same duties as on kickoff.
   2. Ball may be put in play by place kick or punt.
C. Strive to put ball in play without delay.

SECTION 20 - DISQUALIFICATION OF PLAYERS OR COACHES

ARTICLE 1: WHEN A DISQUALIFYING FOUL IS CALLED - (ALL OFFICIALS):
A. ON PLAYER:
   1. Official who called foul shall inform offending player and report his number and type of infraction to Referee, coach and other members of the officiating crew.
   2. If disqualification is for the rest of the game, inform coach, player has five (5) minutes to leave playing facilities or a forfeiture of game may be called.
   3. If there are double disqualifying fouls, Referee may designate another Official to assist in reporting foul to coaches.
   4. The Officials shall not place a hand on offending player, nor accompany or escort him to sideline.
   5. All Officials:
      a. Record player's number and name if known (ask coach).
      b. Observe all other players.
   6. Notify league or tournament director where applicable.
B. ON COACH:
   1. Referee shall notify coach reason for disqualification (accompanied by Back Judge).
   2. Require coach to vacate playing area:
      a. If coach does not vacate, inform captain on field that non-compliance could lead to forfeiture of game.
      b. If tournament or league director present, locate for assistance.
      c. Do not continue contest until coach vacates playing area.

d. Notify league or tournament director where applicable.

ARTICLE 2: ALL OFFICIALS:
    A. Back Judge will accompany Referee to sideline.
    B. Assist Referee if necessary.
    C. Observe all players.
    D. Notify opposing coach of disqualification.

SECTION 21 - ADMINISTERING PENALTIES

ARTICLE 1: REFEREE:
    A. When ball is dead following a foul:
        1. If clock is running inside of two (2) minutes, at end of game, give time-out siqnal.
        2. Get full information from official who called foul.
        3. Give preliminary signal to press box.
        4. Give options to captain of offended team.
        5. When captains most advantageous choice is obvious, quickly inform him.
        6. When captain does not respond, his silence shall be considered acceptance of obvious choice. once made it cannot be revoked.
        7. Make note of enforcement spot for penalty.
        8. After ball marker has been spotted, give final signal to press box side of field only.
    B. When penalty is declined:
        1. Go to spot of ball marker.
        2. Give foul signal followed by penalty declined signal.
    C. When there is a double foul:
        1. Signal each foul, facing press box.
        2 Follow this with penalty - declined signal to press box.
    D. When two penalties are enforced, give proper signals following each enforcement.
    E. When penalty is to be enforced on kickoff or extrapoint attempt:
        1. Indicate proper foul signal.
        2. Point to offending team.
        3. Point toward succeeding spot.
    F. Accepted penalty for foul by either team during the last timed down of a period, play continues with an untimed down.
    G. Announce down and distance to go for lst down if over 20 yards, give proper signal for more than one zone to gain (clenched fists, arms crossed).

ARTICLE 2: LINE JUDGE - (3/4 MAN CREW):
    A. Secure ball marker.
    B. Make note of enforcement spot for penalty.
    C. Proceed with measurement.
    D. On properly marked field, avoid stepping off distance between yard lines, except to the first and for the final yard line.
    E. Walk briskly, use an arm signal to point to each yard line you cross.

ARTICLE 3: ALL OTHER OFFICIALS:
    A. Mark spot for end of run.
    B. Do not permit trainers, attendants or coaches on field.
    C. Relay penalty information to appropriate coach.

ARTICLE 4: ALL OFFICIALS:
    A. Observe live ball foul:
        1. Withhold whistle.
        2. Drop flag at spot and continue to officiate.
        3. When ball becomes dead:
            a. Give time-out signal if inside two (2) minutes at end of game.
            b. Sound whistle.
            c. Verbally report information to Referee.
            d. Make mental note as to whether or not clock should be started on ready or on snap (if inside 2 minutes at end of game).
    B. Observe dead ball foul:
        1. Sound whistle.
        2. Give time-out signal if under 2 minutes at end of game.
        3. Follow procedures outlined above.
    C. See that Line Judge assesses penalty properly.
    D. Calling Official:
        1. After calling foul and ball has been declared dead:
            a. Sound whistle.
            b. Give time-out signal if inside two (2) minutes at end of game.
            c. Get Referee's attention by giving short blasts on whistle.
            d. Make sure spot of foul is marked.
            e. Verbally report information fully to Referee:
                1. Identify foul.
                2. Identify offending team including jersey color and offense/defense or kicking/receiving team.
                3. Identify offending players number or position.
                4. Indicate spot of foul, end of run or end of kick.
                5. Indicate status of ball when foul occurred, loose, in possession or after change of possession.
    E. Assist in locating captains.
    F. Recover ball markers.
    G. Enforcement:
        1. Stay clear of spot of foul.
        2. If enforcement spot is different from spot of foul, go to enforcement spot.
        3. When Line Judge begins enforcement, check for correctness and distance.
        4. Avoid visiting while penalty is assessed.

SECTION 22 - BETWEEN HALVES PROCEDURE

ARTICLE 1: REFEREE:
- A. Signal time to start clock to time intermission if scoreboard clock is used.
- B. If keeping clock on field, start clock.
- C. Request captains presence at center of field.
- D. Determine which team has SECOND HALF CHOICE.
- E. Relay choices to team benches and press box with appropriate signals.

ARTICLE 2: ALL OFFICIALS:
- A. Stay on field together, or leave field together.
- B. Discuss any problems in private area.
- C. Help players with their respective kickoff positions.
- D. Start second half on time.

SECTION 23 - END OF GAME PROCEDURE

ARTICLE 1: ALL OFFICIALS:
- A. Regulation Game:
  1. Leave field together.
  2. Neither avoid nor seek coaches.
  3. Do not discuss game on field.
  4. Report any flagrant fouls or disqualifications to league or tournament directors.
- B. Overtime - (20 YARD LINE PROCEDURE):
  1. Referee:
     a. Hold coin toss at center of field, using general coin toss mechanics.
     b. Home team captain shall call toss.
     c. Toss winner shall choose end of field at which ball will be put in play, or go on offense or defense.
     d. Indicate winner by placing hand on shoulder.
     e. Position offensive captain facing goal toward which ball will be advanced.
     f. Facing his opponent and opposite goal.
     g. Give 1st down signal toward goal being used.
  2. If game is still tied after overtime period, repeat above steps and alternate calling of toss with each team captain.
- C. Overtime (USFTL SUDDEN DEATH PROCEDURE):
  1. Referee:
     a. Same as in regulation play

SECTION 24 - PROTEST PROCEDURE
(SEE USFTL RULEBOOK, RULE 15-PROTESTS)

SECTION 25 - U.S.F.T.L. OFFICIAL'S UNIFORM, & EQUIPMENT REQUIREMENTS

ARTICLE 1: - OFFICIAL'S UNIFORMS - (ALL OFFICIALS):
The mandatory U.S.F.T.L. Officials Uniform shall consist of the following items:

a.) Shirt - Black and white striped officials shirt with U.S.F.T.L. patch worn over the heart. Long or short sleeves are acceptable, but if one official in the crew is in short sleeves, then all officials are in short sleeves.
b.) Pants - White knickers with pockets.
c.) Stirrups - Black with three (3) white stripes (Northwestern style).
d.) Socks - White with black "USFTL" in block letters.
e.) Caps - Black baseball style with white "USFTL" logo in block letters.
f.) Shorts - Black shorts with pockets.
g.) Shoes - Black rubber soled shoes.
h.) Shoelaces - Black.
i.) Belts - Black.
j.) Compression Shorts - White shorts worn under pants, shorts, sweatpants, etc.
k.) Sweatpants - Black with pockets and white "USFTL" logo in block letters, on the left leg.
l.) Hoods - Black.
m.) Gloves - Black.
n.) Undershirts - White.
o.) Jackets - Black and white striped with pockets and a U.S.F.T.L. patch worn over the heart.
p.) Headgators - Black, worn under official U.S.F.T.L. officials cap.
q.) Wristband - White.
r.) Patch - U.S.F.T.L. patch.
s.) Whistles - Black, (2).
t.) Lanyards - Black, (2).
u.) Ball Spotter (Puck) - Orange, (2).
v.) Penalty Flags - Yellow, (2).
vv.) Bean Bags - White, (2).
w.) Elastic Down Indicator - Black, (2).
ww.) Goal Posts - At least one (1) set of fold-up portable goal posts.
x.) Watch - Black, (2), Countdown Timer.
xx.) Pencils - Bullet Style, (2).
y.) Bags - Black with white "USFTL" officials logo.
yy.) Score Cards - U.S.F.T.L. score cards (enough for all games).
z.) Cones - Orange, (24).
zz.) Rule Book - "U.S.F.T.L." Rule Book, (2).

(NOTE: The entire U.S.F.T.L. Official's Uniform and Equipment may be ordered through the U.S.F.T.L. National Headquarters).

SECTION 26 - U.S.F.T.L. OFFICIAL'S CODE OF ETHICS

ARTICLE 1: OFFICIAL'S CODE OF ETHICS - (ALL OFFICIALS):

1. Honor all contracts regardless of possible inconvenience or financial loss.
2. Study the rules of the game diligently, observe the work of other officials and attempt to improve at all times.
3. Remember that while your work as an official is important, you must conduct yourself in such a way that spectator attention is directed to those playing the game and not on you.
4. Dress and maintain your appearance in a manner befit-

ting the dignity and importance of the game.
5. Conduct yourself so as to be a worthy example of those playing in the game and to the fans.
6. Be fair, but not companionable; calm, but ever alert.
7. Be prepared both physically and mentally to administer the game.
8. Do not smoke on or in the vicinity of the playing field nor drink any alcoholic beverages on the day of the game.
9. Keep in mind that the game is more important than the wishes of any individual player or coach or the ambitions of any individual official.

U.S.F.T.L. OFFICIAL'S MECHANICS

PART II - 2 PERSON CREW MECHANICS
SECTION 1 - KICKOFF (FREE KICK) - POSITIONS

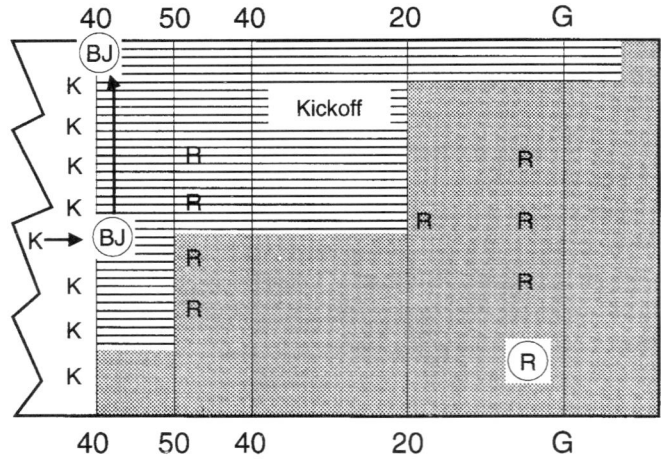

(Diagram Shows 8-Man Team—
Position of Officials shall be the same for 7-man & 9-man teams)

& RESPONSIBILITIES
(NOTE: Assume same positions after a safety.)

ARTICLE 1: REFEREE:
    A. Before Kick:
        1. Position: Near R's 5 yard line, 5 yards from sideline opposite back judge.
        2. Count R's players.
        3. Check for following:

Page 141

        a. Coaches and substitutes are in team box - (dead ball).
        b. Spectators are behind restricted area - (dead ball).
        c. Illegal flags or no flags at all on R players - (flag down).

(**NOTE:** Give warning first - We do not want to call these penalties unless forced to.)

4. Check position of Back Judge.
5. When Back Judge is ready, blow whistle and with arm extended and palm open move arm in direction of kick without turning head.
6. If dead ball penalty occurs, repeat steps 1 through 5.

B. After Kick:
1. Watch for kick going out-of-bounds on your sideline:
    a. Touched - Mark spot.
    b. Untouched - Flag down.
2. Be alert for fair catch signal, if invalid, blow whistle to stop play (flag down) and stop clock if inside two (2) minutes at end of game.
3. Signal clock to start at first touching by R (entire game) and by K (stop inside two (2) minutes) and then start clock.
4. Determine if K touches ball in the air before R - (Flag down - fair catch interference).
5. When kick is caught in end zone:
    a. Determine if player advances ball out of end zone, then runs back in and is downed-(Safety).
    b. Is downed before advancing past end zone - (Touchback).
    c. Steps over end line or sideline (Touchback).
6. Pick up runner and follow until releasing to Back Judge.
7. Observe action behind runner and then in front of Back Judge, especially illegal blocks down field.
8. Sound whistle when ball becomes dead and give time out signal in last two minutes of each game.
9. Mark end of run with ball marker and give first down signal pointing in the direction ball will be advanced, after all penalties are assessed and proper signals given.

ARTICLE 2: BACK JUDGE:

A. Before Kick:
1. Line up R players in their 5 yard front zone 10 yards from K's Free Kick line.
2. Position: 5 yards from sideline on K's Free Kick line opposite Referee-(facing press box if used).
3. Take charge of ball, make sure it is legal.
4. Check legality of kicking tee.
5. Hand kicker the ball and point to position of Referee instructing kicker to wait for Referee's ready whistle - (Dead ball delay of game)

(**NOTE:** Kicking team may kick anywhere on or behind K's restraining line 5 yards from side-lines.)

6. Move into position on K's free kick line.
7. Count K players.
8. Instruct K players to wait for ball to be kicked before crossing K's kicking line (Dead ball - 5 yards).
9. Check for following:
    a. Coaches and substitutes are in team box - (dead ball).
    b. Spectators are behind restricted area - (dead ball).
    c. Illegal flags or no flags at all on K players - (flag down).

(NOTE: Give Warning First - We do not want to call these penalties unless forced to.)

10. Hold arm above head when ready.
11. If there is a dead ball penalty, assess yardage and repeat steps I through 10.

B. After Kick:
1. Watch for kick going out-of-bounds on your sideline:
    a. Touched - Mark spot
    b. Untouched - Flag down
2. Signal clock to start at first touching by R -(entire game) and by K (stop inside two (2) minutes).
3. Determine if K touches ball in the air before R (flag down - fair catch interference).
4. Watch initial blocks by players around R's 5 yard front zone.
5. After ball has been kicked, slide down field approximately 15 yards while watching for fouls in front of the runner.
6. Cover your sideline at all times.
7. Be prepared to take over coverage of runner in your area on a long return and follow to goal line.
8. Sound whistle when run ends and ball becomes dead:
    a. Give time-out signal if inside two (2) minutes of game.
9. Mark spot with ball marker.
10. Get into position for run/pass play unless kick after fair catch is called.

ARTICLE 3: ALL OFFICIALS:
A. Watch For:
1. Muffed ball - (Down at Spot).
2. Laterals - (If forward, flag down at spot-5 yards).
3. Holding on the tag or deflag - (flag down at spot - 10 yards).

B. Carry bean bag or ball markers in hand for spotting.

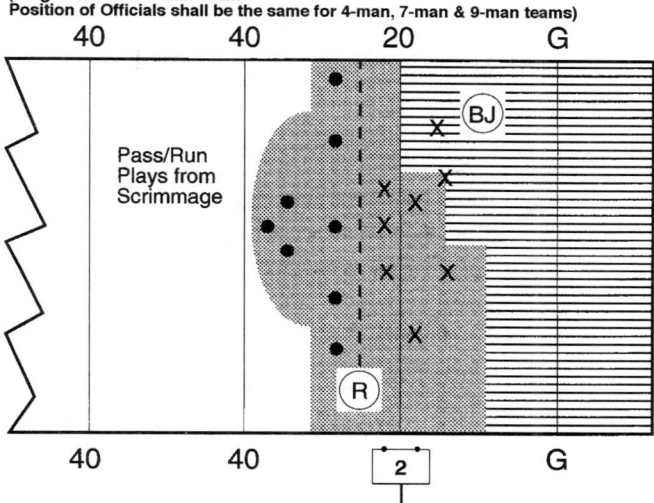

(Diagram Shows 8-Man Team-
Position of Officials shall be the same for 4-man, 7-man & 9-man teams)

SECTION 2 - PASS/RUN PLAYS FROM SCRIMMAGE - POSITIONS & RESPONSIBILITIES

ARTICLE 1: REFEREE:
- A. Before Snap:
    1. Give Ready-For-Play whistle.
    2. Start 25 second clock.
    3. Count team A players.
    4. Position: Five (5) yards from sideline. On line of scrimmage opposite press box.
    5. Switch sidelines at half if there is no press box being used.
    6. Check for following:
        a. Coaches and substitutes are in team box - (dead ball).
        b. Spectators are behind restricted area - (dead ball).
        c. Required number of team A players on line of scrimmage at the snap - (flag down).
        d. Delay of game - announce when ten (10) seconds remain - (dead ball).
        e. Ineligible Receivers Ineligible Lineman Flag-9 man - (flag down).
        f. Encroachment, false starts and snap infractions - (dead ball).
        g. Illegal motion, illegal shifts - (flag down).
        h. Illegal flags or no flags at all on team A - (flag down).
        i. Illegal substitutes on team A - (flag down.)

8. If dead ball penalty occurs, give appropriate signals facing press box, assess yardage and repeat steps 1 through 7.

B. After Snap:
1. Watch initial contact to center.
2. Observe initial charge of linemen.
3. Hold position on line of scrimmage keeping eyes on passer.
4. If run, release from line of scrimmage when runner starts downfield observing action behind runner.
5. When ball comes to your side of field:
   a. If wide run, retreat toward sideline and slide toward team A's goal line to avoid interfering with the play.
   b. Move with ball and cover sideline (responsible for your sideline, end line to end line).
   c. Sound whistle promptly when ball becomes dead.
   d. Be positive of ball location before sounding whistle.
6. When ball goes to opposite side:
   a. Observe action initially behind runner and then in front of Back Judge, especially downfield blocks.
   b. Do not leave line to move down field until certain there is not a reverse or counter play.
7. Do not get boxed in or turn back on ball.
8. Give special attention to contact with passer:
   a. After ball is released, continue to observe passer, not flight of the ball.
   b. Verbally alert rushers and blockers when passer has released the ball.
9. Be alert to observe illegal passes:
   a. Determine whether pass is forward or backward and give appropriate arm signal.
   b. If close, mark spot of pass with bean bag or ball marker, continue to officiate. Use Back Judge for assistance.
   c. If not, drop penalty flag at spot and continue to officiate.
10. Referee is solely responsible for determining intentional grounding.
11. During a run, continue to observe player action behind line before leaving area.
12. Be ready for a kick or pass that may start out as a run.
13. After interception:
    a. Observe action.
    b. Be prepared to take runner to goal line.
    c. Mark spot.
    d. Signal time-out if inside two (2) minutes.
    e. Signal direction ball will be put into play.
14. After incompletion in your area, sound whistle and give signal.

15. After run or catch and ball is dead, look for 1st down and give time-out signal if 1st down and inside two (2) minutes.
16. If there is a touchdown and no foul which would nullify the touchdown, give signal and mark scorecard.
17. Work with down and yardage crew when required.
18. After each play:
    a. Mark spot with ball marker.
    b. Announce down and yardage to go for 1st down.
    c. Give appropriate signals and assess yardage on all penalties.
19. Record all team time-outs, scores, player warnings and ejections, team captains and coin toss options on scorecard.

ARTICLE 2: BACK JUDGE:

A. Before Snap:
   1. Position: 5 to 7 yards from sideline, 15 to 20 yards beyond scrimmage line.
   2. Do not interfere with vision or movement of team B players.
   3. Be alert so receivers do not use you as interference.
   4. Check following:
      a. Coaches and substitutes are in team box - (dead ball).
      b. Spectators are behind restricted area - (dead ball).
      c. Team B players - (flag down).
      d. Illegal substitutes or illegal participation - (flag down).
      e. Disconcerting signals by team B - (flag down).
      f. Illegal flags or no flags at all (flag down).
   5. Switch sidelines at half if there is no press box being used.
   6. If dead ball penalty occurs, help Referee assess yardage and repeat steps 1 through 5.

B. After Snap:
   1. Observe initial charge of receivers.
   2. Watch for illegal contact to center.
   3. Look for illegal use of hands or arms, illegal blocks and other fouls near line of scrimmage.
   4. Defensive holding - (pass plays):
      a. Illegal chucks - more than one, and/or contact made more than 5 yards from line of scrimmage, ball not thrown yet.
      b. Illegal blocks downfield made before pass has been thrown.
   5. Interference - (pass plays):
      a. Defensive - any illegal chucks, blocks or contact other than incidental while ball is in the air (does not have to be catchable).
      b. Offensive - any illegal contact or blocking downfield by team A.
   6. Make sure to continue to move downfield, boxing in receivers and defenders.

7. Do not allow receivers to get behind you.
8. Always move to a position to see between the receiver and defender as the ball arrives.
9. Watch for out-of-bounds plays on your sideline.
10. Be alert for any illegal participation on your sideline and end line.
11. End line is your responsibility.
12. After interception:
    a. Observe action.
    b. Take runner to goal line.
    c. Mark end of run.
    d. Signal time-out if inside two (2) minutes.
    e. Signal direction ball will be put into play.
13. Help Referee with ball marker and assessing yardage on penalties.
14. Record all team time-outs, scores, player warnings and ejections, captains and coin toss options on score-card.

ARTICLE 3: ALL OFFICIALS:
A. Areas of Responsibility:
   1. Keep Play properly boxed in.
   2. Before sounding whistle:
      a. Be certain ball is dead.
      b. Be certain of ball location.
      c. Do not turn back on runner.
      d. When ball becomes dead in your area, sound whistle promptly.
      e. Be alert for:
         1. Dead ball fouls.
         2. Surprise plays or fumbles.
B. Assist in marking end of run with ball marker.
C. Keep track of downs, team time-outs, scores, player ejections, warnings, team captain and options.
D. Watch for illegal substitution and participation.

Page 147

SECTION 3 - PROTECTED SCRIMMAGE KICK - (PROTECTED PUNT) - POSITIONS & RESPONSIBILITIES

(Diagram Shows 8-Man Team—
Position of Officials shall be the same for 7-man & 9-man teams)

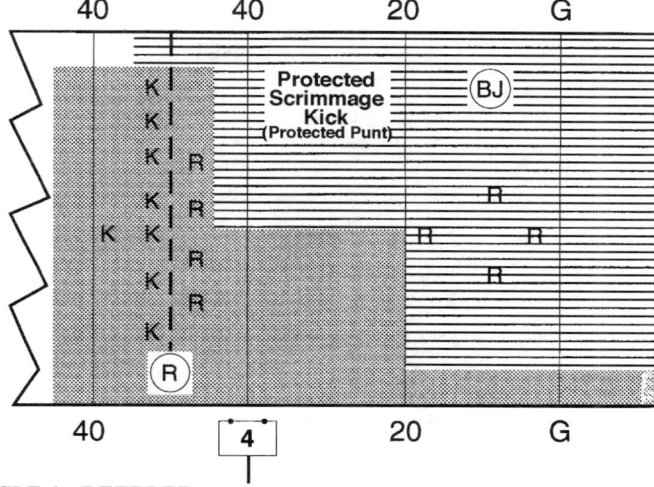

ARTICLE 1: REFEREE:
- A. Before Snap:
    1. Announce to both teams that Team A captain has requested a protected punt.
    2. Position: Same as regular play.
    3. Blow Ready-For-Play whistle.
    4. Count team A players.
    5. Line up players on both sides of line.
    6. Announce to all players that they must wait for ball to be kicked before releasing.
    7. If time-out is called, repeat 1 through 6.
- B. After Snap:
    1. Watch for snap hitting the ground.
    2. Watch for early release - (dead ball):
        a. Mark off penalty.
        b. Repeat 1 through 6 before snap.
    3. Watch for kicker moving backwards from line (flag down).
    4. Watch for kicker not moving in a continuous motion, lateral or toward the line of scrimmage - (dead ball, delay of game).
    5. Watch for fouls that occur on the line of scrimmage.
    6. Move downfield slowly after kick, boxing in players.
    7. Watch for fouls and be ready to pick up runner and follow to goal line.
    8. Mark off all penalties.
    9. Help mark end of run with ball marker.
    10. Give signal showing 1st down and point in direction team with possession will be going.

ARTICLE 2: BACK JUDGE:
  A. Before snap:
     1. Position: Opposite sideline of Referee, 2 yards back from deepest receiver, 7 yards in.
     2. Count Team B players.
  B. After snap:
     1. Watch for valid or invalid fair catch signal and fair catch interference.
     2. Watch for muffed ball - (down at spot).
     3. Be alert for backward laterals.
     4. Watch for ball out-of-bounds on your sideline.
     5. Follow ball carrier and release to Referee.
     6. Observe action behind runner and keep players boxed in.
     7. Be alert for illegal blocks downfield-(flag down at spot).
     8. Watch for holding on tag or deflag.
     9. Mark end of run with ball marker.

SECTION 4 - TRY-FOR-POINT KICK- (EXTRA POINT KICK)& FIELD GOAL KICK ATTEMPT- POSITIONS & RESPONSIBILITIES

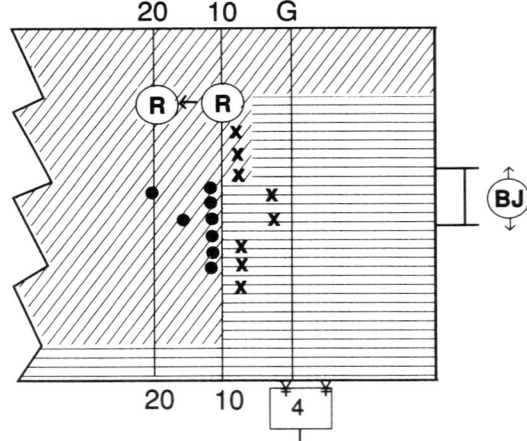

(Diagram Shows 8-Man Team—
Position of Officials shall be the same for 7-man & 9-man teams)

ARTICLE 1: REFEREE:
  A. Before snap:
     1. Announce to all players that we have an attempted kick.
     2. Position on line of scrimmage facing front of holder, 2 yards from farthest defender.
     3. Count team A players.
     4. Blow Ready-For-Play whistle.
     5. Line up center, guards (toe-to-toe with center) and defenders.
     6. Announce:
        a. No rushing between guard/center gap unless guard vacates.

           b. No 3 or 4 point stances.
           c. Whether neutral zone is good or not.
           d. Wait for snap of ball before rushing.
      7. If dead ball penalty occurs, assess, then repeat 1 through 6.
  B. After snap:
      1. Make sure no contact to center by rushers.
      2. Watch ball handling by holder.
      3. Keep eyes on holder and kicker and watch for roughing.
      4. Wait till rushers have stopped rushing before checking to see if kick is good or there is a runback.
      5. If kick attempt is runback, follow runner on your sideline all the way to goal line.
      6. If kick is faked, cover line of scrimmage and watch for illegal pass.
      7. If kick is good, give signal and start thirty (30) second clock.
      8. Mark score on card.

ARTICLE 2: BACK JUDGE:
  A. Before Snap:
      1. Position: Approximately 10 to 15 yards behind goal posts in between uprights.
      2. Count team B players.
      3. Watch for penalties, center to your side of ball.
  B. After Snap:
      1. Watch for 3 or 4 point stances - (flag down).
      2. Rushing guard/center gap - (flag down).
      3. If fake, move toward sideline opposite side as Referee and cover goal line and end line.
      4. If runback, follow runner on your side of field and follow to goal line.
      5. When ball is kicked, you must slide over to side of upright ball is on and give appropriate signal with whistle.
      6. Hustle downfield and line up kicking team for a kickoff.
      7. Mark scorecard.

SECTION 5 - GOAL LINE & TRY-FOR-POINT PLAYS - (SCRIMMAGE PLAYS-NO KICK) - POSITIONS & RESPONSIBILITIES

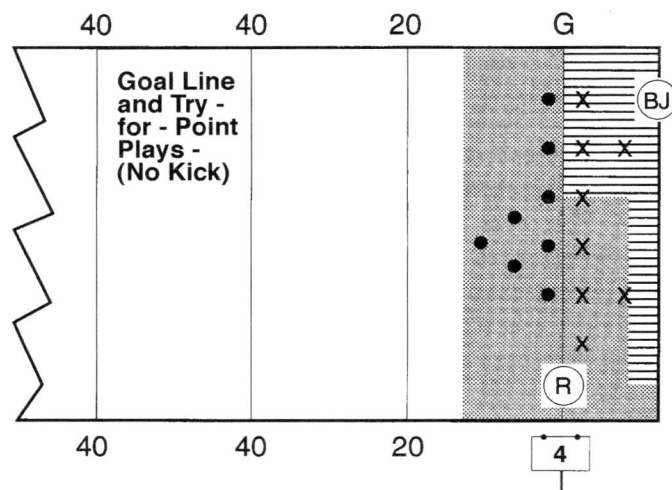

ARTICLE 1: REFEREE:
    A. Before Snap:
        1. Announce to both teams whether team A is going for a one or two point play, no kick.
        2. Blow Ready-For-Play whistle.
        3. Position: Same as regular play.
        4. Responsibilities: Same as regular play.
        5. If dead ball penalty occurs, give appropriate signals and repeat 1 through 4.
    B. After Snap:
        1. Same responsibilities as regular play.
        2. Be alert for interception and follow to goal line.
        3. if there is a penalty against team B or a double live ball foul and no score, repeat all steps above.
        4. if there is a penalty against team A that is or would be accepted, give incomplete signal.
        5. if there is a score and a penalty against team B, give appropriate signals, then touchdown signal.
        6. Move into position for kickoff.
        7. Mark scorecard.

ARTICLE 2: BACK JUDGE:
    A. Before Snap:
        1. Position: 5 to 7 yards from sideline in between goal line and end line.
        2. Same responsibilities as regular play.
    B. After Snap:
        1. Same responsibilities as regular play.

2. Be alert for interception and follow to goal line.
3. Watch for illegal participation, especially at end line.
4. Must cover goal line and/or end line, whichever way play is going.
5. After play, give proper signal then hustle down-field and set-up for kickoff.
6. Assess any dead ball penalties on kickoff.
7. Mark scorecard

PART III - 3 PERSON CREW MECHANICS

SECTION 1 - KICKOFF - (FREE KICK) - POSITIONS & RESPONSIBILITIES
(NOTE: Assume same positions after a safety).

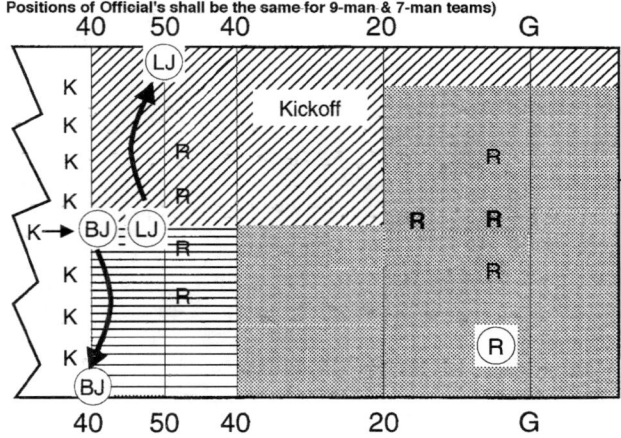

(Diagram shows 8-man Team– Positions of Official's shall be the same for 9-man & 7-man teams)

ARTICLE 1: REFEREE:
 A. Before Kick:
  1. Position: Near R's 10 yard line, center of field.
  2. Count R players.
  3. Check for illegal flags or no flags at all on R players - (flag down).
  4. Check position of other officials.
  5. When other officials are ready, blow whistle and with arm extended and palm open, move arm in direction of kick without turning head.
  6. If dead ball penalty occurs, repeat steps 1 through 5.
 B. After Kick:
  1. If kick is down middle or deep to either side, signal clock to start when kick is touched (entire game) other than first touching by K (last two minutes of game).
  2. Be alert for fair catch signal, if invalid, blow whistle to stop play - (flag down) and stop clock, if inside two (2) minutes in game.

3. Determine if K touches ball in the air before R - (flag down-fair catch interference).
4. When kick is caught in end zone:
    a. Determine if player advances ball out of end zone, then runs back in and is downed - (safety).
    b. Is downed before advancing past end zone - (touchback).
    c. Steps over end line or sideline (touchback).
5. Pick up runner and follow until releasing to Line Judge or Back Judge.
6. Observe action behind runner and then in front of Line Judge and Back Judge, especially illegal blocks down field.
7. Sound whistle when ball becomes dead and give time out signal in last two (2) minutes of game.
8. Mark end of run with ball marker and give first down signal, pointing in the direction ball will be advanced, after all penalties are assessed and proper signals given.

ARTICLE 2: LINE JUDGE:

A. Before Kick:
1. Position: 5 to 7 yards from sideline opposite Back Judge, 10 yards away from K's Free Kick line (face press box if in use) on R's restraining line.
2. Check for following on your sideline:
    a. Coaches and substitutes are in team box - (dead ball).
    b. Spectators are behind restricted area - (dead ball).
    c. Illegal flags or no flags at all- both teams - (flag down).
    d. Proper number of R players in their 5 yard front zone.

  (NOTE: Give warning first - We do not want to call these penalties unless forced to).

3. Help line up R players in their 5 yard front zone, 10 yards from K's Free Kick line.
4. Hold arm above head when ready.
5. If dead ball penalty, repeat steps 1 through 4.

B. After Kick:
1. Watch for kick going out-of-bounds on your sideline:
    a. Touched - mark spot.
    b. Untouched - flag down.
2. Signal clock to start at first touching by R - (entire game) and by K (stop inside two (2) minutes).
3. Determine if K touches ball in the air before R (flag down - fair catch interference).
4. Watch for initial blocks by players around R's 5 yard front zone.
5. Cover your sideline at all times.
6. Be prepared to take over coverage of runner in your area on long return and follow to goal line.

7. Sound whistle when run ends and ball becomes dead:
   a. Give time-out signal if inside two (2) minutes of game.
8. Mark spot with ball marker.
9. Assess all yardage on penalties after kick.
10. Get into position for run/pass play unless kick after fair catch is called.

ARTICLE 3: BACK JUDGE:

A. Before Kick:
1. Position: 7 yards from sideline on K's Free Kick line, opposite Line Judge.
2. Take charge of ball and make sure it is legal.
3. Check legality of kicking tee.
4. Hand kicker the ball and point to position of Referee instructing kicker to wait for Referee's Ready whistle - (dead ball - delay of game):

(REMEMBER: Kicking team may kick anywhere on or behind K's restraining line 5 yards from side lines.)

5. Move into position on K's free kick line.
6. Count K players.
7. Instruct K players to wait for ball to be kicked before crossing K's kicking line (dead ball - 5 yards).
8. Check for following on your sideline:
   a. Coaches and substitutes are in team box - (dead ball).
   b. Spectators are behind restricted area - (dead ball).
   c. Illegal flags or no flags at all on K players - (flag down).

(NOTE: Give warning first - We do not want to call these penalties unless forced to.)

9. Hold arm above head when ready.
10. If there is a dead ball penalty, assess yardage and repeat steps 1 through 9.

B. After Kick:
1. Watch for kick going out-of-bounds on your sideline:
   a. Touched - mark spot.
   b. Untouched - flag down.
2. Signal clock to start at first touching by R (entire game) and by K (stop inside two (2) minutes).
3. Determine if K touches ball in the air before R - (flag down-fair catch interference).
4. Watch for initial blocks by players around R's 5 yard front zone.
5. Cover your sideline at all times boxing in players.
6. Be prepared to take over coverage of runner in your area on a long return and follow to goal line.
7. Sound whistle when run ends and ball becomes dead:
   a. Give time-out signal if inside two (2) minutes of half.
8. Mark spot with ball marker.

9. Get into position for run/pass play unless kick after fair catch is called.

ARTICLE 4: ALL OFFICIALS:
    A. Watch For:
        1. Muffed ball - (down at spot).
        2. Laterals - (if forward, flag down at spot - 5 yards).
        3. Holding on tag or deflag - (flag down at spot -10 yards).
    B. Carry bean bag or ball marker in hand for spotting.

SECTION 2 - PASS/RUN PLAYS FROM SCRIMMAGE - POSITIONS & RESPONSIBILITIES

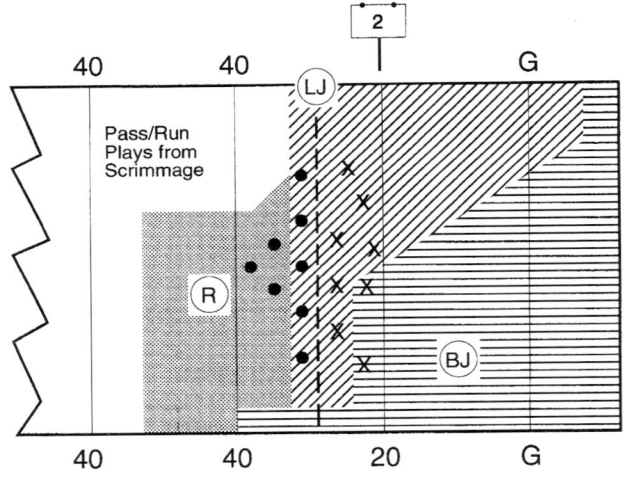

ARTICLE 1: REFEREE:
    A. Before Snap:
        1. Give Ready-For-Playwhistle.
        2. Start 25 second clock.
        3. Count team A players.
        4. Position: one which allows continuous view of ball and quarterback, opposite side from Line Judge at hash mark.
        5. Check for following:
            a. Delay of game - Announce when ten (10) seconds remain - (dead ball).
            b. Illegal shifts - Set one (1) second before snap - (flag down)
            c. Illegal motion - Man in motion moving toward line - (flag down)
            d. Ineligible receivers Ineligible Lineman Flag-9-Man - (flag down).
            e. Snap infractions, false starts - (dead ball).
            f. Team A players simulating a snap - (dead ball).
            g. Illegal substitutes by team A - (flag down).
            h. Illegal flag or no flags by team A - (flag down).
        6. If dead ball penalty occurs, give appropriate signals

facing press box and repeat steps 1 through 5.
- B. After Snap:
    1. Watch initial contact to center.
    2. Observe all blocks behind team A's line.
    3. As passer retreats, remain wider and deeper than passer.
    4. Give special attention to contact with passer:
        a. After ball is released, continue to observe passer, not flight of the ball.
        b. Verbally alert rushers and blockers when passer has released ball.
    5. Be alert to observe illegal passes:
        a. Determine whether pass is forward or backward and give appropriate arm signal.
        b. If close, mark spot of pass with bean bag or ball marker, continue to officiate. Use Line Judge for assistance.
        c. If not, drop penalty flag at the spot and continue to officiate.
    6. Referee is solely responsible for determining intentional grounding.
    7. During a run, continue to observe player action behind line before leaving area.
    8. Areas of responsibilities during a run:
        a. Ball, runner and action around him to neutral zone.
        b. Center of field and your sideline.
        c. Be ready for a kick or pass that may start out as a run.
        d. Do not get boxed in or turn back on ball.
        e. After crossing the neutral zone, check for fouls behind runner.
    9. If there is a touchdown and no foul which would nullify the touchdown, give signal and mark scorecard.
    10. If 1st down has been made or change of team possession has occurred, give appropriate signal if inside two (2) minutes.
    11. After interception:
        a. Observe action.
        b. Be prepared to take runner to goal line.
        c. Mark spot.
        d. Signal time-out if inside two (2) minutes.
        e. Signal direction ball will be put into play.
    12. If penalty occurs, follow proper procedure and let Line Judge assess yardage.
    13. After every play, help spot ball marker and after it has been spotted and other Officials are in their proper positions, give Ready-For-Play signal and sound whistle.
    14. Record all team time-outs, scores, player warnings and ejections, captains and coin toss options on scorecard.

ARTICLE 2: LINE JUDGE:
- A. Before Snap:

1. Position: Five (5) yards from sideline on line of scrimmage opposite press box and Referee.
2. Switch sidelines at half if there is no press box being used.
3. Line up players on both sides of neutral zone and tell them when they have a good line.
4. Check following:
    a. Coaches and substitutes are in team box - (dead ball).
    b. Spectators are behind restricted area - (dead ball).
    c. Required number of team A players on line of scrimmage at the snap - (flag down).
    d. Encroachment, false starts and snap infractions - (dead ball).
    e. Illegal motion, illegal shifts - (flag down).
    f. Illegal flag or no flags at all - (flag down).
    g. Illegal substitutes - (flag down).
5. If dead ball penalty occurs, give preliminary signal and notify Referee.
6. Assess yardage (3 and 4 man crews only) on all penalties.

B. After Snap:
1. Check for contact to center before committing.
2. Observe initial charge of linemen.
3. Action by blockers and ends.
4. If you read run, hold position at neutral zone.
5. If you read pass, slide downfield toward team A's 1st down marker.
   (NOTE: When moving downfield, always keep your shoulders parallel to the sideline and never cross your feet (shuffle feet).
6. Watch for any illegal contact on defensive side of ball on your side.
7. When ball comes to your side of field:
    a. If wide run, retreat toward side-line and slide toward team A's goal line to avoid interfering with the play.
    b. Move with ball and cover sideline (responsible for your sideline, end line to end line).
    c. Sound whistle promptly when ball becomes dead.
    d. Be positive of ball location before sounding whistle.
8. When ball goes opposite side:
    a. Observe action initially behind runner and then in front of Back Judge, especially downfield blocks.
    b. Do not leave line to move down-field until certain there is not a reverse or counter play.
9. Do not get boxed in or turn your back on ball.
10. Be ready to move quickly downfield on a pass or a quick kick.
11. On plays into your side zone, take runner and

ball to the goal line.
12. After run or catch and ball is dead, look for lst down and give time-out signal if lst down and inside two (2) minutes.
13. After interception:
    a. Observe action.
    b. Be prepared to take runner to goal line.
    c. Mark spot.
    d. Signal time-out if inside two (2) minutes.
    e. Signal direction ball will be put in play.
14. After incompletion in your area, sound whistle and give signal.
15. If play continues after an illegal forward pass, drop penalty flag at spot of pass and continue to officiate.
16. Work with down and yardage crew when required.
17. After each play:
    a. Mark spot with ball marker.
    b. Announce down and yardage to go for a 1st down.
18. Record all team time-outs, scores, player warnings and ejections, captains and coin toss options on scorecard.

ARTICLE 3: BACK JUDGE:
A. Before Snap:
   1. Position: 5 to 7 yards from sideline opposite Line Judge, 15 to 20 yards from line of scrimmage.
   2. Do not interfere with vision or movement of team B players.
   3. Be alert so receivers do not use you as interference.
   4. Check following:
      a. Team B players - (flag down).
      b. Illegal substitutes - (flag down).
      c. Illegal flags or no flags at all - (flag down).
      d. Disconcerting signals by team B - (flag down).
B. After Snap:
   1. Observe initial charge of receivers.
   2. Watch for illegal contact to center.
   3. Look for illegal use of hands or arms, illegal blocks and other fouls near line of scrimmage.
   4. Defensive holding - (pass plays):
      a. Illegal chucks - More than one, and/or contact made more than 5 yards from line of scrimmage, ball not thrown yet.
      b. Illegal blocks downfield made before pass has been thrown.
   5. Interference - (pass plays):
      a. Defensive - Any illegal chucks, blocks or contact other than incidental while ball is in the air. (Ball does not have to be catchable.)
      b. Offensive - Any illegal contact made by team A receivers during a pass play past the line of scrimmage.
   6. Make sure you continue to move downfield

boxing in receivers and defenders.
7. Do not allow receivers to get behind you.
8. Always move to a position to see between the receiver and defender as the ball arrives.
9. End line is your responsibility.
10. Watch for illegal participation on your side, especially at end line.
11. After interception:
    a. Observe action.
    b. Take runner until releasing to Line Judge.
    c. Watch for fouls behind runner.
    d. Mark end of run.
    e. Signal time-out if inside two (2) minutes.
    f. Signal direction ball will be put into play.
12. Watch for out-of-bounds plays on your side.
13. When runner steps out-of-bounds, move to spot and hold it.
14. Keep eyes on players out-of-bounds until all action has stopped.
15. Help with ball marker if end of play is 15 yards or more from previous line of scrimmage.
16. Record all team time-outs, scores, player warnings and ejections, team captains and coin toss options on scorecard.

ARTICLE 4: ALL OFFICIALS:
A. Areas of Responsibility:
   1. Keep play properly boxed in.
   2. Before sounding whistle:
      a. Be certain ball is dead.
      b. Be certain of ball location.
      c. Do not turn back on runner.
      d. When ball becomes dead in your area, sound whistle promptly.
      e. Be alert for:
         1. Dead ball fouls.
         2. Surprise plays or fumbles.
B. Assist in marking end of run with ball marker.
C. Keep track of downs, team time-outs, scores, player ejections, warnings, team captain and options.
D. Watch for illegal substitution and participation.

SECTION 3 - PROTECTED SCRIMMAGE KICK - (PROTECTED PUNT) POSITIONS & RESPONSIBILITIES

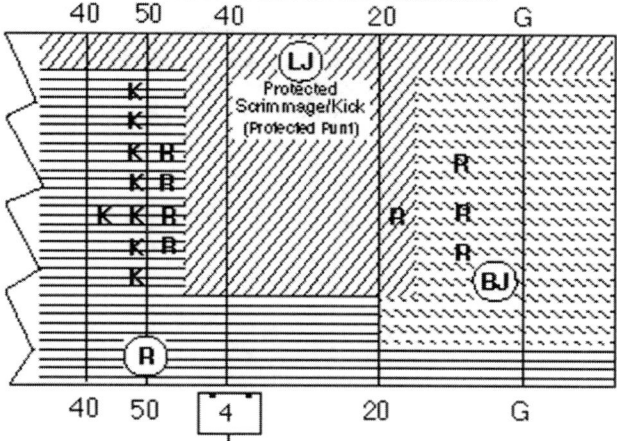

ARTICLE 1: REFEREE:
    A. Before Snap:
        1. Announce to both teams that team A captain has requested a protected punt.
        2. Shift to position on line of scrimmage opposite Line Judge, 7 yards from sideline.
        3. Blow Ready-For-Play whistle.
        4. Line up players on both sides of line.
        5. Count team A players.
        6. Announce to all players that they must wait for ball to be kicked before releasing.
        7. If time-out is called, repeat 1 through 6.
    B. After Snap:
        1. Watch for snap hitting the ground.
        2. Watch for early release - (dead ball):
            a. Repeat 1 through 6 before snap.
        3. Watch for kicker moving backwards from line - (flag down).
        4. Watch for kicker not moving in a continuous motion lateral or toward the line of scrimmage - (dead ball, delay of game).
        5. Watch for fouls that occur on the line of scrimmage.
        6. Move downfield slowly after kick.
        7. Watch for fouls and be ready to pick up runner if there is a long return.
        8. If no foul, give signal showing lst down and point indirection team with possession will be going.

ARTICLE 2: LINE JUDGE:
    A. Before Snap:

1. Move down 15 yards from line of scrimmage.
2. Stay on sideline 7 yards in, opposite Referee and Back Judge.

B. After Snap:
   1. Watch for any fouls in your area - (flag down at spot).
   2. Take runner if in your area.
   3. Follow runner to goal line if on your side of field
   4. Watch for holding by defender on the tag or deflag.
   5. Mark end of the run with ball marker.

ARTICLE 3: BACK JUDGE:
A. Before Snap:
   1. Take a position same side as Referee.
   2. Be 2 yards back from deepest receiver, 6 to 8 yards wide.
   3. Count team B players.

B. After Snap:
   1. Watch for valid or invalid fair catch signal and fair catch interference.
   2. Watch for muffed ball, down at spot.
   3. Be alert for backward laterals.
   4. Watch for ball out-of-bounds on your sideline.
   5. Follow ball carrier to 1st line of blockers, then release to Line Judge or Referee.
   6. Be alert for illegal blocks downfield, flag down at spot, continue to officiate.
   7. Watch for holding on tag or deflag.
   8. Help mark spot with ball marker.

SECTION 4 - TRY-FOR-POINT KICK (EXTRA POINT KICK) & FIELD GOAL KICK ATTEMPT - POSITIONS & RESPONSIBILITIES

(Diagram Shows 8-Man Team
Position of Officials shall be the same for 7-man & 9-man teams)

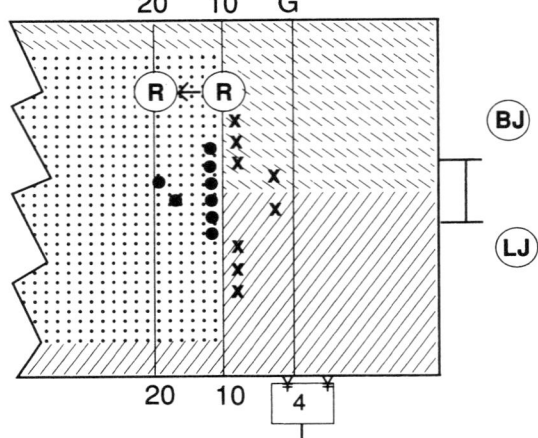

ARTICLE 1: REFEREE:
  A. Before Snap:
   1. Announce to all players that we have an attempted kick.
   2. Position on line of scrimmage facing front of holder 2 yards from farthest defender.
   3. Count team A players.
   4. Blow Ready-For-Play whistle.
   5. Line up center, guards (toe-to-toe with center) and defenders.
   6. Announce:
      a. No rushing between guard-center gap unless guard vacates.
      b. No 3 or 4 point stances.
      c. Whether neutral zone is good or not.
      d. Wait for snap of ball before rushing.
   7. If dead ball penalty occurs, assess, then repeat 1 through 6.
  B. After Snap:
   1. Make sure no contact to center by rushers.
   2. Stay on line of scrimmage and visually follow the ball back to the holder, then watch the ball handling by holder.
   3. Keep eyes on holder and kicker and watch for roughing.
   4. Wait till rushers have stopped rushing before checking to see if kick is good or there is a run-back.
   5. If runback, follow runner on your sideline all the way to goal line.
   6. If kick is faked, cover line of scrimmage and watch for illegal pass.
   7. If kick is good, give signal and start thirty (30) second clock.
   8. Mark score on card.

ARTICLE 2: LINE JUDGE:
  A. Before Snap:
   1. Position underneath upright opposite Referee.
   2. Watch for penalties, center to your side of ball.
  B. After Snap:
   1. Watch for 3 or 4 point stances - (flag down).
   2. Rushing guard-center gap - (flag down).
   3. If fake, move toward sideline opposite Referee and cover goal line.
   4. If runback, follow runner on your sideline all the way to goal line.
   5. If after kick, ball is on your side of upright, let Back Judge know whether it is good or not then walk through inside of goal posts toward the field of play with Back Judge and give appropriate signal with whistle.
   6. Hustle downfield and line up receiving team 10 to 15 yards away from kicking team.
   7. Mark scorecard.

ARTICLE 3: BACK JUDGE:
  A. Before Snap:
  1. Position underneath upright same side as Referee.
  2. Count team B players.
  3. Watch for penalties, center to your side of ball.
  B. After Snap:
  1. Watch for 3 or 4 point stances - (flag down).
  2. Rushing guard-center gap - (flag down).
  3. If fake, move toward sideline same side as Referee and cover end line.
  4. If runback, follow runner on your side of field and release to Referee.
  5. If after kick, ball is on your side of upright, let Line Judge know whether it is good or not, then walk through uprights toward Referee with Line Judge and give appropriate signal with whistle.
  6. Hustle downfield and line up kicking team for a kickoff.
  7. Mark scorecard.

SECTION 5 - GOAL LINE & TRY-FOR-POINT PLAYS - (SCRIMMAGE PLAYS-NO KICK) - POSITIONS & RESPONSIBILITIES

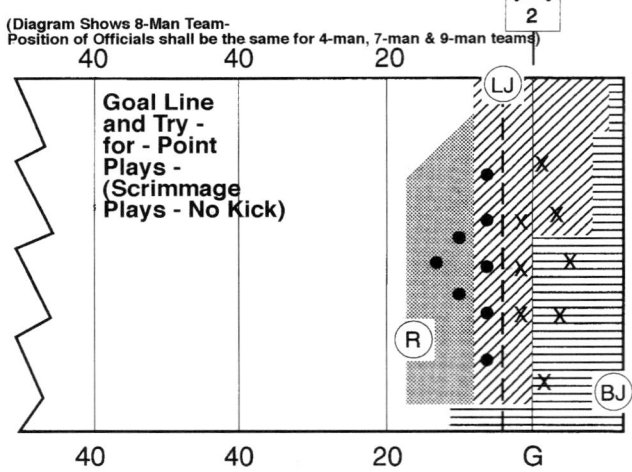

ARTICLE 1: REFEREE:
  A. Before Snap:
  1. Ask Team A captain what choice he/she wants, whether one or two points, kick or no kick.
  2. Blow Ready-For-Play whistle.
  3. Position and duties are same as regular play on one (1) point play.
  4. Position on line of scrimmage on a two (2) point play, cover your sideline. Other duties are same as regular play.

5. If dead ball penalty occurs, assess yardage, give appropriate signals and repeat 1 through 4.
   B. After Snap:
      1. If intercepted, follow runner on your side of field and follow to goal line. Award two (2) points if team B scores and Team A will still kick off.
      2. If point or points no good, blow whistle and give signal.
      3. If point or points good, blow whistle, give signal and mark scorecard.

ARTICLE 2: LINE JUDGE:
A. Before Snap:
   1. Position and duties are same as regular play on one point play except that you must float from line of scrimmage to goal line marker at the snap.
   2. Position on the goal line behind marker and cover your sideline on a two (2) point play.
   3. Other duties same as regular play.
B. After Snap:
   1. If ball breaks plane of goal line before deflag or tag, give touchdown signal and blow whistle.
   2. If intercepted, follow runner on your side of field to goal line.
   3. Hustle down field and line up receiving team.
   4. Mark scorecard.

ARTICLE 3: BACK JUDGE:
A. Before Snap:
   1. Mark initial spot of line of scrimmage - one (1) point try at 3 yard line or two (2) point try at 10 yard line, with ball marker.
   2. Position on endline covering sideline opposite Line Judge on a one (1) point attempt and moving in 10 yards from side line on a two (2) point attempt.
   3. Watch end line and sideline for illegal participation.
   4. Duties same as regular play.
B. After Snap:
   1. If team A scores, give touchdown signal.
   2. If ball is intercepted, follow runner on your sideline, releasing to the Referee.
   3. Hustle down field and line up kicking team.
   4. Mark scorecard.

PART IV - 4 PERSON CREW MECHANICS

SECTION 1 - KICKOFF - (FREE KICK) - POSITIONS & RESPONSIBILITIES

(NOTE: Assume same positions after a safety.)

(Diagram Shows 8-Man Team -
Position of Officials shall be the same for 7-man & 9-man teams)

ARTICLE 1: REFEREE:
    A. Before Kick:
        1. Position: Near R's goal line, 10-15 yards from same sideline as Field Judge.
        2. Count R players.
        3. Check for illegal flags or no flags at all on R players - (flag down).
        4. Check position of other officials.
        5. When other officials are ready, blow whistle and with arm extended and palm open move arm in direction of kick without turning head.
        6. If dead ball penalty occurs, repeat steps 1 through 5.
    B. After Kick:
        1. If kick is down middle or deep to your side, signal clock to start when kick is touched, (entire game) other than first touching by K - (last two (2) minutes).
        2. Be alert for fair catch signal, if invalid, blow whistle to stop play - (flag down) and stop clock if inside two (2) minutes.
        3. Determine if K touches ball in the air before R - (flag down - fair catch interference).
        4. When kick is caught in end zone:
            a. Determine if player advances ball out of end zone then runs back in and is downed - (safety).
            b. Is downed before advancing past

end zone - (touchback).
    c. Steps over end line or sideline (touchback).
 5. Pick up runner and follow until releasing to Field Judge or Back Judge.
 6. Observe action behind runner and then in front of Field Judge and Back Judge, especially illegal blocks downfield.
 7. Sound whistle when ball becomes dead and give time-out signal in last two (2) minutes.
 8. Mark end of run with ball marker and give first down signal pointing in the direction ball will be advanced, after all penalties are assessed and proper signals are given.

ARTICLE 2: LINE JUDGE:
  A. Before Kick:
    1. Position: Near R's 20 yard line, 10-15 yards from sideline same side as Back Judge.
    2. Count R players.
    3. Check for illegal flags or no flags at all on R players - (flag down).
    4. If dead ball penalty occurs, repeat steps 1 through 3.
  B. After Kick:
    1. If kick is down middle or deep to your side, signal clock to start when kick is touched (entire game), other than first touching by K - (last two (2) minutes).
    2. Be alert for fair catch signal, if invalid, blow whistle to stop play - (flag down) and stop clock if inside two (2) minutes.
    3. Determine if K touches ball in the air before R- (flag down - fair catch interference).
    4. When kick is caught in end zone: Look to Referee for proper signal and shadow signal.
    5. Pick up runner and follow until releasing to Field Judge or Back Judge.
    6. Observe action behind runner and then in front of Field Judge and Back Judge, especially illegal blocks down field.
    7. Sound whistle when ball becomes dead and give time-out signal in last two (2) minutes.
    8. Help mark end of run with ball marker and move into position for a run/pass play unless a kick after a fair catch is called.

ARTICLE 3: FIELD JUDGE:
  A. Before Kick:
    1. Position: 5-7 yards from sideline opposite Back Judge, 10 yards away from K's Free Kick line - (face press box if in use).
    2. Check for following on your sideline:
        a. Coaches and substitutes are in team box - (dead ball).
        b. Spectators are behind restricted area - (dead ball).
        c. Illegal flags or no flags at all on K players.

            d. Proper number of R Players in their 5 yard front zone.

        (**NOTE:** Give warning first - We do not want to call these penalties unless forced to).
        3. Help line up R Players in their 5 yard front zone, 10 yards from K's Free Kick line.
        4. Hold arm above head when ready.
        5. If dead ball penalty, repeat steps 1 through 4.
    B. After Kick:
        1. Watch for kick going out-of-bounds on your sideline:
            a. Touched - mark spot.
            b. Untouched - flag down.
        2. Signal clock to start at first touching by R - (entire game) and by K - (stop inside two (2) minutes).
        3. Determine if K touches ball in the air before R - (flag down - fair catch interference).
        4. Watch for initial blocks by players around R's 5 yard front zone.
        5. Cover your sideline at all times, boxing in players.
        6. Be prepared to take over coverage of runner in your area on a long return and follow to goal line.
        7. Sound whistle when run ends and ball becomes dead:
            a. Give time-out signal if inside two (2) minutes.
        8. Mark spot with ball marker.
        9. Get into position for run/pass play unless kick after fair catch is called.

ARTICLE 4: BACK JUDGE:
    A. Before Kick:
        1. Position: 7 yards from sideline on K's free kick line, opposite Field Judge.
        2. Take charge of ball and make sure it is legal.
        3. Check legality of kicking tee.
        4. Hand kicker the ball and point to position of Referee, instructing kicker to wait for Referee's Ready whistle - (dead ball - delay of game).

        (**REMEMBER:** Kicking team may kick anywhere on or behind K's restraining line, 5 yards from side line).
        5. Move into position on K's Free Kick line.
        6. Count K players.
        7. Instruct K players to wait for ball to be kicked before crossing K's kicking line (dead ball - 5 yards).
        8. Check for following on your sideline:
            a. Coaches and substitutes are in team box area.
            b. Spectators are behind restricted area - (dead ball).
            c. Illegal flags or no flags at all on K players - (flag down).

        (**NOTE:** Give warning first - We do not want to call these penalties unless forced to).
        9. Hold arm above head when ready.
        10. If there is a dead ball penalty, assess yardage and

Page 167

repeat steps 1 through 9.
B. After Kick:
1. Watch for kick going out-of-bounds on your sideline.
2. Signal clock to start at first touching by R - (entire game) and by K - (stop inside two (2) minutes).
3. Determine if K touches ball in the air before R - (flag down-fair catch interference).
4. Watch for initial blocks by players around R's 5 yard front zone.
5. Cover your sideline at all times boxing in players.
6. Be prepared to take over coverage of runner in your area on a long return and follow to goal line.
7. Sound whistle when run ends and ball becomes dead:
   a. Give time-out signal if inside two (2) minutes.
8. Help mark spot with ball marker.
9. Get into position for run/pass play unless kick after fair catch is called.

ARTICLE 5: ALL OFFICIALS:
A. Watch For:
1. Muffed Ball - (down at spot).
2. Laterals - (if forward, flag down at spot - 5 yards).
3. Holding on tag or deflag - (flag down at spot - 10 yards).
B. Carry bean bag or ball marker in hand for spotting.

SECTION 2 - PASS/RUN PLAYS FROM SCRIMMAGE - POSITIONS & RESPONSIBILITIES

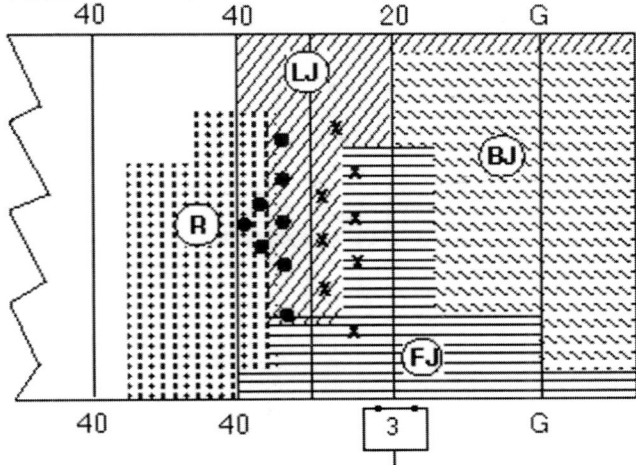

(Diagram Shows 8-Man Team - Position of Officials shall be the same for 4-man, 7-man & 9-man teams)

ARTICLE 1: REFEREE:
A. Before Snap:
1. Give Ready-For-Play whistle.
2. Start 25 second clock.
3. Count Team A players.

4. Position: One which allows continuous view of ball and quarterback opposite side from Line Judge at has mark.
   5. Check for following:
      a. Delay of game - announce when ten (10) seconds remain - (dead ball).
      b. Illegal shifts - set one (1) second before snap - (flag down).
      c. Illegal motion - man in motion moving toward line - (flag down).
      d. Ineligible receivers - (9-Man Ineligible Linemen Flag) - (flag down).
      e. Snap infractions, false starts - (dead ball).
      f. Team A players simulating a snap - (dead ball).
      g. Illegal substitutes by Team A - (flag down).
      h. Illegal flag or no flags by Team A - (flag down).
   6. If dead ball penalty occurs, give appropriate signals facing press box and repeat steps 1 through 5.
B. After Snap:
   1. Watch initial contact to center.
   2. Observe all blocks behind Team A's line.
   3. As passer retreats, remain wider and deeper than passer.
   4. Give special attention to contact with passer:
      a. After ball is released, continue to observe passer, not flight of the ball.
      b. Verbally alert rushers and blockers when passer has released ball.
   5. Be alert to observe illegal passes:
      a. Determine whether pass is forward or backward and give appropriate arm signal.
      b. If close, mark spot of pass with bean bag or ball marker, continue to officiate.
      c. If not, drop penalty flag at the spot and continue to officiate.
   6. Referee is solely responsible for determining intentional grounding.
   7. During a run, continue to observe player action behind line before leaving area.
   8. Areas of responsibilities during a run:
      a. Ball, runner and action around him to neutral zone.
      b. Center of field.
      c. Be ready for a kick or pass that may start out as a run.
      d. Do not get boxed in or turn back on ball.
      e. After crossing the neutral zone, check for fouls behind runner.
   9. If there is a touchdown and no foul which would nullify the touchdown, give signal and mark scorecard.
   10. If 1st down has been made or change of team possession has occurred, give appropriate signal inside two (2) minutes.
   11. After interception:

    a. Observe action.
    b. Be prepared to take runner to goal line.
    c. Mark spot.
    d. Signal time-out if inside two (2) minutes.
    e. Signal direction ball will be put into play.
12. After every play, help spot ball marker and after it has been spotted and other Officials are in their proper positions, give Ready-For-Play signal and sound whistle.
13. Record all team time-outs, scores, player warnings and ejections, captains and coin toss options, on scorecard.

ARTICLE 2: LINE JUDGE:
  A. Before Snap:
    1. Position: 5 yards from sideline on line of scrimmage opposite press box and Referee.
    2. Switch sidelines at half if there is not press box being used.
    3. Line up players on both sides of neutral zone and tell them when they have a good line.
    4. Check for following:
        a. Coaches and substitutes are in team box - (dead ball).
        b. Spectators are behind restricted area - (dead ball).
        c. Required number of Team A players on line of scrimmage at the snap - (flag down).
        d. Encroachment, false starts and snap infractions - (dead ball).
        e. Illegal motion, illegal shifts - (flag down).
        f. Illegal flag or not flags at all - (flag down)
        g. Illegal substitutes - (flag down).
    5. If dead ball penalty occurs, give preliminary signal and notify Referee.
    6. Assess yardage (3 and 4 man crews only) on all penalties.
  B. After Snap:
    1. Check for contact to center before committing.
    2. Observe initial charge of linemen.
    3. Action by blockers and ends.
    4. If you read run, hold position at neutral zone.
    5. If you read pass, slide downfield toward Team A's 1st down marker.
  (**NOTE:** When moving downfield always keep your shoulders parallel to the sideline and never cross your feet (shuffle feet).
    6. Watch for any illegal contact on defensive side of ball on your side.
    7. When ball comes to your side of field:
        a. If wide run, retreat toward side-line and slide toward Team A's goal line to avoid interfering with the play.

b. Move with ball and cover sideline (responsible for your sideline, end line to end line).
   c. Sound whistle promptly when ball becomes dead.
   d. Be positive of ball location before sounding whistle.
8. When ball goes opposite side:
   a. Observe action initially behind runner and then in front of Field Judge, especially down field blocks.
   b. Do not leave line to move down field until certain there is no reverse or counter play.
9. Do not get boxed in or turn your back on ball.
10. Be ready to move quickly downfield on a pass.
11. On plays into your side zone, take runner and ball to the goal line.
12. After run or catch and ball is dead, look for lst down and give time-out signal if Ist down and inside two (2) minutes.
13. After interception:
    a. Observe action.
    b. Be prepared to take runner to goal line.
    c. Mark spot.
    d. Signal time-out if inside two (2) minutes.
    e. Signal direction ball will be put in play.
14. After incompletion in your area, sound whistle and give signal.
15. If play continues after an illegal forward pass, drop penalty flag at spot of pass and continue to officiate.
16. Work with down and yardage crew when required
17. After each play:
    a. Mark spot with ball marker.
    b. Announce down and yardage to go for a lst down.
18. Record all team time-outs, scores, player warnings and ejections, team captains and coin toss options on scorecard.

ARTICLE 3: FIELD JUDGE:
A. Before Snap:
   1. Position: 5 to 7 yards from sideline, 10 to 15 yards beyond scrimmage line.
   2. Do not interfere with vision or movement of Team B players.
   3. Check following:
      a. Coaches and substitutes are in team box - (dead ball).
      b. Spectators are behind restricted area - (dead ball).
      c. illegal flag or no flags at all - (flag down).
      d. Illegal substitutes - (flag down).
      e. Disconcerting signals by Team B - (flag down).
   4. Be alert so receivers do not use you as interference.
B. After Snap:
   1. Observe initial charge of receivers.
   2. Watch for illegal contact to center.

3. Look for illegal use of hands or arms, illegal blocks and other fouls near line of scrimmage.
4. Defensive holding - (pass plays):
   a. Illegal chucks - More than one (1), and/or contact made more than 5 yards from line of scrimmage, ball not thrown yet.
   b. Illegal blocks downfield made before pass has been thrown.
5. Interference - (pass play):
   a. Defensive - Any illegal chucks, blocks or contact other than incidental while ball is in the air. (Does not have to be catchable).
   b. Offensive - Any illegal contact or blocking downfield by Team A.
6. Make sure you continue to move downfield, boxing in receivers and defenders in your area.
7. Always move to a position to see between the receiver and defender as the ball arrives.
8. Watch for out-of-bounds plays on your sideline.
9. Be alert for any illegal participation on your sideline.
10. When runner steps out-of-bounds, move to spot and hold it.
11. Keep eyes on players out-of-bounds until all action has stopped.
12. Help with ball marker if end of play is in bounds and in your area.
13. After interception:
    a. Observe action.
    b. Take runner until releasing to Referee.
    c. Watch for fouls behind runner.
    d. Mark end of run.
    e. Signal time-out if inside two (2) minutes.
    f. Signal direction ball will be put into play.
14. Record all time-outs, scores, player ejections and warnings, teams captains and coin toss options on scorecard.

ARTICLE 4: BACK JUDGE:

A. Before Snap:
   1. Position: Hash mark opposite Referee side of field, 20 to 25 yards from line of scrimmage.
   2. Do not interfere with vision or movement of Team B players.
   3. Be alert so receivers do not use you as interference.
   4. Check for following:
      a. Team B players - (flag down).
      b. Illegal substitutes - (flag down).
      c. Illegal flags or no flags at all - (flag down).
      d. Disconcerting signals by Team B - (flag down).

B. After Snap:
   1. Observe initial charge of receivers.
   2. Watch for illegal contact to center.
   3. Look for illegal use of hands or arms, illegal

blocks and other fouls near line of scrimmage.
4. Defensive holding - (pass plays):
   a. Illegal chucks - More than one, and/or contact made more than 5 yards from line of scrimmage, ball not thrown yet.
   b. Illegal blocks downfield made before pass has been thrown.
5. Interference - (pass plays):
   a. Defensive - Any illegal chucks, blocks or contact other than incidental while ball is in the air. (Does not have to be catchable).
   b. Offensive - Any illegal contact or blocking downfield by Team A.
6. Make sure you continue to move downfield boxing in receivers and defenders.
7. Do not allow receivers to get behind you.
8. Always move to a position to see between the receiver and defender as the ball arrives.
9. End line is your responsibility.
10. Watch for illegal participation on your side, especially at end line.
11. After interception:
    a. Observe action.
    b. Take runner until releasing to Line Judge.
    c. Watch for fouls behind runner.
    d. Mark end of run.
    e. Signal time-out if inside two (2) minutes.
    f. Signal direction ball will be put into play.
12. Help with ballmarker if end of play is 15 yards or more from previous line of scrimmage.
13. Record all team time-outs, scores, player warnings and ejections, team captains and coin toss options on scorecard.

ARTICLE 5: ALL OFFICIALS:
A. Areas of Responsibility:
   1. Keep play properly boxed in.
   2. Before sounding whistle:
      a. Be certain ball is dead.
      b. Be certain of ball location.
      c. Do not turn back on runner.
      d. When ball becomes dead in your area, sound whistle promptly.
      e. Be alert for:
         1. Dead ball fouls.
         2. Surprise plays or fumbles.
B. Assist in marking end of run with ball marker.
C. Keep track of downs, team time-outs, scores, player ejections and warnings and options and mark scorecards.
D. Watch for illegal substitution and participation.

Page 173

SECTION 3 - PROTECTED SCRIMMAGE KICK - (PROTECTED PUNT) - POSITIONS & RESPONSIBILITIES

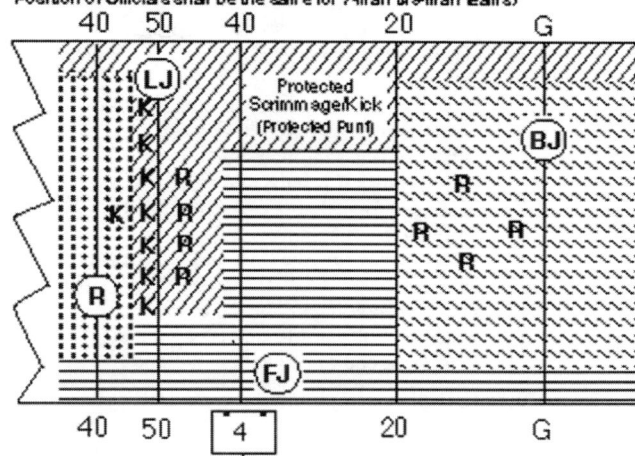

ARTICLE 1: REFEREE:
- A. Before Snap:
  1. Announce to both teams that Team A captain has requested a protected punt.
  2. Position opposite Line Judge approximately 5 yards to the side and 2 yards back of kicker.
  3. Blow Ready-For-Play whistle.
  4. Count Team A players.
  5. After Line Judge has finished lining up players, announce to both teams that they must wait for the ball to be kicked before releasing.
  6. If time-out is called, repeat 1 through 5.
- B. After Snap:
  1. Watch for snap hitting the ground.
  2. Watch for early release - (dead ball):
     a. Repeat 1 through 5 before snap.
  3. Watch for kicker moving backwards from line - (flag down).
  4. Watch for kicker not moving in a continuous motion lateral or towards the line of scrimmage - (dead ball, delay of game):
     a. Repeat 1 through 5 before snap.
  5. Watch for fouls that occur on the line.
  6. Move downfield slowly after kick.
  7. Watch for fouls and be ready to pick up runner if there is a long return.
  8. If no foul, give signal showing 1st down and point in direction team with possession will be going.

ARTICLE 2: LINE JUDGE:
A. Before Snap:
1. Position same as regular play.
2. Announce to bench on your sideline a protected punt has been declared.
3. Line up players on both sides of line.
4. Let Referee know when there is a good line.

B. After Snap:
1. Watch for snap hitting the ground.
2. Watch for early release - (dead ball):
   a. Repeat 1 through 4 before snap.
   b. Mark off penalty - (4 man crew).
3. Watch for fouls that occur on the line of scrimmage - (flag down).
4. Take runner if in your area and be ready to follow to goal line.
5. Watch for holding on the tag or deflag.
6. Watch for ball out-of-bounds on your sideline.
7. Help mark end of run with ball marker.

ARTICLE 3: FIELD JUDGE:
A. Before Snap:
1. Position 15 yards from line of scrimmage, 7 yards in from sideline opposite Line Judge.
2. Announce to bench on your sideline a protected punt has been declared.

B. After Snap:
1. Watch for early release - (dead ball):
   a. Repeat 1 and 2 before snap.
2. Watch for fouls that occur in your area - (flag at spot).
3. Take runner if in your area and be ready to follow to goal line.
4. Watch for ball out-of-bounds on your sideline.
5. Watch for holding on the tag or deflag.
6. Help mark end of run with ball marker.

ARTICLE 4: BACK JUDGE:
A. Before Snap:
1. Position: Same side as Line Judge, 5 to 7 yards from center of field, 2 yards back from deepest receiver.
2. Count Team B players.

B. After Snap:
1. Watch for valid or invalid fair catch signal and fair catch interference.
2. Watch for muffed ball - (down at spot).
3. Be alert for backward laterals.
4. Follow ball carrier to 1st line of blockers, then release to other officials.
5. Observe action behind runner and keep players boxed in
6. Watch for holding on tag or deflag.

Page 175

SECTION 4 - TRY-FOR-POINT KICK - (EXTRA POINT KICK) & FIELD GOAL KICK ATTEMPT- POSITIONS & RESPONSIBILITIES

(Diagram Shows 8-Man Team—
Position of Officials shall be the same for 7-man & 9-man teams)

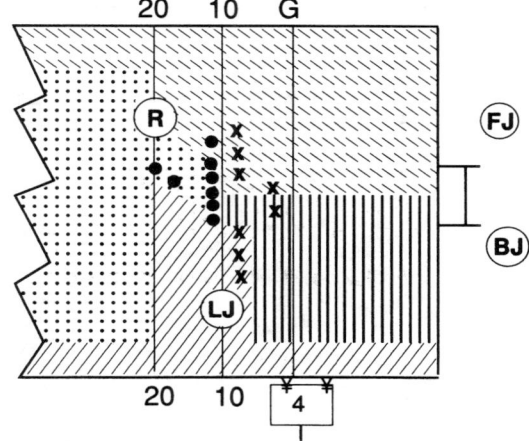

ARTICLE 1: REFEREE:
    A. Before Snap:
        1. Announce to both teams we have an attempted kick.
        2. Position: Facing front of holder in between holder and kicker.
        3. Count Team A players.
        4. Blow Ready-For-Play whistle.
        5. Announce:
            a. No rushing between guard-center gap unless guard vacates.
            b. No 3 or 4 point stances.
            c. Wait for snap of ball before rushing.
        6. If dead ball penalty occurs, repeat 1 through 5.
    B. After Snap:
        1. Watch for muff of snap by holder.
        2. Keep eyes on holder and kicker and watch for roughing.
        3. If fake, watch for roughing on quarterback and illegal forward pass.
        4. Wait till rushers have stopped rushing before checking to see if kick is good or there is a run-back.
        5. If runback, follow runner on your side all the way to goal line.
        6. If kick is good, give signal and start thirty (30) second clock.
        7. Mark scorecard.
        8. Move into position for a kickoff.

ARTICLE 2: LINE JUDGE:
A. Before Snap:
1. Position: Line of scrimmage opposite Referee, 2 yards from furthest rusher.
2. Line up players and make sure guards are toe-to-toe with center.
3. If dead ball penalty occurs, assess yardage (4 man crew only).
B. After Snap:
1. Make sure there is no contact to the center - (flag down).
2. Watch for a muff on the snap.
3. If fake, move toward sideline and watch for illegal forward pass.
4. If runback, follow runner on your side of field all the way to goal line.
5. Watch for any illegal use of hands.
6. Look for roughing on holder and kicker.
7. After kick, hustle downfield and line up receiving team 10 to 15 yards away from kicking team.
8. Mark scorecard.

ARTICLE 3: FIELD JUDGE:
A. Before Snap:
1. Position: Underneath upright, same side as Referee.
2. Watch for penalties, center to your side of ball.
B. After Snap:
1. Watch for 3 or 4 point stances - (flag down).
2. Rushing guard-center gap - (flag down).
3. If fake, move toward same sideline as Referee and cover goal line.
4. If runback, watch for penalties behind runner and cover your sideline.
5. If after kick, ball is on your side of upright, let Back Judge know whether it is good or not, then walk through inside of goal posts toward the field of play with Back Judge and give appropriate signal with whistle.
6. Hustle downfield and line up kicking team for a kickoff.
7. Mark scorecard.

ARTICLE 4: BACK JUDGE:
A. Before Snap:
1. Position: Underneath upright, same side as Line Judge.
2. Count Team B players.
3. Watch for penalties center, to your side of ball.
B. After Snap:
1. Watch for 3 or 4 point stances - (flag down).
2. Rushing guard-center gap - (flag down).
3. If fake, cover end line and your sideline.
4. If runback, watch for penalties behind runner and cover your side of field.
5. If after kick, ball is on your side of upright, let Field Judge know whether it is good or not, then walk through inside of goal posts toward the field of play with Field

Judge and give appropriate signal with whistle.
6. Hustle downfield and line up kicking team for a kick off.
7. Mark scorecard.

SECTION 5 - GOAL LINE & TRY-FOR-POINT PLAYS - (SCRIMMAGE PLAYS-NO KICK) - POSITIONS & RESPONSIBILITIES

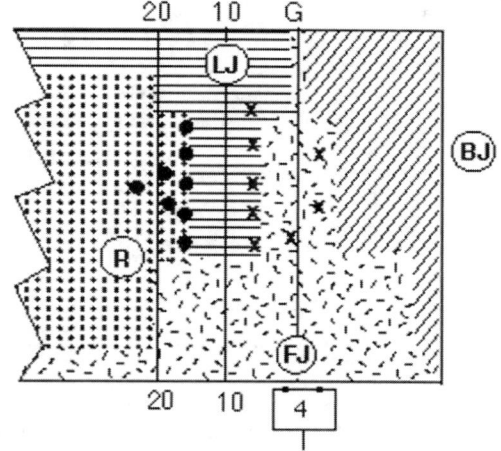

ARTICLE 1: REFEREE:
    A. Before Snap:
        1. Announce to both teams whether Team A is going for a one or two point play, no kick.
        2. Blow Ready-For-Play whistle.
        3. Count Team A players.
        4. Position same as regular play.
        5. If dead ball penalty occurs, give appropriate signals and repeat 1 through 4.
    B. After Snap:
        1. Same responsibilities as regular play.
        2. Be alert for interception and follow to goal line.
        3. If there is a penalty against Team B or a double live ball foul and no score, repeat all steps above.
        4. If there is a penalty against Team A that is or would be accepted, give incomplete signal.
        5. If there is a score and a penalty against Team B, give appropriate signals, then touchdown signal.
        6. Move into position for kickoff.
        7. Mark scorecard.

ARTICLE 2: LINE JUDGE:
    A. Before Snap:

1. Position: 5 yards from sideline on line of scrimmage, opposite press box and Referee.
2. Line up players on both sides of neutral zone and announce when they have a good line.
3. Same responsibilities as a regular play.

B. After Snap:
1. Same responsibilities as regular play.
2. If you read pass, slide downfield toward Team A's goal line.
3. On plays into your side zone, take runner and ball to goal line.
4. Be alert for interception and follow to goal line.
5. After run or catch and ball is dead, look for goal line and signal if touchdown or give incomplete signal if not.
6. After signal, hustle downfield to be in position for a kickoff.
7. Mark scorecard.

ARTICLE 3: FIELD JUDGE:
A. Before Snap:
1. Position: Behind goal line marker opposite Line Judge.
2. Same responsibilities as regular play.
B. After Snap:
1. Same responsibilities as regular play.
2. Hold position at goal line at all times.
3. When ball goes toward goal line on either side of field:
   a. If ball is over goal line before tag or deflag, signal touchdown.
   b. If ball is not over goal line before tag or deflag, signal incomplete.
4. Be alert for interception and release runner to Referee, watching for fouls behind runner.
5. Hustle downfield and take position for kickoff.
6. Mark scorecard.

ARTICLE 4: BACK JUDGE:
A. Before Snap:
1. Position: One (1) yard behind end line, next to goal post, opposite side from Referee.
2. Same responsibilities as regular play.
3. Count Team B players.
B. After Snap:
1. Same responsibilities as regular play.
2. Be alert for interception and watch for fouls behind runner.
3. Watch for illegal participation, especially at end line.
4. Hold position at end line at all times.
5. After play, give proper signal, then hustle downfield and set up for kickoff.
6. Assess any dead ball penalties on kickoff.
7. Mark scorecard.

U.S.F.T.L. CODE OF OFFICIAL FOOTBALL SIGNALS

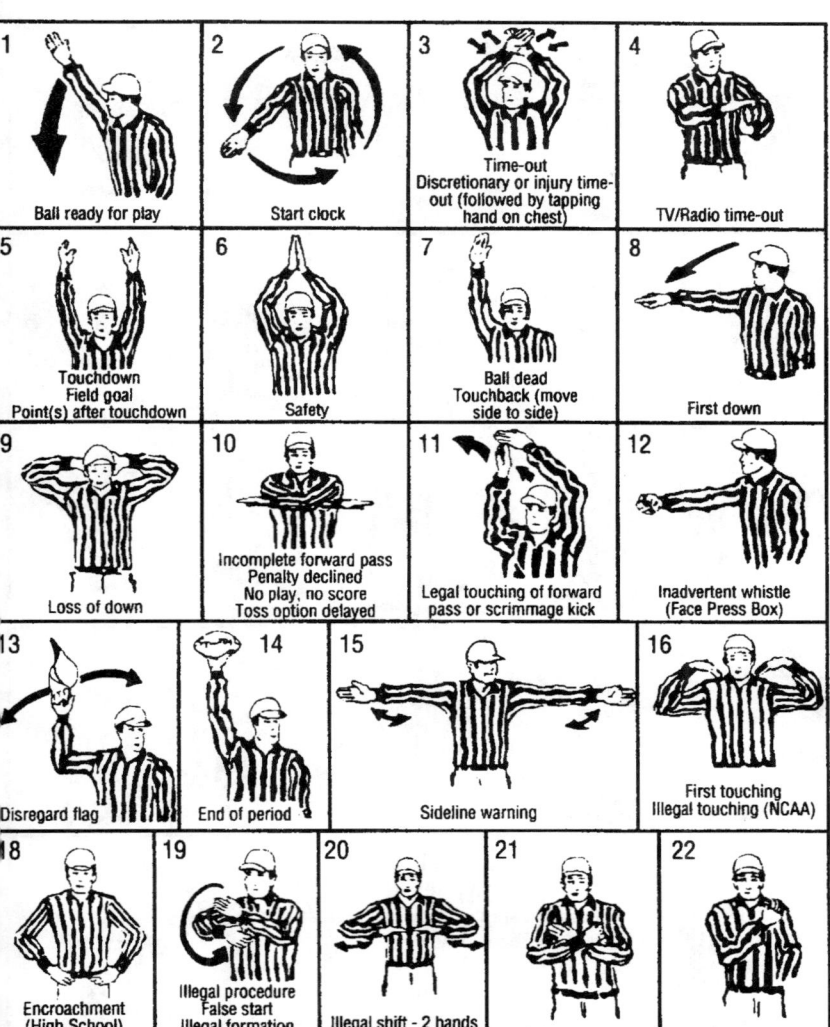

U.S.F.T.L. CODE OF OFFICIAL FOOTBALL SIGNALS

Note: Signals number 17, 25, 26 and 45 are for future expansion.

SUMMARY OF PENALTIES AND FOULS

LOSS OF 5 YARDS	**PAGE**	**RULE**	**SECTION**	**ARTICLE**	**SIGNAL**
1. Required Equipment Worn Illegally	31	4	3	1-3	23
2. Delay of Game	35	5	4	2	21
3. Unfair Tactics	35	5	4	3	21
4. Substitution Rules Infraction	37	6	1	1-4	22
5. Infraction of Free Kick Formation	47-48	10	1	2	7,19, 22
6. Encroachment of Free Kick Lines	48	10	1	3	7,18
7. Advancement of Free Kick by Male (Co-Rec Only)	80-81	20	1	13	19
8. Free Kick Out-of-Bounds	49	10	2	1	19
9. Infraction of Protected Scrimmage Kick Formation - Line Players	50	10	3	3	19 7.
10. Infraction of Protected Scrimmage Kick Formation - Kickers	50	10	3	4	19,21
11. Advancement of Protected Scrimmage Kick by Male (Co-Rec Only)	80-81	20	1	13	19 9.
12. Encroachment	41	9	2	1	7,18
13. False Start	42	9	2	2	7
14. Illegal Snap	42	9	2	3	19
15. Offensive Player Within 5 Yards of Sideline	42	9	3	1	19
16. Infraction of Scrimmage Formation	42	9	3	2	19
17. Player Out-of-Bounds When Ball is Snapped	42	9	3	2	19
18. Offensive Player Illegally in Motion	42	9	3	3	20
19. Illegal Shift	43	9	3	9	20
20. Illegally Handing Ball Forward (Loss of Down)	43-44	9	4	1	9,35
21. Invalid or Illegal Fair Catch Signal	51	10	4	2	32
22. Intentionally Throwing Backward Pass of Fumble Out-of Bounds	44	9	5	1	9,35
23. Illegal Forward Pass (Loss of Down if by Team A)	45	9	6	4	9,35
24. Intentional Grounding (Loss of Down)	45	9	6	6	9,36
25. Helping the Runner	64	12	5	2	44

SUMMARY OF PENALTIES AND FOULS

LOSS OF 10 YARDS	**PAGE**	**RULE**	**SECTION**	**ARTICLE**	**SIGNAL**
1. Delaying Start of Either Half	35	5	4	1	21
2. Fair Catch Interference	52	10	5	1	33
3. Two or More Consecutive Encroachments During Same Interval Between Scrimmage Downs	41-42	9	2	1	7,18
4. Forward Pass Interference Offense (Loss of Down)	47	9	9	5	9,33
5. Forward Pass Interference Defensive (Automatic First Down & Ball Awarded at Spot)	47	9	9	6	8,33
6. Illegally Secured Flag on Touchdown (Loss of Down)	65	12	7	1	9, 27, 47
7. Unsportsmanlike Player Conduct	59	12	1	1	27
8. Spiking, Kicking, Throwing or Not Returning Ball to Official During Dead Ball	60	12	1	3	27
9. Unsportsmanlike Conduct by Coaches, Substitutes or Others	59-60	12	1	2	27
10. Spiking the Ball into the Ground	60	12	1	3b	38
11. Tripping An Opponent	61	12	3	1h	46
12. Contact With Opponent on Ground	61	12	3	1e	38
13. Throwing Runner to Ground	61	12	3	1f	38
14. Hurdling Any Player	61	12	3	1g	38
15. Contact Before or After Ball is Dead	61	12	3	1j	38
16. Unnecessary Roughness of Any Nature	61	12	3	1l	38
17. Drive or Run Into Player	61	12	3	1k	38
18. Clipping	61	12	3	1l	38
19. Contact to Head, Shoulders, Waist	61	12	3	Ic	38
20. Tackle Runner	61	12	3	1f	38
21. Roughing the Passer (Automatic First Down)	62	12	3	2	38
22. Illegal Offensive Screen Blocking	63	12	4	2	8,34
23. Punter Delaying The Kick	60	12	1	2n	38
24. Illegal Conference	59	12	1	2g	38
25. Illegal Contact Blocking	62-63	12	4	1	38

SUMMARY OF PENALTIES AND FOULS

LOSS OF 10 YARDS, CONT'D.	PAGE	RULE	SECTION	ARTICLE	SIGNAL
26. Roughing the Kicker, Center or Holder (Automatic First Down)	59	12	1	1b	30
27. Holding on a Pass Play (Penalty from line of scrimmage)	62-63	12	4	1	43
28. Guarding the Flag (Loss of Down)	63	12	5	1	24
29. Stiff Arm	64	12	5	3	38
30. Obstruction of Runner	64	12	5	4	38
31. Batting a Free Ball	64	12	6	1	31
32. Illegal Kicking	64-65	12	6	2	31
33. Illegal Participation	66	12	8	3	28
34. Illegal Substitute/Replace Player	66	12	8	3d	28
35. Pretended, Unfair Substitution	66	12	8	3d	28
36. Re-entry of Disqualified Player	65-66	12	8	2	28
37. Illegal Flag Removal	65	12	7	1	38
38. Illegal Use of Hands and Arms	62-63	12	4	1,2	43
39. Diving to Advance the Ball	64	12	5	5	38
40. Rushing the Gap on Extra Point Attempt	54	10	7	8	38
41. Rushing the Gap on Field Goal Attempt	55	10	8	7	38

DISQUALIFICATION ASSOCIATED WITH CERTAIN 10 YARD PENALTIES

	PAGE	RULE	SECTION	ARTICLE	SIGNAL
1. Flagrant Unsportsmanlike Player Conduct	59	12	1	1	47
2. Intentionally Kicking at or Swinging an Arm, Hand or Fist at any Opposing Player	59	12	1	1f	47
3. Flagrant spiking, Kicking, Throwing or Not Returning Ball to Official	60	12	1	3	47
4. Flagrant Unsportsmanlike Conduct by Players, Coaches, Substitutes or Others Subject to the Rules	59-60	12	1	2	47
5. Intentionally Contacting an Official	59	12	1	1a	47
6. Flagrant Personal Fouls	61	12	3	1	47
7. Tackle the Runner	61	12	3	1f, 1m	47
8. Intentional Tampering with Flag (Loss of Down)	65	12	7	1	9,27,47

INDEX TO RULES

	PAGE	RULE	SECTION	ARTICLE
BACKWARD PASS				
Defined	21	1	19	2
Intentionally out of Bounds	44	9	5	1
Caught in Flight	44	9	5	2
Out of Bounds	44	9	5	3
Touches Ground	44	9	5	4
BALL, SPECIFICATIONS				
Change of	30	4	1	2
Responsibility	41	9	1	2
BALLSPOTTER	26	3	1	5
BATTING	19	1	11	3
BATTING	64	12	6	1
CAPTAIN	25	2	2	2
CASH PRIZE	17	1	3	1
CATCH	17	1	4	1
CLIPPING	19	1	5	1
CLOCK				
Starting	33	5	2	5
Stopping	33	5	2	6
Last 2 Minutes	33-34	5	2	6-7
COLORS, CONTRASTING	31	4	3	1
COMMUNICABLE DISEASE PROCEDURES	76	17	1	1
CONDUCT OF PLAYERS				
Unsportsmanlike	59-60	12	1	1-3
Unfair Acts	60-61	12	2	1-2
Personal Fouls	61-62	12	3	1-2
CONTACT BLOCKING	62-63	12	4	1
CONTACT FLAG FOOTBALL				
Definition	23-24	2	1	1
Removal of Flag	65	12	7	1
Guarding of Flag	63	12	5	1
DARKNESS	32	5	2	2
DEAD BALL				
Ready for Play	16	1	1	3
Declared Dead	37-38	7	1	2
DELAY OF GAME	35	5	4	2
DELAYING A HALF	35	5	4	1

INDEX TO RULES

	PAGE	RULE	SECTION	ARTICLE
DISQUALIFIED PLAYER	22	1	28	2
DOWNS	19	1	8	1
Unit of a Game	39	8	1	1
First	39-40	8	1	5
DOWNS, Cont'd.				
Series	39	8	1	2
After a Foul	40	8	2	2
ENCROACHMENT	19	1	9	1
Scrimmage Foul	41-42	9	2	1
EQUIPMENT				
Illegal	31-32	4	5	1
Required	31	4	3	1-3
Optional	31	4	4	1-6
Missing	32	4	6	1
FAIR CATCH	51-52	10	4	1-4
Definition	18	1	3	6
Interference	52	10	5	1
Signal - Illegal	18	1	3	7
Signal - Invalid	18	1	3	8
FIELD DIAGRAM	26-29	3	1	1
FLAG BELT	30	4	2	1-3
FORFEITURE	59	11	8	1
FORWARD PASS	21	1	19	2
Legal	44-45	9	6	1-3
Illegal	45	9	6	4-6
Illegal (co-rec)	81	20	1	16
Complete	46	9	7	1
Incomplete	46	9	8	1
Interference	46-47	9	9	1-6
FOUL	19	1	10	1
Personal	61-62	12	3	1-2
Between Downs	67	13	1	2
Double	70	13	3	8
Clean Hands	70	13	3	8
Multiple	71	13	3	9-10

INDEX TO RULES

	PAGE	RULE	SECTION	ARTICLE
FOUL, Cont'd.				
Procedure After	66-67	13	1	1
During Loose Ball Play	67-68	13	2	3
During Running Play	69	13	2	5
FORCE	58	11	6	1
FREE KICK	47-49	10	1	1-12
Out of Bounds	49	10	2	1-3
FUMBLE	19	1	11	1
GAME (LENGTH OF)	32	5	2	1
Shortening	32	5	2	2
Extension	32-33	5	2	3
HANDING BALL				
Backward	44	9	4	2
During Free Kick	44	9	4	3
Forward	43-44	9	4	1
HANDS AND ARMS				
Use of By The Defense	62-63	12	4	1-2
HELPING THE RUNNER	64	12	5	2
HUDDLE	20	1	14	1
HURDLING	20	1	15	1
ILLEGAL PARTICIPATION	65-66	12	8	1-3
INADVERTENT WHISTLE	38-39	7	1	3
INELIGIBLE LINEMAN FLAG FOOTBALL	24	2	1	3
INJURED PLAYER	35	5	3	7
INTERCEPTION	17-18	1	4	2-3
INTERFERENCE				
With Fair Catch	52	10	5	1
With Forward Pass	46-47	9	9	1-6
INTERMISSIONS	32	5	2	1
JERSEY	31	4	3	1
KICKING, KICKER, TYPES	20	1	16	1-8
Free Kick	20	1	16	2
Restrictions	47-49	10	1	1-12
Recovery Of	48	10	1	5

INDEX TO RULES

	PAGE	RULE	SECTION	ARTICLE
KICKING, KICKER, TYPES, Cont'd.				
Foul During	67-68	13	2	3
Into End Zone	49	10	1	9
Out of Bounds	49	10	2	1-3
At Rest	48-49	10	1	8
Co-Rec (male receiver)	81	20	1	16
KICK, PROTECTED SCRIMMAGE	21	1	24	1
Restrictions	49-51	10	3	1-13
Formation	50	10	3	3
Declaration	49-50	10	3	2
Out-of-Bounds	51	10	3	10
KICKER	20	1	16	3
KICKOFF	20	1	16	4
Choice of	32	5	1	1
LOOSE BALL	16	1	1	2
Batting and Kicking	64-65	12	6	1-2
LOSS OF DOWN	20	1	17	1
Penalties	71	13	3	11
MEASUREMENT				
To Ball's Forward Point	39	8	1	3
MERCY RULE	59	11	7	1-2
MOMENTUM	58	11	5	1
MOTION	42-43	9	3	3
MUFF	19	1	11	2
NEUTRAL ZONE	20	1	18	1
OFFICIAL, CONTACTED	59	12	1	1
OUT OF BOUNDS	39	7	2	1-4
PAID BIDS	100-100	30	1-2	
PASSER	21	1	19	1
PASSES	21	1	19	2
PENALTIES	21	1	20	1
Administration	67	13	2	2
Declined	41	8	2	8
Special Enforcements	69-71	13	3	1-14
Philosophy	71-72	13	4	1
Disqualification	59	12	1	1
New Series	39-40	8	1	5

INDEX TO RULES

	PAGE	RULE	SECTION	ARTICLE
PERIOD				
Length 32		5	2	1
Shortening 32		5	2	2
Extension of 32-33		5	2	3
PLACEKICK 20		1	16	6
PLAYERS				
Number of 23-25		2	1	1-4
Designation of 22-23		1	28	1-10
POSSESSION				
Player, Team 16		1	1	4
PUNT 20		1	16	8
PYLONS 26		3	1	7
READY FOR PLAY 35		5	4	2
ROUGHING THE PASSER 62		12	3	2
RUNNER 63-64		12	5	1-5
SAFETY 58		11	5	1
Exception 58		11	5	1
Foul Resulting In 58		11	5	1
SCORING				
Field Goal 58		11	4	1, 2
Touchdown 56-57		11	2	1-3
Try-For-Point 57-58		11	3	1-7
Safety 58		11	5	1
SCREEN BLOCKING 17		1	2	2
SCREEN FLAG FOOTBALL 24		2	1	2
Fundamentals 63		12	4	2
Interlocked Interference 16-17		1	2	1
SCRIMMAGE 21		1	24	1
Line 21		1	24	2
The Start 41		9	1	1
SERIES OF DOWNS 39		8	1	2
Awarding a New Series 39-40		8	1	5
SHIFT 22		1	25	1
Requirements 43		9	3	9
SIMULTANEOUS CATCH 18		1	4	5
Ball is Dead 46		9	7	2

INDEX TO RULES

	PAGE	RULE	SECTION	ARTICLE
SNAP				
Between Legs and Legal	42	9	2	3
Direct Snap	43	9	3	7
STARTING THE CLOCK	33	5	2	5
STIFF ARM	64	12	5	3
STOPPING THE CLOCK				
Two Minute Warning	33	5	2	6
Last Two Minutes	33-34	5	2	7
SUBSTITUTE	23	1	28	9
Eligible	37	6	1	1
Legal	37	6	1	2
Open Wound	37	6	1	4
SUCCEEDING SPOT	67	13	1	2
SUPERVISION	25	2	2	1
TOUCHING	23	1	29	1
TACKLING	59	12	1	1c
TEE	20	1	16	6
TIE GAME	36	5	5	1-5
TIME OUTS	34-35	5	3	1-9
TOSS OF COIN	32	5	1	1
TOUCHBACK	52-53	10	6	1-5
TOUCHDOWN	56-57	11	2	1-3
TOUCH FOOTBALL	24-25	2	1	4
TRIPPING	23	1	30	1
TRY-FOR-POINT	53	10	7	1
YARD LINES	23	1	31	1
ZONE LINE-TO-GAIN	39	8	1	3
4 ON 4	84-89	23	1-2	
5 ON 5	96-100	29	1-2	

NOTES

NOTES

Protect Your Smile!

Vettex model 45 Multi-Sport Mouthguards offer protection, great fit and peace of mind. Double impression design for safety, and pliable rubber for a comfortable custom fit. Choose from eight popular team colors! Order from your local sporting goods dealer today.

MARKWORT SPORTING GOODS COMPANY
St. Louis, Missouri USA
markwort.com
vettexmouthguards.com